The Year I Said Goodbye

Peter Winter was born in Adelaide in 1945 and educated at Adelaide Boys' High School and Roseworthy Agricultural College. He was called up for National Service in 1965 in the 'first ballot', and selected for Scheyville, the Officer Training Unit near Windsor, New South Wales. He graduated as a second lieutenant and was posted to the Infantry Centre at Ingleburn, in preparation for the Vietnam War.

Peter remained in the army until 1986 when, having reached the rank of major, he resigned. He settled with his family in the Adelaide Hills, where he still lives, and worked in the timber and clothing industries. He is now employed at the Woodside Primary School, where his role is to liaise with and support Defence Force families in the school community.

The year I said goodbye

Peter Winter

Wakefield Press

Wakefield Press
Box 2266
Kent Town
South Australia 5071
www.wakefieldpress.com.au

First published 2003

The military photographs in this book were taken by Colonel Andrew Mattay during the 7th Battalion's second tour of Vietnam and are from *Seven in Seventy – A Pictorial History of the Batallion's Second Tour*, published for the 7th Battalion. The cover photograph of Peter Winter was taken by an unknown Associated Press photographer in 1970.

Designed and typeset by Clinton Ellicott, Wakefield Press
Cover designed by Liz Nicholson, design BITE
Printed and bound by Hyde Park Press

National Library of Australia
Cataloguing-in-publication entry

Winter, Peter, 1945– .
The year I said goodbye.

ISBN 1 86254 610 X.

1. Winter, Peter, 1945 – Correspondence. 2. Vietnamese Conflict, 1961–1975 – Personal narratives, Australian. I. Title.

959.7043092

Dedicated To

All who served in Vietnam.

Especially those who toured with the 7th Battalion, Royal Australian Regiment, in 1970–71 and to their families and loved ones who provided comfort and encouragement and remained a source of strength through the most difficult times.

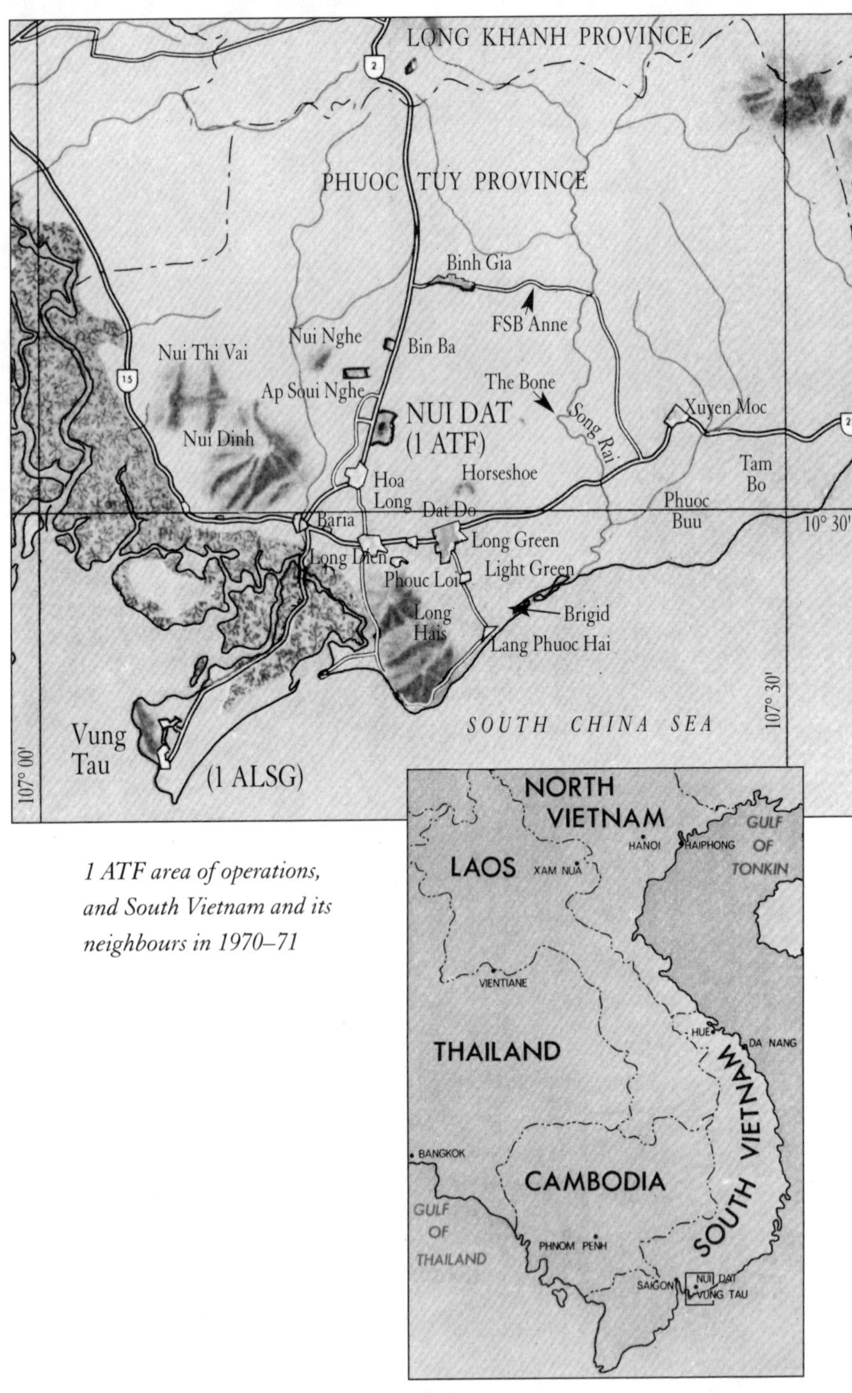

1 ATF area of operations, and South Vietnam and its neighbours in 1970–71

Contents

Foreword

by Lynne Cosgrove

Letter writing and diary keeping are fading arts and pastimes. Our ancestors were prolific, thank heavens, and that is why we know so much about their adventures and everyday lives. Many wrote daily, either letters to loved ones or in meticulously kept diaries into which they could pour out their souls. Often those words, flowing from pen to letter or diary, transcended the thousands of miles of separation between the writer and the reader. This was especially the case with those hundreds of thousands of Australians at war who, often on the opposite sides of the world from their families and friends, bridged the gap with words of love, anguish and humour, with sentiments and records of high drama and of the most commonplace.

Many years ago I married a soldier and thenceforth was known colloquially and affectionately as an 'Army Wife'. Across the years my husband and I have experienced many separations through his job, mostly short but some quite lengthy. In the early days he would write, but increasingly in the age of the ubiquitous mobile phone he would telephone. Even in the most mundane of phone calls there is always a poignant sub-text of concern and love and longing, but in the letters a soldier sends to his loved ones there is often eloquence and imagery and a kind of poetry.

This is what I felt reading the wonderful letters Peter Winter wrote to his wife, his mum and his dad. Whether he was recording an exhausting day on operations in Vietnam or enquiring after family and friends, his letters are redolent with an obvious love and care for those at home and the men in his charge. *The Year I Said Goodbye* is a marvellous chronicle of an exhilarating and poignant year of separation and longing, of anticipation and nostalgia.

My husband and I knew Peter and Raylene some 26 years ago, in Singleteon when we were just married – we see him as an incurable optimist, a man who does rather than contemplates. This is evident from his letters. I loved descriptions of the countryside, the Vietnamese people, the diggers and fellow officers, I loved his poetry and the way he chose a different approach in the style he wrote to Raylene, his mum and his dad. As the mother of three sons, two currently serving in the army, I can imagine my boys taking the soft approach to mum, being very direct with dad and hopefully being very loving and reassuring to their partners, as Peter was.

I met my husband, Peter Cosgrove, about three years after his 'tour of duty' and I must admit that I am pleased I didn't have to go through the Vietnam experience as a wife and mother. Many of my 'army wife' friends did and I have great admiration for them, as I do for Raylene in her new role as a mother with her best friend and lover away for what must have seemed like an eternity.

It was a bonus while reading *The Year I said Goodbye* to find the names of many old friends, many of whom we still share friendships with today.

I feel honoured to have been invited to write this foreword. To Mark-John, thank you for discovering the letters and for learning to understand what your family has been through. I wish James well, and to Raylene, enjoy your adventures, you deserve to! I wish Anne and Ryan a wonderful future. To Peter, thank you for telling an honest story. Anyone who reads it, I'm sure, will want to say 'thank you' for what you did, in that great Aussie tradition, along with all who served in Vietnam.

I hope you enjoy as much as I did this unique perspective of a soldier's 'bridge of words' to those he loved.

Introduction

On 17 February 1970 at the age of 25, I said goodbye to my wife Raylene and our 10-month-old son Mark-John and left with the 7th Battalion, Royal Australian Regiment, to serve my tour of duty as an infantry platoon commander in South Vietnam.

I had been in the army for four and a half years (two as a National Serviceman) and during that time Raylene and I had become accustomed to frequent separation and associated hardships. Because of this we were well aware that the coming year would put a severe strain on both of us. However, being young, idealistic, in love, and perhaps a little naive, we felt we were experienced enough to handle what was before us. Besides, I was a professional soldier, I believed in Australia's commitment to Vietnam, and I knew that overseas service, even if it was in a war zone, was part of the deal.

Throughout the year that followed I kept in close contact with Raylene through letters and tapes. I corresponded on a less regular basis with my mother and her family, my father and relatives and friends. In all, I wrote about 150 letters.

At that time, postage took about seven days to get from Vietnam to Australia, and similarly a week for mail to arrive from Australia. On several occasions, when there were postal strikes, mail was delayed for up to 10 days. I carried writing material with me at all times and wrote whenever the opportunity allowed, whether during a short breather on patrol, sheltering in a bunker in a fire support base, or living in relative peace and luxury in a tent at

Nui Dat. My letters were written on whatever paper was available. In the bush I used my field notebook, a small but essential item used for taking down radio messages and operational orders. I also carried a notepad, provided by The Australian Forces Overseas Fund, in one of my webbing pouches.

Many of these letters were smudged with mud and sweat and even to this day retain the familiar musty smell of the tropics. They were written as I balanced the notepaper on my knee, while sitting with my back against a tree in the deepest part of that unfriendly terrain. When back behind the wire, however, I had access to the battalion's A4-size lined and letterheaded material and wrote in the relative comfort of my sandbagged tent or bunker. The neat and legible handwriting is in stark contrast to the scribble of those written in the bush.

Some readers may question my tendency to switch from imperial to metric measurements. Even though the metric system was officially introduced in Australia in 1970, it had been used by the army for many years before that. So readers will notice that in some paragraphs I express measurements in colloquial feet and inches, but then switch to metres and millimetres.

All letters are still in their original red, white and blue Par Avion envelopes, marked with the words 'Free Forces Mail'. They were numbered in the order that Raylene received them, the first being written on 17 February 1970, and the 108th on 22 February 1971. As each was received, the information was disseminated among friends and relatives and then the letter was placed in a shoe box, together with topical newspaper articles clipped from local papers.

Few of the tapes survived as they were used and re-used over and over until they literally fell apart. Unfortunately, the humid tropical atmosphere played havoc with tapes, electrical equipment and photographs, so much of the associated correspondence was destroyed while 'in country'.

The letters were never intended to be a record of Vietnam experiences. They were simply correspondence between a husband and wife, separated by war. They contain expressions of love and concern, requests for information and general family news; they were an attempt to establish some normality in my life. They were an opportunity, also, to express views about the war and the conflict it was causing back home and to explain how most soldiers serving in Vietnam were feeling. They were a snapshot of my life, as an infantry officer in that strange and hostile environment. Above all, they were an opportunity to unburden my fears and frustrations and shed some of the sadness and horror that I was witnessing.

I didn't know it then, but when I said goodbye to my loved ones in February 1970, I also said goodbye to the life I had known and the future I had hoped for. It was a time of change for all Australians, not just the soldiers in South Vietnam. However, few realised just how dramatic this change would be.

Pre-embarkation leave in Adelaide, December 1969

Chapter One

'33 and Awakey'

22–30 January 1971

22 January 1971 (339 days 'in country')

Dear Raylene, I feel proud to know that after 12 months in this place we are able to call ourselves professionals and stand tall among our famous digger forebears.

I remember looking back across the wide, desolate clearing and the black, baked mud with its sparse shrubs and tufts of grass. Jones's group had broken out into an open formation, covering a width of about 30 metres, each man being spread about 20 metres apart. The eight-man patrol exemplified the strength of our tactics and the modern Australian infantryman and I thought to myself, as I watched them coming toward me, that I wouldn't want to be involved in a clash against them.

My group of 16 had crossed the clearing only 10 minutes before and it was here, in the tree line, that we waited for Jones and his section to 'marry up' with us. My blokes had positioned themselves in the shade of the trees and bushes, not just to escape the heat, but for the fact that in the shade their dark, sweat-stained clothes and shapeless outline were perfectly camouflaged. The machine gunners had been carefully positioned. They lay behind their deadly weapons to appreciate the ground before them and identify the most likely target areas. My signaller was talking in whispers, notifying the moving patrol that we had them 'visual' ... all was ready for the rendezvous.

Jones's crew were alert as they crossed the clearing. Each flank man was searching his arc of responsibility for possible trouble spots. His rifle always pointed in the direction he was looking; always ready for action. The 'Tail-End Charlie' was keeping a careful check on the area they had just passed, in case anyone was following. Their fatigued shoulders were hunched beneath the weight of their equipment, rations, water and 'ammo'; all infantrymen move in this stooped manner. The sweat rags tied around their foreheads created a menacing look, as did the three-day beard growth on their grimy, strained faces. Each one appeared to be a shuffling robot whose progress couldn't be stopped, even if a brick wall was placed in his way. Their steady, relentless pace would be maintained and bricks and mortar would shatter as the Green Machine continued on its way, stopping for nothing or nobody.

As Jones's group quietly passed through our position, my scouts joined on and the platoon, now complete, headed off on a bearing of 6300 mils to our next navigational check point. Everybody automatically adopted the exacting routines of patrolling: searching, listening, checking and thinking. We certainly think a lot as we patrol. We're not switched off by any means.

Thoughts of home, girls, and cool water rarely override the need to search your area of responsibility or keep an eye on your mate in front and the one behind. I tend to think about navigation, you and cool water as I move directly behind the lead section; a position which allows me greater control of our direction and movement and has me up front, should anything suddenly occur.

Our bearing took us through more swamp. Thick, sucking, smelly mud that traps aching legs and refuses to let go. A muffled curse was often heard as a tree root sent another face down in the muck. Surprisingly, our weapons remained clean and operational.

We moved in single file now, walking in the forward man's steps, except where it could be seen that he had gone down to his balls in the ooze. Vines that tangled around our knees were quietly snipped away with pruning secateurs; the robots kept pushing through whatever barriers were in their way.

I'm really proud of my platoon. They amaze me with their special strength and character. Take, for instance, the time we set up ambush on the last night of the latest operation. Without any detailed orders from me, each man prepared for the night by clearing his own area, laying out his ammo and grenades and setting out a bank of four claymore mines to cover the designated ambush zone. They laid down with their rifles, checked that they could observe the area and then each one cleared his personal space of leaves, twigs and anything that may cause an unnecessary noise, should he roll on it during the night. After clearing small paths between each other, so they could move silently at night while checking positions or changing sentries, they then settled down to enjoy one last smoke before 'stand to'. All was completed within 20 minutes and if you stood five metres away you wouldn't know anyone was there. That is until one lazy bastard coughs without fully smothering the sound with his hat. A grunt and glare expresses my annoyance and once again, all is still.

Things look like they're building up. The other day a patrol found an 82 mm mortar with 27 bombs, just north of the Horseshoe. It seems that Charlie had intentions of shelling the 'Shoe over Tet (26–28 January, New Year celebrations). Only about half a mile from Brigid, at midday yesterday, a grenade was thrown at a group of Australian Engineers who were working on a windmill in Hoi My. One soldier was seriously wounded and two slightly. Two 15-year-old kids have been arrested – you never know when it will come your way. Also, yesterday an eagle-eyed armoured personnel carrier driver spotted an M16 mine with a trip wire, set up on a bush track they were about to cross. That makes about a dozen M16 mines that have been found since we've been at Brigid. (We'd used that track only the day before.)

Tonight three ambush patrols are out, while I rest in my musty, claustrophobic bunker. When will we clash with Charlie again? We hope it's soon and we hope it's never again. Time is getting too short to wish for action. We've done our bit. Throughout this campaign we've lost one of our own for every 12 VC we've killed, but that is of little comfort as I prepare for what I hope is a decent night's sleep.

Good night my love.

23 January 1971

The VC planted a flag and spread propaganda leaflets in the centre of Lo Gom last night, a small hamlet about 400 metres from Brigid. Tet begins in two days and you can bet that they will continue to step up their activities. We are limited in our ambushes as Pioneer Platoon has gone bush, leaving only Reconnaissance Platoon and Coy HQ, plus our mortar and artillery crew to defend Brigid. I send out two ambushes a night, which reduces the defence to only 20-odd. If the enemy realised how thin we were on the ground I'm sure he'd have a go at us, although he'd want to be quick, because the fire support from the Horseshoe and Nui Dat would be immediate and deadly.

We've just been informed that we will be going bush from 29 January to 4 February, to check out a bunker system that 6 Platoon had a major contact in recently (grid reference 651 633) and then south to the coast.

I'm carrying an automatic self loading rifle now. I've done a bit of work on the firing catch so that instead of it firing one round each time I pull the trigger, it fires a burst. This is ideal for these conditions, as apart from providing extra fire power in times of crisis, it helps to boost my confidence knowing I've got such a great weapon to protect me. It's like having an elephant gun, compared to the American armalite (M16), which looks and feels like a plastic toy rifle and fires a 5.56 mm round compared to the thumping great 7.62. I remember in my first contact, I squeezed the trigger of my M16 and in a split second or so all my ammo was gone, without me realising it. With the self loading rifle, the kick it gives you makes you realise that you've got one hell of a weapon in your hands. It demands your respect and I'm sure the Viet Cong feel the same way.

The battalion doesn't like the idea of dickying up weapons but Captain Thompson, our company commander, says it's OK because it gives us a lot more fire power, so Recce Platoon now has four automatic self loading rifles in its armoury.

With that cheery bit of news, I'll sign off till next time.

24 January 1971

I received your letter of the twentieth, when you were at Mum's place. You seem much happier and no doubt the change of scenery is the reason. I'm sorry that we have to wait several days before reading about what each is feeling or doing. Mental telepathy would be a wonderful thing because we could converse without this 'waiting for a reply' delay.

I know we've been through some hard financial times, but we are really very lucky. Mark-John is healthy and isn't in need of anything. There is always food in the fridge (even if some of it comes from left over ration packs), we have a roof over our heads and our little Morris 1100 doesn't do a bad job getting us around. The bank manager doesn't greet us with a smile (come to think of it, he probably doesn't even know our names). However, there will come a time when we won't have to scrape to make ends meet, when you won't feel ill for not knowing where the next payment will come from, when you won't have to pray for a miracle to get us through till next payday.

I'm sorry for leaving you with such burdens, but I'm sure the future holds good things for us.

After reading your last letter I felt so very close to you. I wish I could be with you right at this moment to explain just how I feel. I'd sit beside you, look deep into your brown eyes and I'd say:

> You know how much I love you, I'm completely under your spell and I'm amazed at your strength and wonderful outlook on life. Your outlook as a mother, housewife, friend and lover. If I were able, I'd deepen my love for you but I just can't find any more room to put extra love in my heart for you.
>
> As a mother, all I need do is look at M-J. He is my life too and I could wish for no more than he grows up with the love and understanding in his heart that his Mum has and that he loves and respects others, as his Mum does.
>
> As a housewife, all I need do is look at our little home. From one of those ticky tacky little boxes on a hillside you have created a castle; a home full of peace and love.

> As a friend, I consider you are my best mate because you've stuck by me through everything, given me encouragement when I've been down and kicked me when I've needed it. You listen when I need someone to talk to and you accept my shortcomings. You are my beacon on which I set my sights for the future. Without your shining light I'd be lost.
>
> As a lover, I certainly can't complain even though we're both still learning. As long as we continue to share our loving I can't see why we shouldn't graduate with honours in this subject.
>
> You're an angel because you're so very understanding and lovely. A gypsy with so much mystery and passion and a mistress who shares my fantasies and secrets.

It's been such a long time since we've shared a tender moment and as I write, I must admit my surroundings don't lend themselves to any romance. Here I am in my musty, smelly bunker, surrounded by sandbags, steel pickets, corrugated iron and weapons of war. I hope you can understand these confused ramblings from your very lonely soldier.

27 January 1971

Dear Mum, the battalion has commenced its Return To Australia procedure, with our advance party already back at Holsworthy. The 3rd Battalion takes over our area of operations at 3.00 pm on 23 February; a date I'm looking forward to very much. Actually, I've already packed my trunk and could and would leave tomorrow if they called for me to go.

By the time you receive this letter Raylene and Mark-John will be settled back in our Holsworthy home and you'll probably be pleased at having fewer mouths to feed, especially with the constant demands from four growing males with appetites like Rex, Rob, Greg and Peter.

It has been a great comfort knowing that my family have had you to care for them whenever they were in Adelaide, this last long year. Thank you for everything, although I'm sure you wouldn't have had it any other way. Raylene has looked forward to each of her stays in Adelaide, catching up with family and friends, escaping Sydney's weather and showing M-J off to doting grandparents. It's helped break up the long and lonely separation and given her comfort to have you all there.

From what I've been hearing M-J is certainly talking his head off nowadays and is growing up very fast. Raylene always mentions his latest amazing sayings and doings and I'm certainly looking forward to getting to know him again.

To think, that within four weeks I'll be starting my journey home and shortly thereafter will be adapting to life in Australia and hopefully, beginning to feel at ease again. It's as if I've spent my lifetime in this place (if not, then at least a lifetime of emotions) and it won't be all that easy to settle back into a 'normal' routine. There are so many readjustments I'll have to make.

Reconnaissance Platoon has been going out bush for about five days at a time (we next go out from 29 January to 4 February). I enjoy the bushwork much more than living in bunkers and filling sandbags, which is all we seem to do at the Horseshoe or at Brigid.

Have you heard about CS gas that is used over here? (Yes, Australians do use gas warfare.) These crystals, called CS, create heavy chlorine-like fumes when in contact with air and we use them to stop the Viet Cong going back into their bunkers, caves and areas we can't closely patrol. My last patrol took us into an old CS area and we came across several large bags of crystals which had been air dropped back a few years. We were lucky that their effect was all but gone. Even so, we felt a burning sensation in our eyes when we disturbed one and were down wind from several others. The areas will have to be re-seeded or we'll need to boost our patrolling, if these areas are to remain free from enemy activity.

We've done quite a lot of swamp patrols lately. These are pretty interesting because we spend all our time up to our thighs in black smelly ooze, trying to check the area out before the incoming tide drowns us. The tidal rise is about six feet along the swamp area and at one time we were almost caught by a rise of four feet in 20 minutes. Are there any crocodiles in Vietnam?

Hope all is well at home.

28 January 1971

Happy Anniversary, my love. May the following years be as fulfilling as the last four. Only joking. When they say 'You're married to the army now', and give you a regimental badge that demands 'Duty First', they really do expect total commitment. The army has seen more of me than you have in our first years of wedded bliss, what with unaccompanied postings, courses, exercises and weekend duties, not to mention this bloody war.

I'll send this letter to Holsworthy for your arrival at 501 Lighthorse Parade and hope you can quickly settle back into the routine of family life in an army village. I guess there will be a fair bit of work to do on the place, especially on the lawn and garden, which probably looks like some of the places I've been in during this last year.

We're so busy with packing, rebuilding and renovating that I have little time to respond to all the letters and cards I've received recently. I must admit I would have forgotten that my birthday was only a week away. I have so many more important things to think about, including our next operation, which commences tomorrow. I've received two cards from you, and others from Mum and Rex, Lesley [Raylene's younger sister], your Mum and Dad and Aunt Ethel. Then there are the letters from you, Mum and Rob. The photos of you and M-J are beaut and with only a few weeks to go they've made me feel very homesick.

Surprisingly, Tet has been very quiet with only one or two small contacts in an area to the north-west called DeCourtney Rubber Plantation. D Company found 8000 pounds of polished rice in caches just south of the hills in the same area. They reckon it had been collected as taxes from the local farmers, so we may find some other caches in our travels. Support Company has been informed that we will go on our final operation from 9 to 19 February; then thank God, it's all over except for the packing and administration.

Life at Brigid has been a bit slow because we're restricted by numbers to only two ambushes every second night and one ambush on alternate nights. This means my sergeant and I don't go out, instead we spend several hours on duty in the company command post and leave the ambushes to our very competent section commanders.

At nights we have the luxury of playing chess, toasting tomato sandwiches and drinking coffee. It's a good break from what we've experienced in the past. We even find time during the day, when we're not reconstructing our wind blown bunkers, to play volleyball. It's a great game when played in the soft white sand. You can throw yourself about, making some rather spectacular attempts at getting the ball.

Well my love it'll be the twenty-eighth in five hours. My thoughts are with you on our fourth anniversary. Give M-J a big kiss for me and tell him it won't be long till Dad will be playing footy with him and saying our God Bless's together.

God bless Mummy and M-J.

29 January 1971 – from Raylene to Peter's mum

Just a wee note to let you know we had a good trip home. We saw you all as the plane taxied off. M-J had eaten half a packet of chips and two chocolate frogs before we had left the ground and although he got a bit scared when we started to climb the back steps by the jet engines, he was as good as gold on board.

Guy and Robyn met us. What a lovely couple they are. They are very excited because Guy is doing very well in his studies and is considering entering the field of marine biology as his future career. It's amazing to think that only a few years ago he was with Peter at the Infantry Centre at Ingleburn, as first intake National Service officers. Guy spent a year in Vietnam in 1967–68, so he and Robyn are very understanding and supportive.

It hasn't stopped raining since we arrived and last night was particularly heavy. I can't let M-J outside to play, as the grass in the yard is three feet high and none of the paths can be seen. Everyone in the neighbourhood is the same, as the weather has been very wet and steamy, somewhat like our men are experiencing in Vietnam.

All the wives are keeping in contact and today we had tea at Bev's. They come to our place tomorrow night. My hectic social life continues, but we gain so much support from one another in these difficult times, that I am most grateful for their friendship.

I had two letters from My Love today. He's fine and the latest news is that HMAS *Sydney* leaves Vietnam on 25 February. I can hardly believe that after this eternity we have only three weeks to go before he is safely on his way back to us.

30 January 1971

My darling, a little time back you wrote that we have gained nothing from the last 12 months. Financial problems plague us and you are constantly faced with the burden of making ends meet. Similarly, you have had to care for M-J on your own and that has been extremely difficult, what with all his ailments and illnesses.

Your insecurity, especially at nights, is a real worry as I had no idea you felt that way. The 'peeping Tom' episode was pretty terrible, but I thought it had been resolved satisfactorily, so I wasn't aware of your continuing fears.

Then unfortunately, there are those in the Government, media and in the community who'll do and say anything to discredit our involvement in Vietnam. We've had to put up with that since I was enlisted, but to have someone confront you at a party and say those kinds of things to you, is absolutely the lowest. You handled it very well but even so, it worries me that you have to take the brunt of these ignorant comments. I'm not sure I will be able to control myself as well as you, if someone makes a similar statement in my presence.

It reminds me of an incident that occurred during 7RAR's first tour (1967–68). After one of our lads had been killed in action and the news had been reported in the papers, some bastard rang the soldier's family and said 'he got what he deserved'.

This war has changed many people. I've seen what it has done to some over here, but we're not the only ones. We've become a divided country.

I probably haven't helped by writing all that I have in my letters to you, but as I've said before, I'd prefer that you know everything that is happening, so there is no misunderstanding about what we are doing over here and particularly what I'm involved in. It's been an enormous help to me, to unload my burdens in my letters. To have kept all my experiences and feelings to myself would have been unbearable.

Of course I've been very worried about you, especially of late, as you have seemed so unhappy and I can't do anything to help. Please be patient, we've been through so much and I'll soon be home to help and comfort you.

Looking back, time has gone quickly, at least from my perspective. I guess at times the days crawled by. We've both had some terrible low points and I certainly wouldn't like to go through such a separation again. But now, with only a few days to go, it seems to have gone quickly. Perhaps it's just the way your mind shuts out all the heartache and horror.

Remember when this whole saga began? Our last week together before my departure …

Chapter Two

The Beginning

1–19 February 1970

1 February, Holsworthy, New South Wales

Dear Mum, the days seem to be dragging a bit, however I guess the time will come soon enough. I'm leaving at 9.30 pm on the seventeenth by Qantas. As you know, a group will be leaving a week earlier to fly into Vietnam and get our area at Nui Dat ready. They will receive most of the stores and equipment 5RAR have been using during their tour. Then the main body, made up of some officers, most of the NCOs and all of the diggers will sail in HMAS *Sydney* from Garden Island on the sixteenth. Our flight out on the seventeenth will complete the battalion's departure. I will get into Vietnam after a 10-hour flight and a stopover in Singapore and will move straight to Nui Dat, where we will set up our own company areas, attend briefings and prepare for the arrival of the troops, which I think will be on the twenty-sixth.

It's hard to believe that after all our training and preparations that the time is almost upon us and while it will be very hard leaving Raylene and M-J, I'm very excited about it all.

Before I left Adelaide I wanted to explain a few things to you, but just couldn't find the right moment. However, it's important that I say them to you now.

Firstly, you've got to understand that I want to go to Vietnam for both professional and personal reasons. I've trained long and hard for this moment and I've got a bunch of blokes that I'm very proud of and we all want to prove to ourselves that we're as good as anyone for the job ahead.

Raylene and M-J outside 501 Lighthorse Parade, Holsworthy (our Army home), February 1970

I'm a regular soldier now, so I need this experience if I'm going to make a career of the army. Most of our senior officers and NCOs have been overseas at some time; Korea, Malaysia, Borneo and Vietnam and their outlook has been shaped by their experiences. A regular soldier without any kind of overseas service considers that he's missed an important part of serving in the army. We've been trained by some of the best and we're ready to be put to the test.

Personally, I believe that this next year will set Raylene and me up financially. Not just the extra money we'll get from the various allowances, but from the future opportunities that will come our way, like promotion and postings. The War Service Loan will also be a great help when we come to buy our first home. I know it's going to be hard on both of us, especially Raylene, but I think it will be worth it in the long run.

I know that you don't understand much of what I'll be doing and perhaps that's best. But you need to know that I'll be very careful ... no heroics. Although it may sound awful, I also have to say that if anything does happen to me, the army will help Raylene. Also, don't go off the deep end every time you see the TV reports or read the newspapers. A lot of what is seen and read is about American actions and we aren't operating anywhere near them. Our training and tactics are different. They might have all the flash equipment, but we are far better prepared for this kind of warfare.

The media also tends to focus only on the dramatic actions, which distorts the true picture. Anything to sensationalise, sell papers and get better ratings.

If you want to know more about Vietnam I'll get Raylene to lend you a little book that every soldier gets before going. It explains about the country and the people; their culture, religions and way of life.

Remember not to worry too much. I'll keep in touch as much as I can, if not direct then through Raylene.

Taken at Manly, New South Wales, February 1970

Dear Folks, Raylene here. Before we all retire for the night I thought I'd add a few lines to Peter's letter. We have been to the beach today and M-J, the surfie, loved the big frothy waves. He's a real water-baby and now slides up and down the bath on his tummy, kicking his feet. When I take out the plug he plays around the hole, watching the water disappear and isn't afraid of the gurgling noise it makes anymore. He has taken his first steps from me to Peter and is becoming very adventurous.

We attended the Officers Mess Farewell Dinner last Thursday night. It was quite a lavish affair, with the men in their 'blues' and all the ladies in their best evening wear. We were entertained by the Eastern Command Band and were served a marvellous four-course meal. The tables were very fancy with candelabra and special silverware and while it was a very formal affair, it was a really lovely evening.

We have the Farewell Parade on Wednesday, the fourth, and Peter doesn't have to go back to work until the Monday. I've bought a new dress for the big occasion. We'll be going to Sydney on our last weekend together and while we haven't decided what we'll see yet, we are both keen on *Hair*. M-J will stay with the neighbours.

We've now been told that Peter's flight won't be leaving until 11.30 pm on Tuesday, the seventeenth. I'll be going with him in a bus taking the officers and their families. M-J will again stay next door.

On the nineteenth, I leave here for Adelaide with another officer's wife who will help with the driving. She will be staying with her mother who lives on Gladstone Road, Brighton.

We have been taking photos of each other and when this film is developed you can pick out what you like. I took a candid one of Peter and M-J in the surf today. Hope it turns out.

We aren't doing too much during these last few days; beach, sleeping, reading and playing with M-J. Lazy, family things. We've got to make the most of our time together.

Don't worry about your younger son, he's fine. He's about to do what he's been wanting to do for a long time. So, let's try and be happy for him.

Lots of love from us three.

17 February – telegrams

GOOD LUCK AND GOD BLESS.

Nana and Grandpa

MY LOVE AND PRAYERS WILL FOLLOW YOU WHEREVER YOU ARE.

Auntie Ethel.

17 February – letters

Just to let you know that we will do everything we can to look after Raylene and Mark-John in your absence. Our prayers are with you until you are together again for always. The time will go surprisingly quickly; that, Dad and I know. Take great care of yourself.

God bless you Peter dear.

Mum and Dad Greenslade.

My thoughts are with you. I know this is what you want, so I'll not wallow in sentiment, but I want you to know my love, my thoughts and my prayers will be with you every moment, in the following year.

Your loving mother.

17 February – the departure

Darling, so far it's been a quiet trip except for the huge ovation given to Bev Harrell and the concert group when they came on board. After taking off we were given a beer and then everyone settled down to reading or sleeping. All of us were feeling pretty awful about leaving and there weren't too many excited conversations going on, until later in the flight when they brought us a beaut meal and we began to contemplate what was before us.

Our farewell wouldn't be from a movie classic, would it! I found it difficult to say anything appropriate or carry on with passionate embraces. However, in our own way I reckon we both understood what each other was feeling and actions weren't needed to express the emptiness inside.

Please extend my sincere thanks to Guy and Robyn, Ron and Carol and Ron and Gill for seeing me off and for being there to support you. I feel comfort from knowing we have such wonderful friends to help you at any time.

It's now 6.00 am and we've just changed into civvy shirts for our clandestine stopover in Singapore. It seems silly that we have to make a pretence of being tourists and it must look pretty weird because we are all wearing the same green summer dress trousers, black shoes and military style haircuts. Perhaps we're being passed off as a large gathering of salesmen or an all-male religious sect.

We'll be here for about two hours and will be able to freshen up with a shower. The time difference has been interesting because as we've been flying west we've been constantly changing our watches back. I'm not sure what the 'real time' is.

As I expected, my excitement has been slowly fading the further I get from you. Twelve months is a hell of a long time to be apart.

We spent two hours in Singapore which included a breakfast of scrambled eggs and bacon. Although we only stayed in the airport terminal it was strange to be among so many Asian people. The bus driver, flight attendants, hostesses, bartenders, cleaners, stewards and the general population were all non European. It's the first time I've been in such a situation. I guess I'll have to get used to it, won't I!

We took off at about 7.30 am and flew to Saigon. What a shock to the system ...

It's the busiest airport in the world, with every kind of aircraft you could ever expect to see. International airlines like PanAm, Qantas, Air Vietnam were mixing it with military aircraft; Phantom jets, Hercules transports, helicopters and all shapes and sizes of craft, loaded up with all kinds of military cargo and ammo. Planes coming and going, on all sorts of missions. Vehicles of all kinds, racing here and there. The noise was deafening. People everywhere, coming and going for all sorts of reasons too. Vietnamese and Aussies and the overpowering presence of the Yanks.

No doubt there was someone controlling it all but to me, it seemed like 'one hell of a brothel'. We stayed around for about three hours, changing money and organising our equipment, then around 12.30 got loaded onto some RAAF aircraft and flew to our new home in Phouc Tuy Province, called Nui Dat.

My first impressions aren't very favourable, but I'll keep them to myself. Darling, I'm in a war zone and there is no doubt about it. We carry loaded pistols and rifles everywhere we go, even to the showers and toilet. We sleep in sandbagged tents. Sandbagged bunkers and weapon pits are everywhere and miles of barbwire, about 100 yards to our front, encircle the whole area to help protect us from enemy attack. Every minute of the day and throughout the night, artillery and mortars fire at some remote target, aircraft and helicopters fly over constantly and the sounds of battle are ever present.

When we arrived and at this very moment, three companies of Aussies are in contact in the Long Hais (mountains to the south of us). Two armoured personnel carriers and a tank have been destroyed and there are reports of several casualties. It's one of the biggest contacts for some time and yet life in this old rubber plantation goes on, as if nothing was happening. In the tent next to me Nancy Sinatra is singing and to my right the film *Far From The Madding Crowd* is being shown in an open-air theatre.

We are not too impressed with the state of the area and equipment we've inherited from 5RAR. They've been pretty busy during their tour and care of their base camp equipment obviously wasn't high on their agenda. The lucky bastards have only got nine days to go.

Thursday evening, 19 February. Today was pretty exciting in a peaceful sort of way. At 7.30 am, wearing steel helmets and flack jackets and carrying our personal weapons, we boarded two trucks and with a number of jeeps mounted with machine guns for added protection, we did a guided tour of the province roads and villages. Off we went to Hoa Long (south of Nui Dat) then to Baria and on to Phou My. Then back to Baria and on to Long Dien, Dat Do and on to a feature just north of Dat Do, called the Horseshoe. From there back to Nui Dat and up to Binh Ba.

All these places have been scenes of heavy fighting (particularly during the 1968 Tet Offensive) and many of the buildings show the signs of battle. As we drove around jets, helicopters and other military hardware raced to and fro about their business. The former were pounding the Long Hais where 8RAR were in action yesterday (a total of three dead and 31 wounded).

The locals are going about their daily business as if nothing is happening. We're told that most of the people in the area dislike our being here and while the kids smile, call out and make rude gestures to us, the adults go about their business (food stalls, farming, gardening and just surviving) as if we weren't here. There are soldiers everywhere; Aussies, Vietnamese and Yanks in all kinds of vehicles, travelling along narrow, poorly maintained roads at breakneck speed, dodging ox carts, motor cycles, motor buses, people on foot and each other.

Our Engineers can be seen in the towns and hamlets fixing up drains, grading roads, building houses, schools, windmills and other necessities of life and generally doing a great job. But deep down you can't help but believe the people don't want us here. You can't blame them after years and years of conflict.

I've talked with several 5RAR diggers and they are very happy to be going home. Many of them reckon being here has been an experience they wouldn't have missed, and while most agree they don't want to ever come back, there are one or two who have extended their duty and will be staying another year, serving with 7RAR.

I often think about the next 12 months and wonder if I'll be able to handle the responsibility and whether it will change me in any way. But only time will tell. We've just been told that we'll be going out on a patrol with some 8RAR blokes in a week or two. So I'll soon know what it will be like.

Nui Dat consists of an area about 4000 square metres, surrounded by barbwire and mine fields, with a hill (the actual Nui Dat) on the western boundary. A squadron of our Special Air Service live on the hill. There is also an airfield in the middle (known as Luscombe Field) which is a hive of activity during the day, particularly with troop carrying, helicopter traffic. Tanks, APCs, trucks and Land Rovers are forever moving this way and that. It's a very busy place.

Although much of the area has been cleared of vegetation, all tent lines are protected from the weather by rubber trees; thousand upon thousand in neat rows. The canopy gives good shade, but the falling leaves lay very thick on the ground and I can imagine we'll be forever cleaning them up. Vines and shrubs grow wild unless kept chopped back and it's a never-ending problem to keep the undergrowth clear, especially from our defensive wire. In our area we'll have to do a lot of work to clean up, so when the diggers arrive they'll have to spray the area with weed killer and then burn it off in order to get it under some control.

Periodically, during the day and evening a Land Rover moves slowly through the area with a huge, motorised spray on behind, sending a fine mist of who-knows-what into the canopy of the trees and over everything within range, in an attempt to keep the mosquito population down. Even so, we still have to have our daily pills, use army-issue repellants and sleep under netting to keep them from getting to us.

The weather is surprisingly cool, although humid. We get up at 6 am (still very dark) and those not on duty get to bed around 10 pm (so it's a pretty long day).

We've got a lot of work to do to get the place in a reasonable condition before our troops arrive. I've been allotted my area which includes sandbagged tent lines, bunkers and fighting pits, showers, long-drop toilets and a section of defensive wire about 100 metres long. We will be starting work on cleaning it up, from tomorrow.

My darling, thank you for your first letter. It was a comfort to know that you wrote so soon. I hope your trip back to Adelaide was completed without trouble. I was worried you know.

18 February – from Raylene to Peter's mum

Well, Peter has departed and M-J and I are coming to grips with our situation. He's terribly frightened of losing his Mum. If she happens to go into another room or worse, outside without him, he just cries and cries. I wonder how he knows. I think he's scared that I might go away too. Bless him.

He's got three double teeth now. I wish the fourth would come through so we could both get a full night's rest.

Everything seems to be in such a whirl. It's like a dream. I hope soon I'll wake up and everything will be back as it was before.

Chapter Three

New Experiences

23 February–3 April 1970

23 February

My love, I've been out on my first two-day/two-night operation with a platoon from 8RAR. We went up to Binh Ba (about seven kilometres north of Nui Dat) and into the rubber plantation to the west of the village. We searched creek lines and ambushed tracks and while we saw plenty of signs, there was no action. I felt nervous at times, but overall I am quite confident. I guess it'll be when shots are fired that I'll know whether I like the place or not.

Every minute of the day something is occurring. Artillery firing, military aircraft of every shape and size fly over, helicopters swoop low, convoys of trucks with Americans, Vietnamese and others I don't recognise, heading in all directions, not to mention the civilian traffic.

When our patrol finished this morning, we waited for an hour at the northern end of the village until the armoured personnel carriers picked us up. I couldn't help but think of Elcho Island [an Aboriginal mission off Arnhem Land], because of the way the children hung around and reacted to our presence. They asked for cigarettes and chocolate as we had breakfast and were eager to try our biscuits, cheese and bully beef. It was all smiles and light hearted and they sang a song in Vietnamese:

> Australian is Cheap Charlie
> He won't buy me Saigon Tea.

Another similarity with Elcho is the way the adults whisper among themselves as we pass, and then look at us and laugh. You don't know what they say but can't help feel you're the butt of their jokes. Many of them squat by the side of the road and watch us pass, without any expression on their faces and you get the impression that all they want us to do is leave them alone.

Actually Binh Ba is around 60 per cent pro-Communist and a few years ago was the setting for a large Australian attack, including tanks and all. The scars are still obvious on most of the houses. Several burnt-out houses remain and the surrounding area is littered with bomb craters, spent ammunition and all the rubbish of a battlefield.

During our return to Nui Dat, our APCs had to negotiate through all the local traffic which included ox carts laden with wood, straw and farm produce. The oxen don't like us either and get agitated if we get too near.

Lambretta motor scooters carry a whole family; Dad riding, Mum on the pillion seat with a baby in her arms and junior sitting on the handle bars. Somehow they manage to carry all their shopping goods too. Some Lambrettas have a cabin attached and these act as local taxis which are terribly overloaded, taking people to and from village markets. Buses, too, have people sitting inside, up on the roof, hanging off the sides and even on the rear bumper. Bicycles, hand carts and luggage hang from the bodywork and it's a wonder that the vehicle keeps its load, as it manoeuvres through all the traffic.

People walk a lot from village to village as well as to and from their fields. It all seems so casual that you sometimes forget there is a war on. They often carry very heavy loads hanging from both ends of a pole which is balanced over one shoulder. They move along at a quick pace, keeping in rhythm with the bounce of the flexible pole. It's not uncommon to see quite young kids carrying produce in this manner. It's a hard life for everyone.

The people seem to age very quickly, no doubt because of the hardships they face. The young girls are very pretty and the elderly could be anyone's grandparents, but there doesn't seem to be many middle aged ones.

A lot of the diggers distrust the locals and don't want anything to do with them. But I guess I'm a little more tolerant and can understand how tired and resentful they must be after scores of years of warfare. All of the young males will be called up to fight; whether on the Government side or with the Viet Cong – depends on who gets to them first. Every family is affected in some way and there is no guarantee that tomorrow will not bring some terror to their lives. The war is all about them and they can't escape it, so they're making do as best they can.

It would be too simple, however, to say: 'To hell with it, let's get out of here and let them sort it out themselves.' They have been trying to make a go of it for hundreds of years but something or someone always seems to spoil it for them. We've heard of some terrible atrocities that have occurred when the VC take control of a pro-Government community, so despite the hardships these people put up with on a daily basis, I have no doubt that however limited their support for us is, they prefer the stability that our presence has brought to their lives.

Enclosed you will find Chieu Hoi leaflets dropped in their millions throughout the countryside, to encourage VC soldiers to surrender. Anyone carrying these leaflets has a free pass and will be handed over to the Government authorities safely. If they bring in their weapons and equipment, or give information of value they are given cash rewards or grants of land. Some have been recruited by the military to lead them back into the VC area they operated in, to find bunker systems and caches.

I hope this letter gets to you without too much delay. However, with the postal strike in full swing I expect it may sit around in a post office for a while. Every digger returning from Vietnam is vowing to 'Punch a Postie on RTA', until the strike is over.

Thanks for sending the telegram informing me of your safe return to Adelaide. What a sneaky way of beating the postal strike.

28 February

My darling wife and son, I'm pleased to hear that you are both feeling happy and well. There's no need to feel anxious about my being over here as I'm growing in confidence and I've got a great platoon of blokes to look after me. They have only just arrived and are a bit shell-shocked, but should settle in quickly. They will need to, because we've got a four week operation planned soon. Listen to me, I'm sounding like a veteran already.

The letter from the Bidstrups was a great surprise, as was the news that Marg is expecting their first child.

I'm concerned about our OC, Major Warland. He's got some strange ways and has, on a few occasions when on exercise in Australia, questioned my leadership style and the efforts of my platoon. Now he's making similar comments about us in front of the other platoon commanders and it's becoming quite annoying. He's not what I'd call a role model, but as he's the boss I'll have to watch how I react. I'm not too worried what he says about me, as the CO, Lieutenant Colonel Grey, continues to acknowledge me in much the same friendly manner as he did when we were together at Canungra. Even so, I'm not too pleased when 'the Major' makes unfair comments about my corporals and diggers.

I'd like to think though, that we're all adults with considerable responsibility and after a year of solid training we have earned his respect. But, I think 'the Major' is from the old school and he's having trouble coming to grips with the modern generation of soldiers. He often stops our conversation by saying 'no excuses' and refuses to listen any longer. In this day and age of National Service he may find his old ways will be in conflict with many of his soldiers and some of his officers.

Our daily routine while in Nui Dat is like any other base camp:

0600 – Reveille and Paludrin [an anti-malaria tablet] Parade
0700 – Breakfast
0730 – Lines Inspection
0800 – Training
1200 – Lunch

1300 – Training
1645 – Paludrin Parade
1700 – Area Clean-Up
1800 – Evening Meal
1930 – Films
2130 – Lights Out

You ask if I need anything. Well, the only thing I could do with is pimple cream, as the humidity and sweat has aggravated my skin problem especially on my back and chest. It's not that I'm worried about my complexion, it's just that I wouldn't like to get some skin infection. You'll have to send me a whole truckload if it's going to do any good.

The weather has actually been quite cool even though the humidity is high, especially around midday to mid afternoon. The wet season will be on us in another month or two which will change the look of things around here quite a bit. Right now it's very dry and everything is covered in a fine layer of red dust.

Raylene, if you need any money let me know and I'll be able to arrange to send you some within a week of you asking, postal services permitting. I'd prefer sending you everything in my pay book or at least $50 a pay extra to ensure you don't have any problems managing on the allotment I've made to you.

5 March

Tomorrow the whole company will go out on a 24-hour patrol. It'll be the first time my blokes have been outside the wire and been on patrol with live ammunition.

We'll be going with tanks and APCs and each platoon will be dropped off at different locations to set up ambushes. Three APCs will stay with each platoon who will be about 1500 metres from each other. The tanks will stay with company headquarters, who will be in an ambush of their own.

We've worked with tanks and APCs before, so it won't be strange having these great metal monsters with us. They make a lot of noise and attract their share of enemy attention and we'd prefer not to have them so near, but then again, they have a lot of extra fire power, which is welcomed. Unfortunately, the 'tankies' have had a hard time of it lately, with mines and being fired upon by rocket propelled grenades, so I'd really prefer to go out on our first operation without them.

7 March. We're back from our first patrol and while nothing exciting in the way of enemy activity occurred, we have a good story to tell.

The armoured column, with us inside the APCs, made its way for five kilometres through scrub and rubber plantation. At a designated spot my APCs broke off and as quietly as possible disappeared into a patch of thick scrub. We stayed there for two hours while I worked out my orders and plan for the ambush. I went on a reconnaissance and sorted out the lay of the land before giving my orders and getting everybody prepared. We waited till last light before moving into the selected position, which was the junction of three tracks.

It only took half an hour to prepare the position, which included setting our machine guns and claymore mines to cover the tracks. We then made little tracks between each group so that at night we could move to and fro without noise. Finally, we each set out a blanket on which we would lay and put our ammo and grenades within reach. At 7.30 on the night of 6 March, 6 Platoon was ready and waiting for its first lot of unfortunate enemy.

We have been given section radios (commercial walkie-talkies) to trial. These allow me to communicate with my section commanders, without having to move about too much.

For the first two hours the whole platoon was alert, but from 10 pm until sunrise we had a roster whereby two people in each area were awake and on gun duty. That made at least 10 people ready for action at any time. If any enemy was to come by, the claymores were to be fired (this would wake everyone who hadn't been warned of their presence). Each machine gun would fire 200 rounds into its designated area and every rifleman would fire 20 rounds into their areas of responsibility. In addition, three soldiers armed with 40 mm grenade launchers would fire several rounds into likely escape areas. The APCs who were covering our rear area were to be used to follow up the demoralised enemy, should that be necessary. So the stage was set. I felt sorry for any poor bastard who came into our area.

At about 2200 we heard an unfamiliar sound. Those who were able to sleep were wakened and we lay there with tingling skin and sweat forming on our brows. A familiar smell came from the track only 10 yards to our front. Corporal Riddett spoke quietly to me on the section radio:

> 'Did you hear that?', he asked. 'Yes', I replied, 'Keep very still. Spring the ambush when you're ready.'
>
> Then a few minutes later he spoke again: 'I can see movement. It's coming toward me.'
>
> At 2230 I whispered over the radio: 'How are things, anything to report?' 'It's OK', he replied, 'It's gone.'

So ended our meeting with a tiger. Only four and a half feet long, but a tiger all the same. It wasn't till some time after that I recognised the smell as that which comes from the big cats cages at the zoo. It apparently came right through our position and eyed off Corporal Riddett and his mate for a few minutes before casually moving on its way.

Although I didn't see it, I could smell it very strongly. That's all that disturbed us during the night, but I guess it's just as well. By 0600 we had gone from the area, leaving the friendly bush to the tiger and her/his mates. Below is a diagram of the ambush.

By the time you receive this letter the whole of 7RAR will be out in the north-east of the province on our first battalion operation, which is to last about six weeks.

Your letters tell me that you've been keeping very busy. I'm wondering if you don't find work in Adelaide will you be heading home sooner?

I've been swamped by your letters. Seven in such a short time. I'm really being spoilt.

I'm very happy and well, although I miss you terribly.

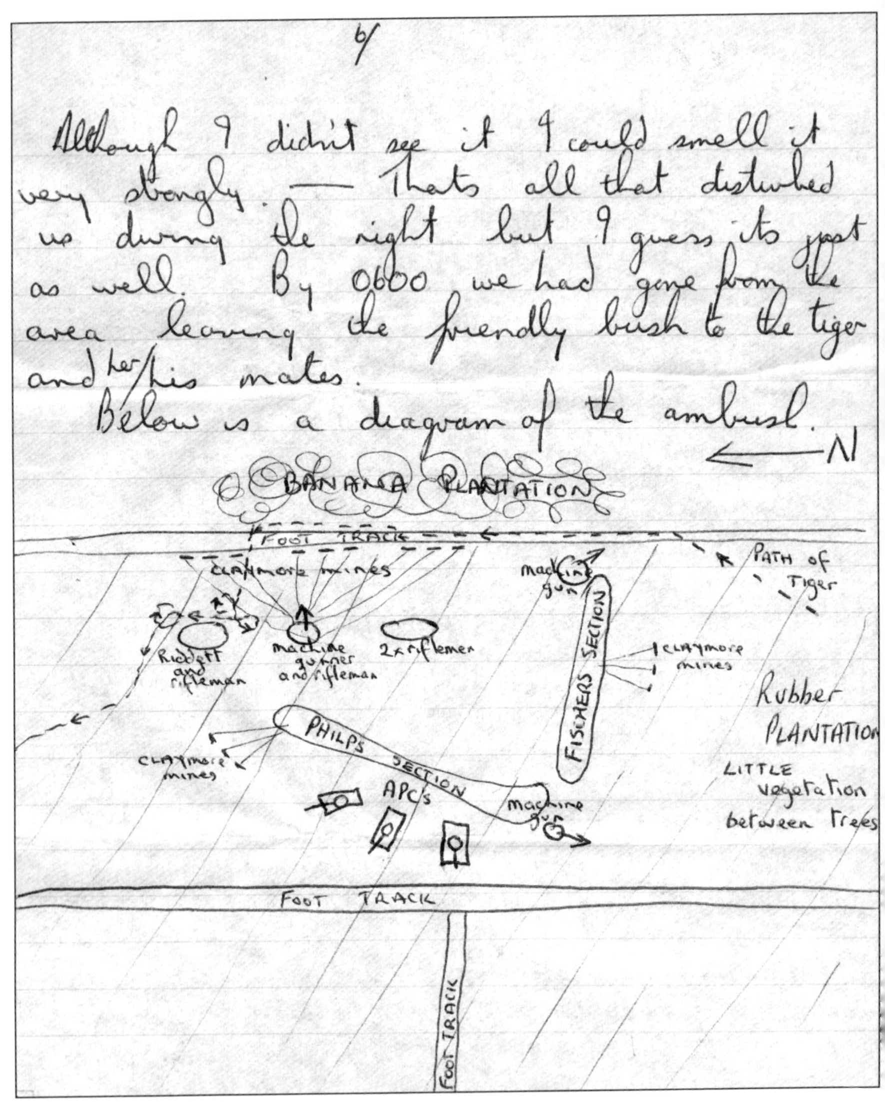

6/

Although I didn't see it I could smell it very strongly — Thats all that disturbed us during the night but I guess its just as well. By 0600 we had gone from the area leaving the friendly bush to the tiger and her/his mates.

Below is a diagram of the ambush.

6 March

Dear Pop, very soon 7RAR will be going bush on its first big operation. Everybody is anxious to get on with it, especially since the other battalions are having such a hot time.

8RAR has had a very rough time of it and since I've been here have lost 16 killed and 30-odd wounded. They've been in the Long Hai mountains, a bad area for mines and booby traps, but are taking the fight right up into the VC stronghold and are hitting them very hard. We've been told that the Government has ordered that their operation be stopped, because the casualty rate is too high and it's causing too much adverse publicity. What a way to run a war.

The VC and North Vietnamese Army are really on the run in Phouc Tuy. All reports show that we've caused heavy casualties and disrupted their supply lines so much, they have had to move further north. Their morale is pretty low too.

Every night we go to sleep with the sounds of artillery firing. The 155 mm and the 105 mm guns fire several rounds at any place, at any time, to harass the enemy and keep him on the move. All day the artillery and mortars give support to the patrols and armed helicopters (gunships) and jet fighters strafe and bomb enemy positions. The sounds of war keep ringing in my ears.

There is no doubt that we're winning the war militarily. However, I wonder whether our politicians can sustain their part of the bargain. There are no votes to be won from this kind of war and I can't see any of our illustrious leaders having the guts to continue their support for us, when so many people are against it.

Don't think that we are involved in the type of actions you read about in the papers or see on television, because most reports have nothing to do with Australian activities in Phouc Tuy Province. Further north the huge American war machine is seen in all its glory. They move in force, looking for trouble, asking to be hit, so that they can bring in all their fire power to overwhelm the opposition. We on the other hand, use jungle fighting tactics, patrolling and ambushing in small groups; taking control of the countryside so the enemy is restricted in their movements.

After all of our thorough training, it is quite funny to see how the Yanks have to resort to comic books to get the message across to their soldiers about keeping their weapons clean. With each M16 rifle issued, they provide a booklet which has a big, busty blonde in skimpy clothing, showing how to strip, clean and assemble the weapon. She reminds me of a character from *Li'l Abner* [an American cartoon series]. What a laugh. I can imagine what the regimental sergeant major would say if it was suggested that we should follow the same idea for our weapons training.

The Australian military are better trained for this kind of warfare, are doing an extremely good job and I'm proud to be part of it. It's going to be interesting to see how we go when we get into our first real action. I'm confident we'll all handle the situation well. I feel we will know in the next few weeks.

7 March

My darling, I've just come from the open-air theatre after seeing a film. I can't remember its title but the theme tune is haunting me. It brings to mind a long, white sandy beach, blue skies, wild surf crashing and waves rolling swiftly up towards the shore. I picture the wind blowing your long, dark hair across your face as you make your way slowly along the beach. Periodically, you stop and gaze out to sea. The relentless waves swirl about your feet and wash away your footprints from the sand. It is such a lonely scene.

I remember the wonderful times when we were alone. I mean before we settled down. Our wandering days, when our love was new. I feel terribly alone at this moment and I long to be with you. I want so much to tell you how much I love you. How much I hate being without you.

The film had a few love scenes that were very real for me. Not a lot of talking, no fancy words, just a silence that explains everything.

Darling, I felt that I had to write. Perhaps it's pre-op nerves, but right now I hate this place for causing us to be apart.

If only I could hold you tight, kiss you, feel your body and love you as I've never done before. It's times like this that I feel so awful about the days I've wasted. Remember that when I go into my quiet periods, I don't mean to hurt you. I feel so locked up inside and I don't know how to escape from the loneliness I create for myself.

Why can't I express my love for you more clearly? To love you is my only aim. To make you happy and care for you and M-J is all I want to do with my life.

Now, as I go to bed I'll try to remember how we lay together and made love so easily on that last night. How I long to be with you now. If I feel this way now, how can I survive 12 months without you.

You mean everything to me. You are the only one who helps me to bear what's going on here. All I see, all I hear and all I do is involved with aggression. You are my only link with our real life, our beautiful, peaceful days at home.

Please think of me tonight and every night for the next six weeks. Watch the moon and think of me because I'll be looking at the same moon and thinking of you.

16 March

Just a short note written during a break, while waiting for re-supply. All is well, although I'm feeling tired, dirty and a little frustrated. Our first five days on this first operation has proved fruitless, except for a few unoccupied bunker systems and three enemy who were very lucky to escape unscathed.

It's very difficult for me to find time to write as we're always on the go. However, as we get re-supplied every three days, it will give me a chance to jot down a few words and get the letter sent back to Nui Dat by chopper, where they will post it off to you.

6 Platoon is working very well. I could ask no more of them.

I hope all is well at home. I got your letter three days ago and I'm not sure whether I can arrange any money for you till I get back to the Dat and right now I don't know when that will be. The photos of you and M-J were great but unfortunately, because I've had to carry them with me, the sweat and humidity have ruined them.

18 March

This is a strange place to write a letter to you, but as it's a half hour till stand to, I'll jot down a few lines. Actually, 6 Platoon are in ambush on the Song Rai, a large river running north/south in the eastern part of the province.

We found an enemy water and crossing point which has been used by about six people in the last 24 hours, so we'll stay here till 0800 tomorrow to see if anyone else comes along.

We've been patrolling for eight days now and have covered a hell of a long way but as yet have only come across signs, thatched resting places and some bunkers. We've demolished the huts and bunkers and are hoping these latest signs will bring us in contact with the enemy. 7RAR has yet to open its account and everyone is a bit edgy. This operation is due to go on for another four weeks and it'll be a relief when the first action comes.

I received your letter on our last re-supply and am anxious about your financial position because I'm not sure if I can help you until I get back from this operation. I'll see if someone back at the Dat can arrange to get something to you. The trouble is that it takes so long to get anything done when we're out bush. I pray you can manage until I get something to you.

Thank M-J for writing his few lines. I'm afraid that after I read your letters I have to burn them so somewhere deep in the jungle of South Vietnam, the remnants of your letter lies in the brown dust. Actually, I use the ash to blacken my face and help with my camouflage, so probably all your dear words are embedded in the pores of my skin ... how romantic. I'll seal this letter with a loving kiss and hand it to the pilot tomorrow.

19 March

This won't be the neatest or cleanest letter, my love, as I'm balancing my notepad on my rifle butt and as I haven't washed in 10 days, my hands are leaving greasy marks all over the paper.

Nothing eventuated from our ambush at the river crossing last night and I was able to get my last letter off just a few minutes ago, when the chopper came in with our rations. We don't need any water brought in this time because we're next to the river. He brought in some extras that certainly have raised our morale ... an orange, a can of soft drink and a frozen carton of milk for each person.

I received another letter from you and I'm amazed how quickly

M-J is growing. I'm afraid he won't know me at all when I get home. How long do you intend staying in Adelaide? You seem to be pretty busy. Hope you don't tire yourself out.

I've arranged for our adjutant to send you $100 and he's already got back to me saying it's on it's way to you. Better service than a bank!

We'll be heading off shortly in a northerly direction. The boys are getting tired, mainly due to the heat and humidity and the fact that Charlie keeps avoiding us. Shouldn't be long though. North of us there was a large contact last night. I suspect it was an American unit in the neighbouring province. We could hear the firing and explosions going on for hours.

Time goes very fast out in the bush. We were standing to at 0500 this morning and it's now 1400. All we've done is secure the landing zone, receive our re-supply and are now waiting for the chopper to return to backload the rubbish and unnecessary items. When that's over, well move off 1000 metres and set another ambush for tonight.

We've had one incident involving Karl and Doug's platoons who were moving in the same direction about 500 metres apart. 5 Platoon saw movement across a clearing and began firing. They'd fired about 300 rounds before it was realised it was the other platoon. The result was two shaken up platoons and one lad with a bullet scar across his left cheek and the tip of his nose. I'm pleased to say that my group are still pretty calm. They've kept their heads whenever there have been some jumpy moments.

Another platoon in another company fired 1000 rounds and called in 20 rounds of artillery on movement to their front, one night. In the morning they found one very large, very dead, porcupine. It may seem unprofessional for these things to happen, but it gets scary out here, keeping in mind that Charlie is around in groups of five to 50.

When we found some bunkers the other day (6 Platoon has found four systems, each of about 10 bunkers) we were inside the system before we knew it. If anyone had been there we'd have been in some strife, however we've learnt by this and know how he sights his bunkers and where to expect them He's very good at camouflage … then again everything is so dry right now and the ground is covered by three inches of dead leaves, that it would be easy to conceal anything.

The following are a few thoughts and my impressions of Vietnam …

Vietnam is Phouc Tuy. It is the Song Rai on my right and the grassy clearing on my left. It is the bamboo thicket to my front and the palms to my rear. At night it is the cicadas and frogs but always, day or night, it is the sights and sounds of war.

Vietnam is a million silver stars in a black sky, framed by the dark shadows of tree-tops. Night-time is a time for thoughts of home and peace. It's the only time that you feel so very lonely.

Vietnam is a whispered joke in an ambush position. A smile and a silent laugh when your mate gets hopelessly tangled in a bamboo thicket or stumbles into a nest of green ants and struggles to get clear of the thousands of swarming, stinging insects, without making a sound. The understanding, when the faces before you reflect your own tiredness and frustration.

Vietnam is hot, dirty, sweaty, smelly bodies in torn, untidy, ill-fitting green clothing.

Vietnam is unfriendly. Everything seems to be covered in sharp thorns, growing just so it can grab and hold, tear and cut, leaving fine splinters that soon fester in arms, legs and faces.

Vietnam is something scampering across the jungle of dead leaves, sudden fluttering movements from the tree-tops and a muffled cough from a darkened form in the undergrowth.

Vietnam is the sound of cracking bamboo, which reports like a rifle shot any moment of the day or night. It's the sound of bushes, grasses and branches being carefully parted to let a darkened form pass quietly through. At night it is the sight of fire-flies in the darkness, flashing their torch light tails and convincing you that they are a column of enemy making their way through the jungle, with the aid of small lights.

Vietnam is … This one will be left until our first action or perhaps on the final day here, as I pack my bag and climb on the truck that will take me home.

What is the food like? Back at Nui Dat it's OK. Plenty of fruit, and lots of potatoes and all kinds of meat. Unlimited fruit juice and milk. In the bush it's what you make of it. We get one 1-day Australian pack and two 1-day packs of US rations to last the three days between each re-supply. The Aussie pack consists of three tins of meat, with packets of hardtack biscuits which taste like straw.

It's very filling and together with a pack of rice, some margarine and cheese and a tube of jam you can make quite a decent meal of it. The brew material (coffee, tea, sugar and condensed milk) are worth their weight in gold.

The US rations consist of nine tins for one day which is far too bulky and heavy for our patrols, but all the same they provide an excellent assortment. Their tinned fruit are a collectors item and the tinned turkey, chicken and ham beats our corned beef hands down. Their brew material is lousy. So we mix and match with the best out of each.

Weight is the main problem. We're carrying up to 80 pounds on our backs and in this climate and the distances we travel, it's very telling. I'm carrying eight water bottles, three to four days rations, 12 magazines of ammo, assortment of webbing, knife, bayonet, secateurs, small shovel, maps, compass, codes, notebooks, plastic explosive, spare socks and bedding, not to mention my rifle. Pity my poor signaller, he has to carry the radio and spare batteries, as well as all the usual gear.

Habits are hard to break, so I hope after a year of living like this, when I'm back home, I don't grab my shovel and head out to the backyard every time I want to relieve myself. Squatting over a 'cat hole' is much simpler than going to the little room. Standing anywhere and pissing, is very easy and takes no time at all. It's all done so very casually. To live in the bush you have to live with it and that means no comforts and no embarrassment.

Sleeping is the same ... spread out your ground-blanket, lay down and close your eyes. Easy. It's only what crawls over you during the night, that takes some getting used to.

20 March. Another long night with no results. We ambushed a

sandy corner of the river. It was a good position but all to no avail. While we're still on our own, 4 and 5 Platoons are with company HQ west of us, all heading north.

It's now 1300 on the twentieth and we've been on the move all morning. We've seen quite a few good signs. Two tracks (really they are foot pads) linked up and followed a creek towards the river. I'll send out a recce group soon, to follow the tracks and find a good position for tonight's task.

Night of the twenty-first. Our ambush position was a success in layout only. No one came, however it was such a good position and obviously a well used area that 4 Platoon and company HQ are there now, while we are another 1200 metres north. I'm trying to write this by moonlight so please excuse the scribble. This afternoon I decided to boost the platoon's flagging morale, so we stopped an hour early and as tactically as possible, organised a wash in the river. Well not so much a wash as a chance to sit for a few minutes in the cool, still water and scrape off some of the grime with the rough river sand. It was very welcoming after almost two weeks without any kind of a wash. Six blokes at a time sat up to their necks for 10 minutes, while the rest kept guard. It would have been quite pleasant had it not been for the war.

Tomorrow is our re-supply day but as we are in very thick jungle we will have our gear dropped from tree-top height. That means we won't be able to backload anything, including this letter.

Last night we had a quiet time, just harboured up in the jungle without worrying about ambushing.

I'll finish this letter now because there's a chance that they will winch our supplies to us tomorrow, so I may be able to get some gear back out. If so, I'll try and send this letter out.

I love you so very much. I hope that these coming 11 months go quickly. Love from somewhere deep in the jungle on a very moonlit night.

Your lonely soldier.

22 March

My darling, the chopper arrived at 1030 and dropped our supplies from 50 feet. We received three days rations (tins bounce, you know) plus a handful of bread crumbs (rolls ... don't) and a cup full of orange squash (oranges bounce too, but don't keep their shape) and last of all our mail. It took an hour to gather all the letters which scattered across the canopy after the sandbag they were in split open and the downwash from the rotors spread them to every corner of the countryside.

We are now in the process of burying 20 sandbags of rubbish and unwanted rations (we tear open the packets and puncture the tins, so the Viet Cong can't use it).

Your letter arrived and you didn't seem too happy. If it's money worries I'll try and send some more as soon as I can. You don't seem to be enjoying your work so far. I hope by the time you receive this letter things have improved.

It was beaut hearing of M-J's latest activities. I bet he's being terribly spoilt by all his grandparents, uncles and aunties.

Things have been very quiet and the pace has slowed down since the enemy signs have become less. We've been moving in thick jungle for a day and a half. It's much better than fighting a path through the bamboo scrub, even if visibility is down to 15 feet. Tonight thankfully, the strain is off a bit because we have harboured away from the river and unless Charlie stumbles over us, we don't expect any action.

At times I feel that this is all so unreal ... I expect to head back to camp at Holsworthy any day and mark down another exercise as completed. We've been out for almost two weeks now and when you think that this is only one quarter of the time we'll spend on this operation, the reality of the time remaining for the whole tour has yet to hit home. It's a bloody long time to be away from you and M-J.

23 March. Another lazy day. We only moved 700 metres as we had to wait for another company to get into position up north.

The worst part of all of this is the constant sticky feeling of grime oozing from every pore, of perspiration dripping from your body and saturating your clothes, making it all very uncomfortable. Pimples are a constant problem especially on my shoulders and across the small of my back where the pack and webbing rubs. My copper dog tags are leaving a green stain on my chest and the front of my shirt.

Our medic, Private Ryan, is very busy treating ticks, bug bites and the runs. Splinters, which cause small festering sores and headaches brought about by the heat and exertion are also a problem. I've remained free of all illnesses, but am feeling very tired.

It's now 11 minutes to 3 pm, I wonder what you are doing right at this minute. If I knew, it would make things easier to bear. I guess this is part of the hardship they talk about. When I get time to dream about you, I see you on the front steps of our home, with M-J crawling on the lawn and trying to turn the tap on and off. I suppose he'd be able to do that quite well by now.

My dreams are silly ones, like yours, and are quite mixed up; but I do dream of you. I'm sure the good fairy will grant me my wishes one day in the not too distant future.

The scribble on the bottom of this page is an encoded position sent to me by Karl – 'fposvgxh' – which means he's now at grid reference 582 745. If you look at the map in the spare room you'll see where he is, right at this moment.

The next day. I'm in a poor mood and I'm getting tired of it all. One of my blokes is being sent home on compassionate grounds in a couple of days, so I'll get him to drop off this letter when he gets back to the Dat.

28 March. We have all come together to regroup and receive new orders, in a fire support base called Anne. This is a dug in position about 500 metres square surrounded by barbwire and occupied by six 105 mm howitzers and six mortars and a company of infantry. The base provides us with artillery and mortar fire support when we are in the bush, especially when we're a long way from our main support base, Nui Dat.

As we entered through the wire we were instructed to drop our gear, take all valuables out of our clothes and strip off. We then had to dump our clothes in a heap and get straight into the showers they had set up for us. After that they gave us a new set of greens, underwear and socks and fed us in great style on 'hot box' meat and potatoes, a quart of milk and two cool drinks. I'm not sure what they did with our dirty gear but if it didn't crawl away by itself, I wouldn't be surprised if they just dug a hole and buried it. It was very tattered, dirty and smelly (as were we), and that's probably why they had us go through all of this well away from the fire support base troops.

It was a great relief to have a full night's sleep too, without having to worry about ambushing and doing machine gun and radio picket. We're now sitting around a landing zone waiting to be picked up by choppers and flown into a new area for the second part of our first operation.

Our last two weeks were not fruitful, except for finding a few bunker systems, so we're changing areas and have been told to take our time and get results.

We've heard that our Government is considering withdrawing all troops from South Vietnam. This hasn't gone down too well with most of the blokes. Even though at this stage it's just talk, most of us want to see out the whole tour. If we pull out, all the effort and sacrifice over the years will have been to no avail. What a waste of young lives. [Two years later in 1972, the last of the Australian troops would depart with 49,211 having served, 3131 wounded, and 501 killed.]

The days are going pretty fast here in the bush, but I'm finding them physically and mentally demanding.

The choppers are arriving but I'm on the last slick out, so I'll have a little more time to finish this letter. I'm sorry I couldn't send M-J a birthday card, or you and the folks an Easter greeting. I've received cards from your family, so please send them my best wishes.

Your work at the babies home seems a drag, but I'm pleased you like that other job. How long do you expect to stay in Adelaide?

This paper comes from my field notebook. You never know what I'll be writing on next. I've even tried the ration pack toilet paper, but it's Government issue and isn't any good for the job it is supposed to do, let alone being used as writing paper.

I'll have to go now ... just in case you want to know what's in store for me in the next few days, check out these grid references on your map in the bedroom: 558 674 to 571 670, to 573 707 to 577 731 to 582 750 to 578 756 to 580 772.

Night of the twenty-eighth. We landed OK and immediately moved off about 1000 metres into an ambush position, which is covering a creek and track crossing.

Midday of the twenty-ninth. The days are very hot and humid and as we sit here among the bamboo, ants and flying insects, I'm perspiring so much that even my trouser legs are wet. Each day there are more clouds in the sky and they reckon it'll be raining in a month.

Water is usually our main problem, but right now we're only 200 metres from a creek, so we can replenish our bottles each day. The whole company is separated about 1000 metres between platoons and we're sitting and waiting. I've now got a track to watch but it doesn't look very promising. Intelligence reports say that all major enemy units have split into groups of two or three. This makes it difficult to be at the right spot at the right time. However, nights are pleasantly cool and I often stay awake till 10 watching the stars and moon and listening to the sounds of the bush. It's a nice time to think of home and other pleasant things.

Night of the twenty-ninth. We moved again, under orders from the company HQ. This time 1400 metres south to a large clearing. It looks very promising but has added a problem ... one of water. We'll have to move every day to and from the creek to get our supply and the movement may compromise our position. What I might do each time is move to the creek and return to a different part of the clearing and ambush in a new spot.

Our next re-supply is on the first, another three days of rations. We all look forward to our little luxuries; the mail, milk and soft drinks.

It's now 7.30 and getting dark. I'm thinking of you constantly and I love you so much, darling. At this time I also think of M-J, our parents, relatives and friends. Everything about home seems so secure and peaceful. Even the bad times don't seem so bad after all.

Another day. It's just as well we're flexible. It's now 5 o'clock on the afternoon of the thirtieth, and the company is complete and we will be receiving new orders in an hour. Apparently the commanding officer wants us further north quick smart, so we all moved to this central location. 6 Platoon moved 2000 metres through some very difficult terrain in one hour, in the heat of the afternoon; so we were given permission to bathe in the creek (swift flowing, clear water and two feet deep). Now we have settled down and I've had a huge meal of spaghetti and mince (US rations) and three mugs of Australian coffee.

After tomorrow morning's re-supply we'll be moving north as a company. I hope we stick by the creek because eight bottles of water doesn't last long in these conditions.

I'll end this letter now and have it go back to the Dat in the chopper tomorrow.

All my love and thoughts are with you.

PS I reckon I'm losing weight because I buckle my trousers on hole 4 now instead of 1.

PPS Happy Birthday to you, Happy Birthday to you, Happy Birthday dear M-J, Happy Birthday to you.

Happy Birthday Wishes to my son on his First Birthday . . . Sorry I'm late.

31 March

Dear Mum, sorry I've left it so long to write but as you can imagine, it's a bit difficult to find the time when we're on the move so much. I've been writing to Raylene quite a bit, so I hope she keeps you informed of my goings-on.

It's very hot and humid but I'm pleased to report that we're all handling it very well. Morale is high and despite a few problems, we're settling into the task.

Last night 7RAR had its first success when 3 Platoon of A Company ambushed and killed two VC. It has taken three weeks of hard slog to get this result and we are now all on our toes, as we expect this will be the start of some major activity.

Right now we are about four kilometres inside Long Khanh Province and involved in a task force operation which includes all Australian battalions and some Vietnamese units. It's been an interesting, tiring, hot, frustrating, thirsty, dirty, unrewarding and at times boring, operation.

We went 19 days without a wash or decent clean-up, until an opportunity came to bathe in a creek. It was a most wonderful experience.

So far the platoons have been independent and moving about 1000 metres apart. We come together now and then, as we are now, awaiting helicopter re-supply (in about two hours time) after which, we'll split up again for another three days. I prefer it this way because you can plan your own tactics and be more independent than when you're with company HQ and two other platoons.

Thanks for all your news. I'm a little sorry to hear that Rob and Greg are hanging up their shanghais for long hair and lace. At least Peter is keeping the traditions going.

It reminds me of my younger days at Waymouth Street, when I first got rid of my pets, lost interest in 'my gang', bike racing and bitsers and found that I was attracted to girls. Warn the boys that shanghais are less trouble.

Give my love to Grandma and Grandpa. When I'm resting at night I often think of life back home; peaceful and contented. I think of them because their lives represent a good, long and loving life; a real pioneering story, one full of struggle and heartaches and yet one which achieved so much. They can look back on their lives with pride and savour many wonderful memories. I only hope I can be like them, when I'm their age.

This country is strange. I haven't seen a lot of it or its people, but we've flown over it, travelled through it, slept on it, fought in it, and crapped on it. It's hot, humid, thorny, prickly and a wild, cruel place. It's also very beautiful, but unfortunately, we don't have a lot of time to admire the countryside.

I must sign off now because the postman (Possum, is the name we give to the helicopter) is due soon and we will be on our way once again. It's been a pleasant opportunity to spend some time writing to you. Till next time.

Ooroo.

1 April

I'm not in Phouc Tuy any more, my love, I'm in the province to the north called Long Khanh. We walked here yesterday covering 4500 metres in three hours, again in the heat of the day. B Company is part of a 7RAR block (southern) while 6RAR blocks to the north and South Vietnamese forces block the west. Two companies of 6RAR will sweep through the area today and tomorrow and our job is to hit any enemy trying to escape from them.

We were moved on very quick orders and my feet are still throbbing from the pace. Right now I've only got 10 men with me. All the others are with company HQ, 400 metres away preparing a landing zone for the mortars to be flown in today.

My breakfast consisted of five cereal blocks, made into a porridge and a tin of US apricots, a mug of Australian tea and four US biscuits covered in peanut paste. This made up for my dinner last night which was a block of chocolate and a mug of coffee.

The weather seems to be getting worse. I hope we stay in this position for a few days to give us a chance to rest. We've been constantly on the go since it started and the pace has been so hectic in the last few days, we're all starting to feel a bit washed out.

I wouldn't be surprised if this operation finished in about 10 days because we've heard that B Company has been booked into the Badcoe Club (the Rest and Convalescence Centre, in Vung Tau) on the twelfth. We'll get a couple of days at our beachside resort, which is located on the sunny shores of southern Phouc Tuy, overlooking the South China Sea.

It's now 8.30 in the morning and the sun is already beating down on us making it very uncomfortable. Yesterday's bathe in the creek is a long forgotten memory as our perspiration and body muck sticks to clothes and I'm sure I stink as much as my signaller, who seems to be keeping his distance from me.

Last night I was on radio picket from 9.00 pm to midnight. I lay in the cool air, my burning feet smothered in foot powder and covered by fresh socks (not new ones, just the same pair I've worn for two days, but turned inside out). This means that my two pair of socks can last eight days. Anyway, I lay there and gazed at the stars and moon again. My thoughts went crazy when a plane flew over. It was very high and the sound made me remember the times I was on an exercise in Queensland. Whenever I heard one, I use to fantasise that I was on that plane, flying straight home to you. For a brief moment I really thought I was back in Australia.

It's now 10 o'clock, same day and A Coy have killed two Viet Cong. 6 RAR is into their sweep and it looks like we've got them bottled up. In the next day or two they'll be trying to sneak between our platoons who are only about 500 metres apart. The 7RAR barrier stretches for 10,000 metres and with 6RAR and the South Vietnamese forces, they'll have a difficult time of it.

It's now 11 o'clock and a Voice Aircraft has been flying over jibbering away in Vietnamese to inform the enemy that they are encircled. Actually the voices are those of VC who have given up. Those who have surrendered under the Chieu Hoi program. I must admit, if I heard my mate saying 'give up' I'd tend to consider my options.

We've been told that there is a company of women VC in the north of our area. They are fully equipped and quite a strong unit. There are a few jokes going around about getting stuck into them, but it's a bit weird to think that we could be fighting women.

Despite the jokes, I don't think any of us would want to be involved in an ambush resulting in women casualties. What a strange war this is.

It's now half past two and just this instant it began to spit with rain. That's all it did, for about two minutes. I'm sure it can't be bad being wet, because it won't be cold and it'll be a relief from the heat and humidity that we've had to put up with.

Lunch today consisted of a tin of US meat balls and beans in sauce, followed by a US date pudding, then US biscuits and chocolate and to finish off with, a mug of Australian tea.

All very satisfying and filling. When we're static like this we eat like kings. However, when we're on patrol or in ambush we'd be lucky to get one meal a day and that is usually cold.

What's home life like? It seems like ages since I've sat down to a meal prepared by a loving wife. Actually it's been 41 days if my calculations are correct and that means another 324 days to go. Shit.

Things have brightened up a bit. B Company have found a machine gun, two grenades, eight anti-tank mines and 150 pounds of explosives, hidden in caches within our area of responsibility.

2 April. It rained last night, enough to wet all clothes and dampen the top half inch of soil, but it wasn't cold. There's no breeze this morning and everything seems so fresh and cool. There are dark clouds overhead so it looks like the change we've been waiting for has finally arrived. Once again 6 Platoon is idle. Yesterday and today I've had to provide working parties for company HQ, which leaves me with only 10 men. We can't do much in the way of area searching or ambushing, so we just man the machine guns, keeping a look out and hoping something will come along to brighten our day.

Breakfast was a tin of US turkey loaf, a tin of Australian camp pie and I'm on my second mug of cocoa with US biscuits and jam. As we are next to a creek we can really indulge in a full mug of brew, however when on patrol we rarely get half a mug. It's funny how these little luxuries can make you feel somewhat spoilt.

Our next re-supply is in two days time. We call them 'maint-dems'. We missed out on our mail, bread rolls and cool drinks last time, so I hope this one will make amends. You know, when you think about it, today's field soldier travels further, much quicker, has more support and better equipment, communications, rations and accessories, than any in our history. Even so, he has the same character as those that served in past wars.

I feel there is a closer relationship between officers and their troops than ever before. When you've got a platoon of regulars and National Service, you have an interesting mix. Some of our 'Nashos' have tertiary qualifications and therefore leadership skills have to be particularly tuned to their maturity, questioning attitudes and life experiences. However, regardless of all our equipment and technology, the basic Aussie soldier hasn't changed. Private Coote was in the Boer War, at Gallipoli and Tobruk and he's now doing his duty in Vietnam.

The other day after a particularly hard four-day slog, 'the Major', in one of his moods, confronted Corporal Fischer about his section's appearance. 'Why haven't your soldiers shaved, Corporal? You look like a mob of bushrangers.' Since then, we've adopted the tag, and are now known as 'The Bushrangers'. 'Fish' has designed a plaque for us and at long last we've got ourselves a nickname to match Doug's 'Gibbon's Gorillas' and Karl's 'Metcalf's Marauders'. I don't expect the blokes to shave every day. It's a waste of water and the beard helps darken the face and therefore give some form of camouflage. We have a general clean-up every third or fourth day to coincide with our re-supply.

It's now the third of April. Nothing much has happened and as I lay here in the heat, I keep saying to myself: 'At least I'm getting paid for this.' It's boring and I'm trying to keep the blokes interested by sending out patrols and water parties, but they're getting slack and the sentries are finding it difficult to stay alert. This means a lot more effort by the section commanders and Jock Henderson, our platoon sergeant, is working overtime to keep everyone switched on.

I wish we would move somewhere, do something, get something, anything, except sit around like this.

I wonder what the Hit Parade tunes are nowadays. It's been over a month since we've listened to a radio. I was thinking last night of the tune *Love is Blue*. Remember how we first heard it in the train, coming home from Alice Springs and how I described the picture of a horseman riding across an open field, that it brought to my mind.

Well, I've now got another scene to go with the tune ... The large, international jet liner takes off from the Saigon airport and as it lifts gracefully into the clear blue sky, the tune begins ... 'Da Da, Da Da Da Da'. Next you see the jet from the clouds above, as it makes it way over a vast landscape ... During the part where the harpsichord goes ... 'Deedle, Deedle', you see me in the plane looking very tired and drawn, but with an air of expectation. I gaze out of the window at the clouds and think of the one I love, the one who I'm flying home to. Finally the aircraft begins its descent and taxis slowly towards a large terminal where only two people stand. A woman with long dark hair holds the hand of a small blonde-haired boy of about two. The tune continues and fades as the passenger, the only one on the airliner, alights and slowly walks towards them. At last he is home.

I'll close now my love with all my love and kisses.

PS

Take the misery of loneliness
The tears of sorrow too
Add the sadness of a parting
And a pinch of missing you
Stir them all together
And keep them in your heart
Now you know just how I feel
Since we've been apart.

Chapter Four

Changes

9 April–8 June 1970

9 April

My darling wife, we arrived back from the first op on the seventh and I was extremely pleased to get back and settle into base camp routine again. Well, not so much the routine, just the opportunity to get a full night's sleep and regular meals, without the constant pressure of patrolling, ambushing and wondering what was waiting around the next bamboo thicket.

The last week tended to drag by because we were stationary for most of the time and I was beginning to have problems with my health. I was getting stomach cramps and pains and headaches that came and went throughout the day and night. My section commanders were also a handful at times, as they were getting a bit fed up with the inactivity and tended to slacken off a fair bit. The whole platoon were feeling the affects of the weather, exertion, boredom and lack of enemy activity. I'm sure the limited ration pack diet may have had something to do with our overall malaise too.

Shortly after returning, Major Warland informed me that I was to take up the position of company second-in-command, as Owen Cairns was being moved to the Mortar Platoon and George Wenhlowskyj would come in from Support Company to command 6 Platoon. I'd like to think it's a promotion, as in Australia it holds the rank of captain, but here of course, it's just a reshuffle of people. I'll be responsible for the whole company's administration and that means bookwork and piddling jobs. I know it will be good experience, but I'll have to work more directly with 'the Major' and put up with his tantrums ... so altogether, I'm not feeling too excited about it all.

Chris Johnson was promoted to lieutenant the other day. He's doing a superb job. Ian Dunn was involved with one of the battalion's first action in which his platoon killed a VC officer and captured 190,000 piastres ($A16,000). Dave Chitty is still the same little terrier. Greg Lindsay has also had success in the field and is earning himself quite a reputation. Karl Metcalf and Doug Gibbons have also received good reports and I'm pleased that I'll still be working closely with them.

Over all, the battalion worked very well during the first operation, however we've unfortunately had our first soldier killed, a South Australian lad called Ron Smith who was shot during a contact with five Viet Cong on the evening of 3 April. We've also had a few blokes injured and some others succumb to illnesses.

B Company will be going to Vung Tau for R and C (rest and convalescence) from 17 to 19 April and I intend to relax as much as I can, so that I can approach the second operation with a clear and refreshed mind. We will be going out bush again a week after we get back, so all in all we'll have about three weeks to recuperate, iron out our problems from the first operation and prepare ourselves for the next onslaught.

I've placed my name down for R and R (rest and recreation) in November. It's a long way ahead I know, but I feel it'll be best keeping it to the latter part of the tour.

I received a letter from you yesterday in which you explained that you'd be leaving the job at the babies' home. You also mentioned that M-J hadn't been too well. I hope all is OK now. Please look after yourselves for me.

I saw a beaut film last night called *Me, Natalie* starring Patty Duke. It's almost like a female *Graduate* and I'd recommend anyone to see it because it has all the emotional stuff that makes you feel good in the end. I guess I'm just a romantic slob when it comes to these sort of films.

I'm glad that the car isn't giving you any trouble. It really has served us well and will need to do a few more trips across the Hay

Plains before this year is up, so keep me informed of any problems. We might have to consider another, if this one starts to play up.

Every now and then I get a strong urge to write verse. After a few lines I usually give up, but I haven't felt like that for a long time. I think my last masterpiece was when I was at Roseworthy College. I wonder why difficult experiences bring out the poet in me?

The days are getting longer. First light is about 6.30, whereas when we first arrived it was still dark around 7.00. Last light is about 7.30. This tells us that the wet season is pretty close. I expected the humidity to be a lot worse. It's bad, but it's not yet unbearable. The rubber trees here in camp provide excellent protection from the sun and also allow some breezes to circulate.

Thanks for the offer to send over a goodies pack but honestly, we are in need of very little. We get plenty of cigarettes, toothpaste, soap, and shaving cream from our ration supplementary packs. The food we get includes plenty of fruit, bread and the usual vegemite and jams. Perhaps I can send you something from this smorgasbord.

Let me explain some of the responsibilities I have in this new job of mine.

The Boozer Monies: During the last operation we had almost 100 cartons of cool drink delivered to us in the bush. Two drinks per-man – per-maintdem. Some of the blokes ordered special items such as boot polish, curry powder and tins of fruit. I had to go through the orders and the receipts from the canteen and find out how much to charge each man. The job took about six hours because I had to find all the maintdem lists, some of which had been misplaced.

Stores and Ammo: I have to order ammo, stores and transport for the daily training activities here in camp. I'll also have to do this for operations, but at this stage it's all very simple stuff.

Book Checking: I'm now in the process of going through numerous books, files and registers to check every soldier's personal details. This includes their regimental number, religion, next of kin, birth and discharge dates. I'm bored telling you about it. I do other 'exciting' jobs too, like being Fire Officer, which means I have to look after the fire equipment and practice the soldiers in fire protection drills.

It seems the only way to get a good job around here is to stuff up, get dragged in before the commanding officer and be sent somewhere else. The last officer to have this happen is now in Vung Tau as Duty Officer at the Peter Badcoe Club, our R and C motel. (And that was a punishment?)

Darling, I'm not very happy just now. My platoon was taken from me and I've been given a desk job that has a glorified title. My bum is sore from sitting too long at a desk and from the kicks I get from 'the Major'. The biggest thing to come to grips with is that I'm now the closest thing you can get to being a Pogo.

12 April

My love, another day of paper, scribbled notes, rushing around checking and re-checking ... and what for? I can't see any results for all this effort and yet I realise that without it the company, or at least all the diggers, wouldn't get the necessary things that make life more bearable.

Darling, the 2IC of B Company woke at 0530 and worked through till 2030, spending nearly the whole time at his desk where his tired fingers and exhausted mind must now concentrate a little longer to do the thing he has waited all day for ... to write to you.

To write to you, is to talk with you, to be with you and to love you. So come closer my love and share some more tender moments.

Life here is pretty dull, as it revolves around training and area maintenance. It seems we're just on hold until the next operation and most of us would rather be out in the bush than being cooped up here. I must admit though, it's great to be able to switch off at night without the constant worry that patrolling and ambushing brings.

Come with me now on a tour of my desk. On the right hand side I have a large khaki telephone which puts me in contact with the company switchboard (which is located in one of the bunkers nearby). Depending on the ability of the soldier on switch duty, this allows me to talk to any of the three platoons, the OC, the company sergeant major, the store, kitchen and the orderly room. If I'm lucky, I can also get onto the battalion switchboard operator who can put me through to anyone in the unit.

Next I have an ashtray, clear of butts, a half empty packet of Lucky Strike, but alas, no matches. Administration files holding many, many, many pieces of paper, together with a huge folder containing other confusing documents and forms. I've got a whole pad of carbon paper for the triplicate copies that have to be made of everything. Then I have three rulers, 15 different types of pens and pencils (all colours) and three clue boards with unlined paper and scribbled notes on each of them. These are my reminders of tomorrow's activities and tasks; things I need to do in the coming days and queries I have to chase up for the diggers about leave, pay, mail and the like. Then on this side of my desk I have a pipe and some Dr. Pat tobacco, but alas still no matches.

Right at this moment a little bug has climbed onto my letter pad and is crawling towards my pen ... I wonder if it makes its noises in Vietnamese? I think I'll christen it 'Nguo'.

I've done my good deed for the day because little Nguo had cobwebs all over its back legs and I've been able to clear them away. What an ungrateful little bug(ger), he/she has just flown off into the darkness and not even a single thank you.

It's now 8 pm (2000 hours) on 13 April and I've only just settled down following eight hours of violent illness. I vomitted so much my stomach hurts and it feels like the diarrhoea has burnt the skin off my bum. I'm totally exhausted. There are several others suffering a similar fate, including the commanding officer.

Last night I had a dream where we met, following my return from Vietnam. I can clearly remember saying: 'The time went really quickly, it seems no longer than two months.' You can imagine how I felt when I woke up. It's hard knowing that we've got another 10 months to go. Never mind darling, we'll see it through and will be the stronger for it.

I often think of you sitting in the garden at home, with

Mark-John playing nearby and wish that I could be there to share him with you. How I miss you both.

I'll sign off now. The guns are firing again.

16 April

R and C begins tomorrow, my love. We will be heading off to the sandy beaches of Vung Tau for two days of total relaxation and while there is a lot of excitement building up, I'm more concerned with arranging everything and ensuring it all goes off like clockwork. You can imagine what they'd all say if their first break was spoilt by my shoddy planning.

We haven't been given any definite orders about our next operation yet, so we won't have to worry about anything for the next few days.

I've just sent off a tape to you so you will soon have caught up with everything from my part of the world. My only complaint at this time is that I'm feeling very lonely. My letters and tapes only seem to make it worse. I know there is nothing I can do except bury myself in work and try to get through each day at a time. But my darling wife, it is getting harder. *The Impossible Dream* is playing on the radio . . . Quite apt.

Here's another verse to add to 'Vietnam is':

Vietnam is sadness, loneliness and heartache
The kind only brought about by separation
It's a land of tears. Tears that are hidden deep inside
'cause soldiers aren't allowed to cry.

26 April

R and C was relaxing, but didn't last long enough to have any long lasting benefit.

We arrived at the Peter Badcoe Club at about 1530 and had settled into the motel style rooms by tea time. The place is like those in Surfers, with a large swimming pool, bar, beer garden and an area for outdoor pictures. There are plenty of activities to keep people amused including surfing, skiing, yachting and speed boats. The shared rooms were very clean, cool and comfortable.

That night Karl, Doug and I went into Vung Tau. It's a filthy, smelly, corrupt hole. We couldn't go anywhere without being approached by men wanting to exchange MPC (the monopoly money that the Government has issued) for piastre (South Vietnamese currency), or women wanting 'boom boom'. I was approached by several young kids who said their sisters wanted 'boom boom' and when I said I wasn't interested, one of them said his brother would do it.

I was just coming to grips with the seedy side of life when five big, loud, black and chrome motorcycles ridden by white Americans, roared down the main street as if straight out of *The Wild One*. The riders were dressed in denim and leather and wore Second World War German helmets. Their passengers were local tarts hanging on for dear life as the bikes raced noisily towards some well known dive. This was my introduction to the culture being brought to this sad world by the American military. I was absolutely dumbfounded. I must say that most of the US soldiers I've seen over here leave a lot to be desired. They're scruffy, loud and act as if they are the saviours of the world. No wonder the locals don't respect them.

We couldn't even get away for a quiet drink in the best hotel in town. No sooner had we entered when we were surrounded by young bar girls wanting Saigon Tea. They were all dolled up with make-up and Western-style clothing and kept demanding that we buy them a drink. They sat next to us and acted as if they were really keen to get to know us, but their only interest was to keep ordering drinks for us, even if we hadn't finished what we already had. In the end it was just too much, so I went back to the Badcoe Club and spent the evening reading John Wyndham's *Rebirth*. The others rolled in at all hours with many weird, wonderful and funny stories to tell.

Next day was beaut. I spent my time by the pool drinking cold coke (at 5 cents a can) and going for a dip whenever the sun got too hot. The beach was out of bounds because of a rip, so I relaxed completely all day and had a very good deep sleep that night.

By 1000 the next morning we were on board the trucks heading back to the Dat. It was time to switch back on again.

Then our whole world fell in. We were jumping off the trucks back at our lines when the word came that we had an hour to get ready to move out. One moment we were joking about the Vung Tau experiences and the next we were racing to get everyone fully operational. By midday we were fully equipped and moving out through the wire on our second operation.

One moment I was feeling cool, clean and relaxed and the next I was keyed up, sweating, had 100 pounds of gear strapped to my body (we were told to carry five days rations, not the usual three) and was struggling to push through the familiar bamboo bush environment.

Major Warland was as concerned as all of us, so he called a 'company harbour' [a defensive formation] a few kilometres outside of the Nui Dat perimeter, to fully brief us. It was also an opportunity for many of the troops to sober up a bit because, as we had been expecting a couple of days back at the Dat before going out bush again, many of them were still a little hung over from their night in town. In fact, it wasn't until later that I realised that 'the Major' wasn't in the best shape either. Such was his confusion that he had left his weapon back at Nui Dat and he spent the first few days with just a knife strapped to his belt, as his only protection.

After quite some time resting up and preparing, we set off at last light to travel about 12,000 metres to a place we know as 'the Bone'. The idea was that we would move as quietly as 100 soldiers can in the dead of night, through jungle, across very rough terrain and be into the suspected enemy area by dawn, without anyone knowing.

The only way this could be done was to get the whole company in single file and just follow the leader. The leader in this case was Karl. He was responsible for getting us to the right place at the right time, so he literally led the way with map and compass and 99 of us followed. Few knew where we were or what was happening, but just followed the shadow in front, hoping that in the pitch black, he too kept in contact with the shadow in front of him. We moved along a dry creek line for quite some way but it was very hard going, stumbling over the rocks and boulders as quietly as we could. It was a very stop/start journey that had us all feeling frustrated, tired and very exposed. It would have been a real disaster if we had stumbled into an enemy ambush.

It must have been really tough to lead a group in such difficult conditions, but by first light Karl had got us to the exact position on the small bone shaped hill. Everyone was feeling very relieved, although tired and footsore.

Operation 2 has been going for seven days now and we've had some pretty scary things happen right throughout the area. There's been a marked build up of enemy activity and nearly every company has been involved in some way.

We've been involved too and at this moment are still following up a series of actions that started on the twenty-second. We've killed two VC, wounded four and captured several weapons and a quantity of documents. Unfortunately we've had one lad killed in action (Private Hughes) and another (Private Kavanagh), died in the field of suspected cerebral malaria.

Lieutenant Bob Pothoff was killed last night. He was the bloke with the tall, thin, blonde girlfriend that sat next to us at the Farewell Mess Party at Holsworthy. He was in an area well to the south of us, when the APC he was in hit a mine.

Karl has been sent back to Nui Dat after catching a bit of shrapnel in the bum. He's OK, but can't sit down. He'll be back with us in a few days. Three others have also gone back with minor wounds, so I've had a lot to do with bringing in choppers and completing the required forms that result from these kinds of incidents.

It's all been a bit of a shock to the system. To be one minute relaxing beside a pool with a can of coke and the next laying in a stinking hot, bamboo jungle with an M16 in your hand. It's times like this that make you realise that this is the real thing.

The days are extremely hot and humid and everyone is caked with sweat, grime and filth. My job is much the same out here as it is in camp. I miss not having any soldiers. I take care of re-supply, casualties and the general demands of 100 men in a war zone. Everything from providing ammunition to getting advice on how to treat venereal disease in the field. Still, I'm sticking to it despite my own personal feelings or the demands of an ungrateful boss.

Now that I'm with company HQ, I tend to eat more and because I'm less active, I feel I'm getting fat and lazy. I've even had time to compose this poem:

In Vietnam, the land of hatred
There's a soldier serving there
His face is gaunt, his features haggard
His eyes reflect a saddened glare.
Although this soldier is only twenty
He's seen a lot of life this year
He's witnessed death and caused destruction
He knows what's meant by pain and fear.
Many months of dreary working
Patrolling, searching, constant strain
Dirty, sweaty, unhappy boredom
Wondering when *it* will come again.

Dreams of home dashed every morning
Long and dreadful days ahead
Times of danger best forgotten
Feeling nothing for the dead.
There is something you must remember
Forget the stories that you've heard
There's no glory for the soldier
Who thinks this war is so absurd.
There's a saying in Vietnam
Comes from the diggers, I've heard tell
'When I die I'll go to heaven
'cause I've spent my time in hell'.

30 April

It's only 20 past seven in the morning. I've already eaten (a US date pudding, eight biscuits with peanut butter and a mug of tea) and I've cleaned my rifle and packed my gear. Now it's just a matter of waiting to see what the morning Orders Group brings.

We got our re-supply yesterday and they continue to make us carry five-days rations. With all the rest of the stuff (ammo, water, clothes, equipment) it weighs about 100 pound. The signallers and machine gunners have to carry even more. It's a real art to lift and swing these loads onto your back, but once they're there it's just a matter of balance; keeping your pack high on your back and moving with stooped shoulders. What a relief it is to rest the pack against the trunk of a tree or better still, to sit with the full weight of the pack being rested on the ground. The difficulty then is to get yourself up to a standing position. There's skill required in this manoeuvre too, but usually it can only be done with the help of one of your mates.

The area we are in is almost the same as in our first operation. The enemy were here when we first moved in but we've pushed them south, where they've been hit quite a few times. We're expecting them to come through this area on their way back to the safety of the north.

We've found several new bunker systems and places where they could be unloading barges and pontoons from the Song Rai.

Back a few days ago, B Company was involved in quite a stoush. It all began early one morning when several enemy were seen by one of our sentries and fired upon. Their reaction was very aggressive and I can remember taking cover in a small depression, feeling very exposed to the heavy automatic fire that they were pouring into our position. Karl, in his typical fashion, grabbed his platoon and took off after them, reporting that he was following a heavy blood trail which was leading down to the river. Company HQ followed soon after and Doug's platoon went to cut-off the enemy's likely route. George's platoon remained in location, ready to back any of us up, if need be.

Karl reported that they had found the body of a VC, but as company HQ began closing up to the position another fire-fight began. Apparently the first group had carried their comrade to the river bank where he had died, so they went off to their camp nearby to get some help. They were returning to retrieve the body when they clashed a second time with 4 Platoon and quickly withdrew.

5 platoon had moved into a block position to the south and we were with 4 Platoon blocking their escape to the north. What, with 6 Platoon to the west and the Song Rai, a considerable barrier to

their east, our guess was that they were holed up somewhere in-between. Where, we weren't sure. How many, we also weren't sure.

As the morning progressed I had to recover and search the body of the dead Viet Cong and arrange to bury him. Unfortunately the ground was so hard that we couldn't dig more than a shallow grave which barely covered his body. It wasn't the most pleasant task but I was pleased that the three diggers that helped, treated the job with respect. I guess this was the first dead body they had seen and in a strange way we all felt that 'there, but for the grace of God ...'

No sooner had I completed this task when Jock Henderson, 6 Platoon sergeant, requested a chopper to take out one of his soldiers who had collapsed with heat exhaustion. I was reminded of the commanding officer's directive, following the first operation, to reduce the number of requests for air support unless it was life threatening, so I asked Jock to look after his soldier as best he could for the time being. At the first opportunity, after we had worked out what to do with the enemy situation, we would be able to call in the casevac (casualty evacuation) helicopter.

Shortly thereafter I was sent off to do a particular task and it wasn't till after that I heard that Jock, with increasing urgency, had continued to request evacuation. Finally, this was arranged, but as the chopper came in to pick the lad up he collapsed and died. Early reports are that he died from cerebral malaria which may have been picked up in the previous week.

7RAR has certainly been in the thick of things of late. There have been 13 contacts in the past 10 days. One of the platoons to the south of us, ambushed a group estimated to be 70 strong. It was thought that they were on their way to attack Dat Do.

It's spitting with rain right now which means that the wet season is close at hand. It doesn't change our efforts nor do we care much, because whether it's the dry season or the wet, we're constantly wet through with perspiration. We only moved 500 metres today, but in that short time I was soaked.

As I prepare for our next move I'm rearranging my gear. I'm carrying five days rations, eight water bottles, a small roll of bedding, 15 magazines of 5.56 mm ammo, a bandolier of 160 additional rounds, three high explosive grenades, four smoke grenades, assorted maps, papers, an M16 rifle, a knife, bayonet and a shovel. All in all, quite a load.

The webbing hangs heavy but is worn with ease
His rifle, well used, is oiled to please
Though tired and sore
He will take much more
He's an Infantry soldier and proud of his Corps
He'll grumble and bitch, but go on with his war.

Look close at this man, look deep in his eyes
See the mateship and laughter, hatred and lies
Deep down there is pain
But who is to blame
He's an Infantry soldier and proud of this claim
He'll fight to the end, 'cause that is his game.

He comes from the cities, the small country towns
An everyday lad that you meet all around
A man set apart
One who's proud of his art
An Infantry soldier who must play his part
A survivor because he has hardened his heart.

There are two types of scorpion in Vietnam. One is small, brown and gives a good sting, but isn't fatal. The other is black, a little bigger and is a killer. I was stung twice by presumably the first kind the other day. The bastard must have crawled into my shirt during the night and parked itself on my shoulder. As I was waking up I must have disturbed it, because I felt this terrible pain on my shoulder, another on my bicep and then, as I struggled to get my shirt off, I felt another on my wrist.

I don't know what kind it was because, as I shook my shirt off and it fell to the ground, the great big GP boot of my signaller stomped the scorpion into the earth. In desperation I asked the executioner to check its colour but by then there was little left. The only advice the medic could give was that if I was feeling any worse in 10 minutes to let him know. So I sat nursing a very painful arm for the next few minutes waiting to see what would happen. Nothing did, so we went about our daily duties.

We got a new recruit into the company today. A tall, fit National Serviceman from South Australia named Cornes [Graham Cornes, legendary South Australian footballer and inaugural coach of the Adelaide Crows]. I'm told he's played Aussie Rules for Glenelg, so I'd be interested if Stephen has heard of him. He will certainly be useful when it comes to the Inter-Company Sports Day.

3 May. We had another successful day. 6 Platoon came across four VC bodies (may have been from our previous encounter) and 4 Platoon had a contact which resulted in two very heavy blood trails and a quantity of equipment.

'The Major' and I had another little disagreement today. Company HQ was 200 metres from Karl when he had his contact and as we were waiting to see what support we could offer, I heard two 'whumpfs'. I took a bearing on the sounds and reported them to the OC saying that it sounded like a mortar firing from a bearing of 400 mils. He said: 'Bullshit, they're grenades being thrown by 4 Platoon.'

When Karl finally got back, I questioned him about the contact and he said they hadn't used any grenades, but thought that at one stage they were being mortared. I was going to tell 'the Major', but decided against it as it wouldn't have helped settle our relationship, which is becoming fairly strained at times.

I feel guilty whenever I write to you and all I do is bitch about this and that. I realise that you understand my plight, but perhaps I go on a bit too much. I'm sorry if I sound like a broken record but after all, my world here revolves around a small group of people, all living in one another's pockets and all feeling much the same way about our existence. We can't bitch to each other because we're all experiencing the same difficulties, so we all seek solace by writing to our loved ones and pouring out our problems. In some strange way it helps us to cope.

I've read three books lately. *Orange Wednesday* by Leslie Thomas, *Attack Alarm* by Hammond Innes, and I'm halfway through *Rabble in Arms* by Kenneth Roberts.

The first was a very enjoyable, humorous, spy-come-sex story, with the main guy an everyday, reluctant lover/hero. It would make a good film. The second is about the defence of England during 1940, from the perspective of the gunners who manned the beaches and airstrips around the country. It was an ordinary story but had a gripping finish. The present read is about the American Revolution. All the statesmen and generals are dickheads and the real heroes are those that history has forgotten. It would make my high school history-teacher turn in his grave.

Perhaps one day I'll get around to writing a book about our lives. Perhaps I will call it *A Winter's Tale*. It will be a romantic adventure story with a very happy ending.

Some time I wonder if this experience will change me and my outlook on life. Will I be a partial stranger to you and others when I settle back into normal life again? Will I be tolerant to those who know or care little about what we've been through? Who knows? Our love is strong and M-J is ours and these are the two things that will help me come through this. I'll be much thinner, I hope a lot wiser, I'll be experienced and more knowledgeable in the ways of the army and I'm sure I'll have strong views about a number of Government policies. Even so, I feel that there may be some difficulties in settling back into the routine of life in Australia. We'll have spent a year living in such basic conditions, under constant pressure and knowing that not everybody back home supports us being here. It'll take some adjustment before feeling relaxed and carefree and one of the crowd again.

The next day. Today was maintdem day … hooray. It didn't go off too well … boo. But we finished up with all our gear … hooray. But the 2IC has a headache … boo. But he'll be OK soon … hooray. Till next maintdem day … boo.

Usually four choppers bring in our supplies, each one 20 minutes apart. The time lapse gives us a chance to hand out the gear and ensure that which was ordered, arrived. Today, however, three

APCs dumped all our gear in one hit, mixing everything in one big heap. 'The Major' was in one of his moods which meant we had to clear up the mess, get everything out to the platoons and all the backload ready and loaded, in record time.

To make matters worse someone back in camp thought it would be nice if we had a home-cooked meal, so we were also left with eight large, hot containers of freshly cooked food (meat and vegetables, cake and custard, bread and jam and even an urn of tea). Just like we use to get at Holsworthy when we were doing a day-long exercise in the close training areas, but not a very practical thing to do in the depths of the Vietnam jungle.

In addition, we had 13 lads go back to Nui Dat and seven join us. Their departure and reception required the usual paperwork and administration checks.

I spent the morning scrambling to and fro, organising the breakup of the five days of rations for every platoon and getting them to come in for the hot meal, while maintaining some form of tactical security. All damaged and unwanted equipment had to be recorded and labelled before it went back and then we had to put all rubbish into sandbags, so that it to could be taken back to the Dat.

I'd be in the middle of one task when the OC would give me something of the most urgent nature to do. Well, I did it all and he must have been pleased because he didn't say anything to me for the rest of the day.

I was helping to throw the last of the rubbish bags into the back of an APC, when I realised that in all of the rush, I hadn't had anything to eat. One of the diggers gave me four slices of bread that he had saved, so I did get something in the end, but I certainly don't want to experience anything like that again.

Finally all the platoons struggled off to their new locations, under the weight of their fully laden packs and company HQ did likewise. I collapsed into my night position feeling totally exhausted. Now it's 6.30 pm and I'm feeling a little better. I hope that it's a quiet night. The last thing I need now is something major to happen.

Your concern about the VC activities is understandable, but I can assure you he's not in a position to do too much. He's been hit so hard and so often lately that all reports say he's running out of food and supplies and is exhausted (I know how he feels). We have so many patrols out and we've kept him on the run since we started the operation in April. Don't worry my love, old Charlie Cong won't be doing anything in May, except gathering nuts.

As 2IC, my job is to ensure the protection of company HQ by checking the platoon and our support section, to make sure the sentries are positioned correctly and are alert. Also, I have to keep check on who goes where and for what reason. I enjoy getting around, speaking to the troops and finding out how they're coping. There's always something happening, something being planned, someone needing something, that I'm always in demand. I'm getting to know all of the diggers pretty well. I know who I can joke with, who to have a serious chat with and when it's best to leave them alone.

There's a bird's nest, in a tree, three foot above one of our machine gun positions. In the nest are two small, bald, ugly little chicks. The mother bird comes home several times a day to feed her brood. She sits in a tree nearby and chirps madly. The diggers at first use to move away several feet so that she would go into the nest, but now she flies straight in, with no hesitation. The diggers are crumbling up bits of biscuit and putting them on the side of the nest. They've even started looking around for bugs and grubs so that the mother bird doesn't have to leave the nest so often.

Colonel Grey flies around in a Sioux Helicopter and surveys the operational areas from a height of about 300 feet. He's also flown so low over battle areas that on several occasions he's been fired at. His helicopter has been hit by enemy fire three times. I'm not sure what his pilot thinks about all of this. I wonder if they draw straws to see who has to fly with 'that crazy colonel from 7RAR'.

I received two letters from you and one from Don and Marg Albert. Darling it's so hard to respond when there's such a time lapse between you writing and me receiving your letters. These were posted on 30 April and here it is 5 May. At the time of writing you were very sad and worried. Are you still feeling the same way or has the new week brought a brighter outlook? Has M-J overcome his sore throat or is he still having trouble sleeping? I feel like I'm following my family. I'm a week behind your life.

I've booked my R and R for November and while I know your preference is for August, I don't think I can change it. I'll give it a go, but as everyone in the battalion has registered and had authorised their preferences, it will create a few problems if we start rearranging rosters. Only a certain number can go at any one time, so the only way to change will be to find someone that was scheduled in August, who now wants to go in November.

The other day I read that a certain army major condemned the bush hat we currently wear, suggesting that the slouch hat was more appropriate. 'If it was good enough for Kokoda, then it should be worn in Vietnam'. It's called a 'Hats Ridiculous' and that's what it is. It's little more than a bloody useless piece of cloth. I'm not sure who this major is or what experience he's had, but I doubt whether he's ever used a bush hat the way it's supposed to be used.

> It's tattered, torn, scarred and sometimes burnt. It's always stained with juices from the last few meals, along with grease, oil, dirt and sweat. It's supposed to be green but this varies depending on age, use and the imagination of its owner.
>
> I've seen them covered with names of loved ones, numbers representing months to go, safety pins, grenade pins and even lucky charms.
>
> It's designed to shade the eyes and neck from direct sunlight however, with ingenuity it is used by those with experience for numerous other tasks. For instance, what flannel could soak up sweat, wipe the face of dirt and grime; what serviette could soak up spilt tea or soup better; what oven glove could hold a steel mug full of steaming coffee or a hot can of luncheon meat; what pillow can give a more restful sleep for a weary head and what rag could clean a rifle, boots or even a dusty seat, better. It's also not bad at shading the eyes and neck from direct sunlight.
>
> Although it's made in the same factory as a million others, the final process consists of a heavy grinding, smashing and crumpling machine

that makes each one a different shape, so that you never see any two alike. Each one has its own personality, and somehow adopts the personality of its owner. The styles reflected vary from Cowboy, with the sides turned up; Mexican, with the front and back turned up; and Napoleon, with three sides turned up. Now and then you see one with no sides turned up and wonder what kind of person the wearer must be. Very conservative or perhaps, just wanting to make a statement?

If you pick it up by the crown and place it flat on your head you still never get two that look alike. Some diggers can even spin it on one finger, fling it into the air, still spinning, so that it falls 'flop' onto the owner's head and there it sits, comfortable, casual, but with a 'couldn't care less' attitude that just demands respect.

To own a new one is very embarrassing and you feel like a new boy at school. At nights you soak it in dirty water, stamp on it and roll it around on the floor, hoping that this will bring some respectability. But all to no avail. Then all of a sudden (you can never predict just when) it at last becomes the smelly, dirty, priceless article you've always longed for.

Sadness is losing your old faithful. One that's been through it all with you, one that's become as close to you as your rifle and sweat rag. Soldiers don't cry very often but it's too much when you lose your bush hat . . . utter sadness, hopelessness and humiliation.

One couldn't wish a better fate to one's bush hat than to lose it in the heat of battle. To know that somewhere, in some corner of a paddy field, perhaps tangled up in bamboo, lies your bush hat. One more casualty of this filthy war.

Is it possible to feel love for a piece of cloth? Well whatever it is, I feel very close to that tattered, smelly shape that lays in the dirt before me.

Do you know there's even been a hit song written about the Aussie bush hat. It was written and presented by Dig Richards back in the late 60s, after he had toured Vietnam with an entertainment group.

Well, the battalion has been redeployed except for B Company, who'll remain in the same area for the next two to three weeks. Things have gone very quiet, so all the other companies have gone into the southern areas and will endeavour to push the enemy up into our blocking positions.

It looks like this operation will go on for a few weeks yet. It's a long time to spend out in the bush and we're starting to look more like a rabble in arms, than the bright eyed, eager, soldiers that commenced this operation so many weeks ago.

Boots are unpolished and many are wearing out, greens are a reddish colour that turns black when on the move, due to perspiration. They look and feel stiff and threadbare. They are torn at the knee by the thorns, and safety pins are now holding some together.

Soldiers haven't washed for weeks. Most haven't shaved for days. Their hair is ragged and falls thickly below the ears. It's kept back from their eyes by a sweat rag that is tied around their forehead. Bush hats are secured to the head by an odd assortment of string, cloth and safety pins.

The camouflage blackened faces add to the rag-tag effect. We're an ugly, untidy looking lot. If you get close enough to look into their eyes you see tiredness, but you also see a fierce determination.

We're a far cry from the clean cut lads you saw at the Farewell Parade.

PS I'll send the photos back to you. They will get damaged if they stay over here.

3 May

Dear Dad, just a few lines to let you know what your No. 2 son has been up to.

The following action occurred on 20, 21 and 22 April.

I was just changing my position to ease the pain of some stones digging into my back when an M16 opened up with a burst. This was followed immediately by some further bursts of fire and an explosion. With a quick roll I was in a small depression with my M16 and a bandolier of 10 mags of ammo grasped firmly in either hand. The machine gun nearby began to fire, together with neighbouring M16s and self loading rifles. Despite the noise you could hear the distinctive crack of the enemy's AK47. Then other explosions (two, I think) ripped through the bamboo nearby as the enemy's rocket propelled grenades targetted our machine gun position. A lot of yelling filled the air as the platoon drawing most of the fire tried to sort things out and the OC called for information. Other machine guns opened up to support the one pinned down and give them covering fire, as they tried to withdraw back to a less exposed position.

After about 15 minutes the firing died down so a section swept through the contact area and found one AK47 and a great deal of blood.

The action had been initiated by one of our sentries who had been lying about 20 yards from our main position, observing a foot track. He saw about six enemy, dressed in an assortment of clothing, coming towards us. When the lead man was close enough he fired a burst of 10 rounds at him. The one following immediately retaliated with a burst of automatic fire and a third fired an RPG into the trees, hoping for a good shrapnel effect.

A patrol led by Karl Metcalf took off after the enemy, following the blood trail that indicated that someone had been badly hurt. The rest of the company divided into three; Doug Gibbons taking his platoon to the south for about 2000 metres, George Wenhlowskyj's platoon secured the current position and remained to see where he could best be deployed. Company HQ and the remainder followed up Karl's patrol.

We couldn't catch up with him though because he was literally running after the withdrawing enemy. We were receiving reports from his out-of-breath signaller that they were racing along a well-used track which seemed to be heading towards the Song Rai river. They would move at a cautious trot for about 150 metres then stop and listen, then set off again, just like a pack of hounds after a fox. Finally, they reached a small re-entrant only 100 metres from the Rai where they found a body of a VC wrapped in a plastic sheet. He had been shot in the stomach and head and his mates had carried him to this location, where he had died. The patrol deployed, while Karl searched the body.

In the meantime, company HQ had closed in on Karl's location but stopped about 100 metres short, to establish communications with the other platoons and with battalion HQ. We were in the process of reporting the details of our activity when all hell broke loose.

4 Platoon, B company soldiers warily search an area of recent contact with VC

Apparently while Karl was checking the VC body, movement was heard and a group of enemy were seen coming towards them, no doubt to collect their deceased friend. The section commander waited until the lead man was almost upon them when he stood up and fired, then dropped to a kneeling position and fired again, then he hit the ground and fired a third time. The result was a second VC dead and a mad scramble as the two or three others raced in all directions to get away.

The remainder of the afternoon was spent repositioning and reporting. Little did we know that while company HQ joined up with Karl on the bank of the Song Rai, the enemy were less than

200 metres away, in a strongly fortified bunker system. No doubt he was intent on keeping a low profile because he must have thought that with all the action that had occurred in the past few hours there must be a battalion of Australians in the area.

We stayed in the area for another 24 hours, while 5 and 6 Platoons searched for the enemy to the south and east. Then on 22 April the OC called it quits and directed that they come into his location in preparation for a move into another area.

As Doug's platoon moved towards us, they spotted two enemy on the bank of the river but as they were moving into an attack position they were fired on and Private Tilmouth was badly wounded in the throat. Doug pulled back from the area and called for a 'Dust Off' (a casevac chopper to get Tilmouth to hospital). Within 15 minutes he was on his way to the Vung Tau military hospital and to immediate surgery. (We've heard since that he was stabilised and is soon to be returned to Australia for further treatment.)

The OC obviously thought that this latest incident was unrelated to the previous action because he looked at me and said: 'Do you want to go and have a look?' 'Too right', I said, but was then a little concerned when he told me to take the company HQ support section (a group of six) into the contact area and check it out. By my calculations there were at least six enemy and by now they would be pretty upset. I would have liked at least two sections (18–20 men). Anyway, I grabbed an extra machine gun and as many grenades as I could scrounge and led my intrepid band into the unknown.

We had gone about 250 metres and I was feeling very uneasy, because the bush was quite thick and visability was only five metres or so. We moved in extended line with about five metres between each person and periodically we would lay on the ground and search our front for anything that may be suspicious. I was just thinking to myself that we should strike something in the next few minutes, when I noticed a very well concealed bunker immediately to my front. I signalled to the others that when I dropped a grenade into the bunker they were to open fire and blast shit out of the vegetation to their front.

As planned, the 'whoompa' was immediately followed by such a volley of automatic fire that the bush and bamboo ahead of us was ripped to shreads. The response was also immediate. Return fire from AK47s and RPGs came ripping back towards us and I was thankful that we hadn't proceeded any further than we did. I also heard other explosions that I couldn't recognise but I wasn't about to check them out any further, so I got the group to withdraw back to a shallow depression we had came through on our way in. So began a stand-off which was to last most of the afternoon, resulting in one of our lads being killed and six wounded.

A lot of diggers carry good luck charms; tokens from home or gifts from loved ones. I guess they are reminders of better times and bring comfort when you need it most. Some wear crosses, others rings around their necks accompanying their dog tags. I've heard that Cambodian soldiers wear small Buddhas on a necklace which, when they're under fire, they put into their mouths in the hope that it will protect them. I don't carry any such thing, but I tell you what: I called on my guardian angel a couple of times to help me through the day.

We couldn't see the enemy nor could they see us. You just fired in the direction of the incoming fire or the sounds of voices. It appeared that we were 30 metres from the enemy position which was spread right across our front. Their fire was coming from positions to our front and flanks and it was quite continuous. I was beginning to feel that the OC's estimate of 'just a few VC' was way out.

After only 20 minutes we were very low on ammo, so I put the grenades to good use. We have an attachment that can be placed over the barrel of the rifle which enables a grenade to be launched a considerable distance. In our case it helped to punch the grenade through the thick vegetation and get to places we couldn't have reached by throwing.

A couple of times during a lull in proceedings I inched forward with one or two to see if there was anyway we could get closer to the bunker system, but in the end I realised that such a small group would not be able to do anything, without suffering casualties. So I decided to keep up our actions from the safety of our little depression (no medals for this band of warriors).

During this fairly hectic and somewhat frightening period I felt that the unfamiliar explosions that I'd been hearing were small calibre mortars, but luckily none came close enough for me to verify exactly what they were.

During the action I kept reporting back to company HQ what was happening. When we eventually ran out of ammo, I called for help from Bushranger (Australian helicopters that are armed with machine guns and rockets). They operate in threes and once they had identified our position and I'd given them a description and a direction of the enemy, they came in at treetop height firing their mini guns (5000 rounds a minute). No sooner had one completed his pass, the second was into the action. Then the third would come in with all rockets firing. They made four passes ripping the vegetation to shreads and doing wonders for our morale.

Karl came in with some of his platoon and pushed beyond the area we had previously reached. However, they came under heavy fire and an RPG hit a tree nearby, spraying them with shrapnel. Several were hit, so he pulled back, carrying one of his lads who had been hit in the forehead. I called the gunships in again and as they went into action, we evacuated the wounded and a couple from my group that weren't feeling too good.

We had to continually mark our position with coloured smoke so that the choppers could tell where we were. Now and then we'd fire a phosphorus grenade into the area that enemy fire had come from and call on the gunships to concentrate their efforts in that location. The choppers also kept us going with ammo and smoke grenades by hovering over us and dropping these vital supplies in sandbags.

By 5.15 in the afternoon things had quietened down, with only the odd shot from either side being fired. We had been told to remain in our position and keep the enemy from pulling out because three tanks were trying to reach our location, but were having trouble with the vegetation and terrain. The plan was to attack the bunker system with the whole company, supported by the tank troop. As the day wore on it was obvious that the tanks wouldn't make it before nightfall, so the battalion commander called for a napalm strike.

We had to pull out, rejoin the company and move a safe distance while two Phantom attack aircraft came in to drop their cannisters on the area. The sound of them screaming in and dropping those dreadful fire bombs will stay with me forever. I almost felt sorry for the VC who were on the receiving end.

Throughout the night the artillery added to the devastation. These were firing from Nui Dat and a fire support base and took it in turns to hit the bunker system with all they could, in order to keep the enemy from escaping in the darkness.

At first light the company and the three Centurion tanks pushed through to the bunkers. We were expecting some kind of resistance, but within the battered and burnt jungle we found 18 newly constructed bunkers that had been occupied by at least 30 persons, numerous papers and documents, signs of wounded having been treated, a few discarded weapons, but no enemy. The darkness is his friend and he escaped because we had to wait for the dawn.

By the way, we did find a base plate position for the 60 mm mortar I'd been hearing, too.

So Pop, I've seen my first major action and I'm pleased it's come and gone. During contact a lot of emotions are involved. You don't seem to hear all the noises because you're too busy doing things like, giving orders, firing your weapon, speaking on the radio, checking your position and encouraging your mates. There's a lot of excitement and at times fear, but overall it's just doing what you've been trained to do. When it's all over the feelings of relief and satisfaction are strong.

The shock of being fired at is overcome by a mixture of natural instincts, well-trained actions and a fair concentration of adrenalin pumping through the veins. There are feelings of loss when someone you know is killed or wounded, but for the time that is pushed well back in the mind. There are even feelings toward the enemy. Mostly it is just a desire to defeat him, to get the upper hand and to destroy him and all that he stands for. That obviously means you need to kill him, but in doing so there is no real hatred towards him as an individual. I felt a little sad for one fellow, when I was burying him after one of our earlier actions, because from the papers he had I knew he had a wife and family. Again, you don't keep these feelings too close to the surface.

I haven't written any of these details to Raylene or to Mum as I don't think it would do any good for them to know just yet. I'll probably tell Raylene at a more appropriate time.

Best wishes to you and everyone, from Peter and his guardian angel.

PS I suppose you've heard by now that the Government has decided to reduce the size of our force over here. When 8RAR's tour is completed, they won't be replaced. That means that the remaining two battalions will have to cover the whole province. It was difficult enough with three battalions so will be bloody impossible with just two. Oh well, I guess this is the start of our complete pull out and handing the responsibility back to the local troops. Poor bastards, they don't stand a chance.

9 May

My love, yesterday was another maintdem day and for a while we were surrounded by the usual hurry and scurry, shouts and curses, demands and orders, dust and dirt. However, all settled down when we realised that everything had arrived and was issued out. Surprisingly, people began to smile again.

The first can of lemonade didn't even wet the sides. The second one, 10 minutes later, was a great relief. But the greatest pleasure was the cold carton of milk. What a change from the warm, chlorinated, plastic water bottle flavoured Song Rai water we have lived on for all these weeks. The company cook back in camp had also made two salad rolls for each of us. What luxury. I've no doubt that everyone will buy him a beer when we're back at Nui Dat.

I got a letter from you, one from your Mum and one from my Mum. Your Mum sent a twig of Blue Gum which I've 'stuck in my hat and called it macaroni'. Your letter as usual, was read several times before being tenderly burnt [it was policy that personal mail received in the field be destroyed]. I hope things go well for your trip back to Holsworthy and I'm really pleased to hear that your Mum and Dad will accompany you.

I bet you're looking forward to getting back to our little home. I can picture the place right now and wish I were there too. With your Mum and Dad's help you should be able to get the place cleaned up pretty quickly. That old shed can come down and a new fence would look great. Three fruit trees could be planted in the backyard and the lawn could do with a weeding, seeding and fertilising. Painting the front fence would really make the place look special. But don't try and do it all in the first few days back ... take your time.

Darling, I've said it before and I'll say it again, don't get too worried about my constant reference to my state of unhappiness. I bitch to you because there is no one else to turn to who will listen, understand and reply with tender words of encouragement. I may sound unhappy but please believe me, I'm healthy, safe and contented, although at times a little frustrated. You're my 'one who listens' and I take great comfort from knowing that I don't have to keep my feelings and burdens to myself.

Well darling, for the past week or so company headquarters has sat in little holes on the side of a hill and kept out of trouble. We've spotted torches at night and have heard some strange sounds, but so far we've not come into contact with any Viet Cong.

Doug's platoon is providing the security for our HQ and tonight he'll have two sections in ambush about 400 metres out. During the day the platoons are either ambushing tracks or creek lines or moving through suspected enemy areas, checking for recent signs. Headquarters remains propped on a hill, so that we can guarantee communications back to base. We've got five radio sets (ANPRC25). One is for communications with the platoons, another gives us contact back to battalion HQ. Mine provides a link to the company administration elements back at Nui Dat. Then we have constant communications with our supporting artillery. The other one is held as a spare, but is also used in ambushes.

The other day 6 Platoon plodded past our location, en route to yet another ambush position. All the familiar faces, although hot, dirty, bearded and sweaty, were smiling and in good spirits. The tail end was brought up by Sergeant Henderson who stopped to have a brief chat with me.

Karl said to 'the Major' that 'George will have a good platoon in a couple of months' (meaning that his platoon will be unaffected by the next march out of National Servicemen).

'What do you mean,' I said, 'he's got a bloody good platoon now.'

'The Major' looked at me and laughed and said to Karl: 'Better watch what you say about 6 Platoon while the 2IC's around. He's still a bit touchy about the changes I made.'

Fischer is the only corporal left from the initial bunch as Corporal Riddett was promoted to sergeant and sent to D Company and Corporal Philp was demoted for going AWOL for a while, after the last R and C. 'Fish' is a real good bloke and we still have a few chats now and then, to keep me up with how everything is going. George has settled in well, has the respect of all the diggers and although they have yet to be involved in any contact, they've done their share of the hard slog.

I'm settling into my relationship with 'the Major' with the help of the company sergeant major who has also been on the receiving end of his moods. We've decided to share the kicks and shield the others as best we can, so that the frustrations don't affect too many. Each morning we judge what kind of day it's going to be by his reaction to our greetings. If it's a reasonable response we know all will be OK, otherwise we spread the word to the others to keep a low profile or to ensure any request from him is completed without delay. We've even briefed his batman to prepare extra brews and snacks to help sweeten him up a bit on his really bad days. So far, it seems to be working.

Gee, my back is sore from lying and sleeping in my stony hole. I had to laugh at one of Mum's comments in her last letter. 'How's your complexion?' she asked ... Well, there I was in my dirty little hole in the ground with my sweaty, smelly clothes and filthy hands clasping the clean white pages of her letter. The perspiration dripped from my chin and my hands left grubby marks on the pages. I remembered that my reflection, when I last looked in the mirror, showed a bearded, long-haired, grimy fellow with familiar, but changing features. My copper dog tags have stained my chest green and the face blackening (for camouflage) hides the pimples and blackheads. My arms and legs are covered in scratches and there's the odd festering sore caused by bamboo cuts and 'wait a while' thorns.

My back has been subjected to pack-horse loads. I wear a stiff, dirty shirt that hasn't been changed for five days and I'm suffering the effects of sleeping on stones for the last several nights. I can't feel if I have any pimples on my back because the whole area is numb. It's been 16 days since we had our last 10 minute soak in the river and my dear Mum asks: 'How's your complexion? …'

Things have become very quiet in the last three days. One of the other companies shot a postman the other night and the documents he was carrying were from the leader of the local VC organisation. Our actions over the past month have really got them worried. They've lost a lot of key people in recent clashes with us and they feel that they can't go anywhere, without fear of being ambushed. Their plans have had to be curtailed because there's a shortage of food and ammunition, due to our patrols finding their supply caches. I wouldn't be surprised to see a change in our activities soon because I think we've cleared this area pretty well.

Today is the eleventh, and it's Today. Yesterday was the tenth. No names anymore. No Mondays or Saturdays just today, yesterday and tomorrow – and of course maintdem day. Time also means little to us. You get up, eat and go; then you stop, eat and ambush.

It's time for me to sign off.

14 May

I received your photos and letter yesterday and have been happily studying them by the hour. M-J is absolutely wonderful and the photo of you sends thrills through me. I look at the photos with mixed emotions; love, loneliness, happiness and sadness. How I long to be with you both.

I'll be sending this letter to Holsworthy as you should be back home by the time I get this finished. How does the house look? Does M-J remember it? Please take care when driving around Sydney. It's so much busier and faster than Adelaide.

We got the front two pages of the *Advertiser* the other day and read all about the Moratorium Day activities. It isn't the best news to hear and it leaves us with a real sour taste in our mouths knowing that some people don't support us. I don't mind them having another opinion about the war, but I'm not too happy when they carry the VC and North Vietnamese flags, chant enemy slogans, call us murderers and burn the Australian flag. We got a laugh from the story about the 3RAR diggers disrupting the Adelaide Moratorium march. It would have been quite a sight to see the stand-off between the marchers and the diggers. It's interesting to read that people have supported the soldier's actions. I guess this war has caused a lot of conflict at home as well as over here.

The other day a patrol of ours stumbled onto a group of enemy who were having a midday siesta. There was a brief, fierce fire-fight which resulted in two of the enemy being killed and several large packs of food, clothes and medical supplies being captured. None of our blokes were injured.

It's begun to rain frequently now (every day for at least two hours) with the nights being the wettest. Right now I'm sheltering under my hootchie while little pools form at my feet. When the rain stops the atmosphere becomes very sticky. Remember Elcho?

Perspiration has now turned my greens into damp rags and I feel like stripping off to get some relief from the still air. Now that wouldn't be a pretty sight.

They say we'll be out here for about another week or two.

Morning of the fifteenth. I've just had a brew of coffee and a tin of boned turkey. We'll get an extra re-supply tomorrow because we're heading off to a new area. We've been out for 26 days and the last wash was on day 18. If it rains today I'll strip off and see if I can get some of this grime off. I noticed that I've got a few rashes starting to appear on my body.

It's been a lifetime since I last saw you and it seems an eternity till we'll meet again. Take care of yourself and our lovely son.

17 May

Your news about the trip home sounds as if it went off very well. With the car and M-J behaving themselves and the great company, time must have passed quickly and the journey would have been quite pleasant.

I've just had a dinner of frankfurt pieces and beans in tomato sauce, pecan roll, biscuits and jam, US coffee and two pieces of chocolate ... quite filling. The problem is that when I have anything hot I perspire for hours after. I still haven't washed, still smell and I actually feel slippery to touch.

I have to go on radio watch for two hours soon, so I'll be leaving this letter part way through.

What's it like to be home again after so long? Has the place changed much ... is it still like home? Of course there will be a lot of work needed to get things back into shape but with the extra pairs of hands, it won't take long.

Three months have gone ... nine to go. I certainly hope they go as fast as these first few.

I'll be sending you a cheque for $130 soon. This will be to repay Guy and Robyn's loan. I hope the little extra will cover their patience, as it has been almost 12 months since they helped us out.

It's now almost 5 o'clock and I'm preparing for the night. There's nothing much to tell except that we'll be going on R and C in two weeks then straight back out in the bush again. When this operation finishes, we will be going straight back to the Dat, grab our gear and onto the trucks to Vung Tau for two days, then back out here for another extended operation. What a life; fresh air, exercise, relaxation and the chance to see a beautiful country and meet its people.

It's now 10 am on the nineteenth and we've got one more VC. I'm sitting in another pit (same size as the other) with my hootchie overhead to keep the sun off. My boots and socks are off and my shirt is undone and I'm preparing some rice for my midday meal.

Doug's group has just found 400 pounds of rice in an old bunker system just nearby and it appears it's only just been put there. Things are looking up.

It's now 4 pm and I've just come back from a wash in the river;

soap and all. What absolute luxury. For the first time since this operation began I can write without fear of smudging the page with my dirt and sweat. I feel great. No more greasy dandruff in my hair, my fingernails are clean, my chest is lily-white and I could only find three pimples and six blackheads of any consequence. My feet and legs have been dusted with tinea powder and I've got a half an hour to enjoy my brew of tea before I take over the radio picket. Sometimes we feel so spoilt.

It's maintdem day tomorrow, so I'll sign of with lots of sweet smelling love and kisses and get this in an envelope for Possum to deliver to you.

17 May

Hi Pop, received your letter yesterday and was very pleased to hear from you. Your words of encouragement came at a very opportune time and helped me a lot.

I'm still having trouble coming to grips with some of the issues but with your help and that of my mates here, I'm sure I'll be able to keep my spirits up. But you do get taken to the edge over here. Why, only just a few minutes ago I disturbed two lizards copulating on my gear. Now I know I have to put up with hardships, but the female lizard was a bit shy and she took off leaving her partner very frustrated and his 'old boy' was hanging out too. As he slowly moved off the dirty bugger dribbled all over my equipment. Now I ask you: what is a fellow supposed to do?

As far as my future career goes, I'm still considering taking discharge in 1973. The more I see and hear of the army, the more disenchanted I get. It wouldn't be too bad if I were single but it puts a lot of pressure on a married soldier. Raylene has had a very lonely life and I know it's been very tiring looking after M-J these last few months. We've had so little time together since I've been in the battalion and now I'm missing out on the joys of being a husband and a father.

Anyway, I'll be giving it some serious thought in the next few years. So much can happen in that time. I should be a captain by then and with a bit of luck might swing an interesting posting. Peacetime soldiering is a little easier than what we've had to go through, so I might just wait to see what comes my way, following this tour.

I'm not sure what I would do if I rejoined Civvy Street. I'm still interested in the land and could pursue my agricultural dreams. I'm sure some of my Roseworthy mates would help if there was something worthwhile on offer.

Following the bunker attack, things have settled down to regular patrolling and searching. We are the only company left operating in this area as all the others have moved to the south of the province and are finding a lot of action down there. We've spent a lot of time living in holes in the ground (6 feet by 2 feet by 2 feet) waiting for the VC to come by. While some signs indicate there are a few things brewing, it's most likely that the news has got around about us being in the area and they are keeping well away.

Give my love and best wishes to everyone. I'm looking forward to the time we can sit around, have a few drinks and discuss the future of your youngest son. I'm sure I'd be more rational in my thinking if I were in the front bar of an Adelaide hotel with you and some of my friends and family.

22 May

I haven't had any mail for the past week, my love, so I expect I'll get a fair stack next maintdem (in two days).

I love you very much.

I miss you terribly.

I'm happy and well.

I think of you often.

I hope you've settled into home life again. I wonder if M-J recognises anything.

Yesterday, A Company hit a large bunker system which contained 50 enemy. Chris Johnson's platoon was mainly involved. As I write, they are searching the place and have found a lot of abandoned weapons, gear, documents, food and medical supplies.

I've just prepared a snack of four cereal blocks mixed into a porridge with a tin of apricots added. Quite filling, but I feel it needed something else to hide the cardboard flavour. I'll have to keep experimenting with my cooking until I find the right combinations.

I was thinking last night of how lonely and unhappy you must be at times. If you had married some other 'fancy', back all those years, you'd probably have a nice house and car and a husband that spends all his time with you and your several kids. I'm glad that you didn't of course because I'd still be single, bored and very lonely. You see, there is only one person in this world for me. Thank you my darling for making my life so fulfilled.

I'm in the process of drinking my washing-up water. I cooked the above meal in my steel mug and of course, a lot has stuck to the sides. I've wiped as much off as I can with my finger, but it doesn't reach right down to the bottom, so I filled the mug with water to soak the porridge off. Seeing I can't waste water I'm now drinking it . . . imagine that.

How is our darling M-J?

I sent a form back to the Dat to have $130 sent to you, for Guy and Robyn. However when it gets to you, if you need it, then please use it. I've got about $200 in my pay book (I still owe the battalion $100 from the time you needed the money urgently). However, by the time I get back from this wonderful hole we'll have finalised our main debts and will have enough for a three-course meal at Herman's Haystack [a restaurant/bar in Sydney] with perhaps enough left over to see a film (one of our real big nights out).

I hope the car is behaving itself. No more stopping for no apparent reason. Just keep the garage people informed and I'm sure they will help. The bloke even said he'd drive out to our place if you had trouble. I'm sure if you explained your situation, they would be willing to help.

I wish I could spend some time with you now, to find out how things are. You could tell me all about your stay in South Australia and what you have planned for the coming months.

I'd love to have a quiet meal with you. Candles burning and a typical Holsworthy sunset. I'd love to walk with you and M-J along some quiet street, no need for talking, listening to the peaceful world and enjoying each other's company. These are the things I miss so much.

Possum (a small chopper ... looks like a horsefly with a big glass head) came into our position today to change over a radio that didn't work. He very kindly brought in our mail and I was able to read the latest from Mum and you.

You mentioned showing Guy the letter I sent, dated 30 April ... looking back on it now, that seems ages ago. A lot of water has flowed down the Song Rai since then (an old Vietnamese saying). We've covered a lot of ground since then and although still in the same general area, it's a whole lifetime away.

My handwriting is bad because the knee I'm using isn't very broad and every now and then the paper slips off. Also my hand is very sweaty and slippery.

It was great to hear that you went out with Guy, Robyn, Ron and Gill. I can imagine what a beaut time you must have had. We'll have to arrange a get together on my return, so that I can thank them for being such wonderful, understanding friends.

I'm halfway through a paperback that has been doing the rounds of the company HQ, called *'Chesty' Puller, USMC*. We have several books being handed around and this one looks like I'm the last in line. I don't think it will see out the operation and may very well be left buried in some dark corner of this foreign country.

Darling, how can I find the words to express my love for you? ... I love you more than Chesty Puller loves the US Marine Corps ... Now that is really something.

It's amazing how things change so quickly. You can't afford to get too relaxed and settled. One minute, 'peace and quiet'; the next, pandemonium. At 3 pm Karl's group killed one VC about 700 metres south of us. He was carrying a large quantity of medical supplies, money and documents. At 4 pm our gunners opened up on two people crossing a clearing about 50 metres away. They immediately ran back the way they had come and a search party of ours is now following a blood trail. 'The Major' and the artillery officer are scheming some kind of plan for tonight's ambushes and I'm here, sitting in my hole, writing to you, as if nothing has happened.

It's now 7 pm and all is quiet again. We expect a step up in activity in the next few days as a sweep by tanks, APCs and A Company has commenced in the south with the idea of pushing a tired and harassed enemy towards us. We are in four locations about 700 metres apart. All have prepared 'dug in' positions and feel that the next 24 hours will tell whether the plan will be successful or not.

The night passed quietly except for a very heavy, very noisy downpour that went from 3.00 am to 5.30 am. It's now 7.00 and there's not a cloud in the sky. It looks like it will be a stinker of a day. 'The Major' had a tear in his hootchie and all his gear got wet. He is now walking around with no trousers because they're hanging on a nearby bamboo clump, drying out.

Everything is fresh and green. The bamboo has been cleaned of all its dust, the soil smells rich and productive and the air is so clean and pure.

Another day gone, another day coming, another day to the next maintdem and another day closer to you.

Anything in the papers about the Moratorium? I've heard that in Adelaide the 3RAR commanding officer has received phone calls and letters supporting the diggers that disrupted the protest march in King William Street. Many people, after hearing that the army had charged them for 'Conduct Unbecoming' have offered to pay their fines. It's good to know that some people still back us. But it's a bit of a worry that this Moratorium thing continues to grow.

This morning another Possum dropped in but this time he left behind a Hoi Chanh (an ex-Viet Cong who has surrendered under an official program called Chieu Hoi). This dark skinned, small-framed man left his company a few days ago and he has agreed to lead our blokes to some bunker systems. He was with Chris Johnson when they hit the bunkers the other day. We've been told that there were about 60 enemy occupying the area at the time and of these, 26 were killed. It's possible that in the coming weeks we'll find the graves of those who were wounded and who have subsequently died. I wonder how he feels about all his mates being killed in this action.

The Hoi Chanh is now accompanying Karl and George into an

area about 700 metres south-west of here, so we're hoping to have something come of this pretty soon.

By the way, one of the two who stumbled into us yesterday was a woman. The digger who fired first states that she was about 20-years-old and was dressed in black shirt and trousers.

Walt Disney would have a great time over here filming the wildlife. Just sitting here in my hole I can see three spiders of different size and colours. Two lizards, one with a blue head and the other like our drop tails, but only much bigger. Later in the day the frogs come out. Small ones, fat ones, broad ones, thin ones, long-legged ones, short-legged ones and ants. Red ones, black ones, green ones, little 'eeny-teeny' ones and some huge buggers.

We've seen monkeys, snakes, deer, tigers, wild turkeys and peacocks, and the rivers teem with fish. At night the animal noises sound really weird and it can be a little scary when you're on sentry duty and you're not sure what it is that is moving out there in the darkness. At times you can swear that there are 100 enemy crossing your front, all with torches, but in fact it's just the fire-flies and fungus shining in the pitch black. The blue-headed lizard calls ... 'gooork gaar, gooooork gaaar, gooooroooorooorook gaaaaaaaaark' ... Then somewhere in the distance a reply is heard.

Funny how time seems to drag when there's nothing much happening, but here in the bush there are always interesting things to observe and I find that the days and nights pass fairly quickly. It's now 4 pm and I'd better sign off now and prepare for tonight's activities.

25 May

As you can tell by the paper and the neatness, I'm no longer in the bush. I returned yesterday, 36 days since departing, leaving the rest of the company out in the field for another eight days, while I organise their return, R and C, and general administration.

For instance, they will arrive here on the morning of the third, I'll take all their ammo from them and replace it with fresh stuff. They'll receive two cool drinks, overdue mail and packages. Then they'll get their pay and have some exchanged into piastre, in preparation for their two-day break (some also have to pay off some debts at the PX canteen). Then it's down to the Regimental Aid Post for a series of shots and health checks. We'll also have to issue leave passes, ID cards and other papers, all needing to be individually signed for.

That night we'll have a barbecue which everyone is looking forward to because, for the first time in more than six weeks, everyone can completely switch off and forget about the war. We've arranged 45 cartons of beer (90 dozen) plus 13 cartons of soft drink. In addition, there is one can of rum and coke per man. Our cooks have planned a smorgasbord that reminds me of the Roseworthy parties we use to have at the Botanic Hotel. No one will mind if anyone gets a little drunk, but in fact we've found that many of the soldiers, after a few beers, seem to drift away and prefer to sit in small groups and quietly discuss whatever it is that comes to mind. Few dwell on the past operation, other than to toast missing mates.

Although I'll be heading down to Vung Tau early in the morning to prepare for the company's arrival, the main group will get on board a convoy of trucks for the drive to Vung Tau at about 10 am.

R and C lasts till the afternoon of the sixth and by midday on the seventh, B Company will be in the field again.

This last operation has in military terms, been quite successful. After 40-odd days, B Company had nine contacts, resulting in 15 enemy killed, an estimated 10 wounded (blood trails) and numerous weapons, medical supplies and documents. We've destroyed 800 pounds of rice and other food supplies as well. We received one killed, another died from a tropical disease and eight were wounded. All of the latter returned to duty after two weeks, except one who was RTA for treatment.

With the latest operation (codenamed Concrete 2) drawing to a close, the battalion has killed more than 50 of the enemy, with only four of our own being killed. I know these are terrible, hard-hearted statistics, but it's what is happening over here. Another way of looking at it is that when it comes to the likelihood of me being a casualty, the percentages are all in my favour.

I was told this morning by one of the other company 2ICs that I should be getting captain's pay, but due to a technicality I can't. That's a loss of about $40 a pay. The more I hear of this type of thing the more I realise that Catch-22 is alive and well in 7RAR. This doesn't help my feelings towards the army or my long-term career possibilities.

Now is the winter of my discontent.

The first thing I did on my return was to pick up my mail and long awaited parcels.

Your escapades of late have left me breathless. You'd better slow down a bit or else you'll need to go on R and C too. Thanks for all the special goodies, however I'm not sure whether I'll give those roasted caterpillars a try. We may be in an exotic part of the world but I've got to draw the line somewhere. The Russian Crab was devoured in one sitting in the officers mess tonight. I tried to camouflage the caterpillars among a bowl of peanuts but I noticed that they were still there when it was time to leave.

The books will be great. I'll take two with me to Vung Tau and I'll put the others into circulation in our unofficial bush library. I'll hand the toys over to the chaplain (Father Teefey) who will no doubt find some little ones down at the orphanage to love them.

I won't say anything more on my dates for R and R because as I've tried to explain, any changes mean that the whole roster has to be altered and that may cause someone else's plans to be upset. The other thing is that now that Mum has said not to worry about anyone else, I've been planning that we spend the time together, just the three of us. We've got such little time to share that we should just keep it to ourselves.

I've also received two books from Rex: *Good Ol' Charlie Brown* and *D-Day, Book No. 1, Purnell's History of the Second World War*.

It's now 7.15 pm on the twenty-sixth. I had to leave the letter unfinished last night due to a practise stand to. Everyone within the Nui Dat Base was called to arms by the warning siren, so we all grabbed our weapons and gear and raced to our allotted pits and bunkers to repel the threat. Everybody, including cooks and bottle washers, man the trenches and I must admit, that even though I had a rag-tag army to command, I was pleased with the way in which they carried out their tasks. After a while the all-clear sounded, but by then it was too late to go back to what I was doing before, so I turned in for the night.

One of the diggers (ex-6 Platoon) who is now doing clerical duties has bought himself a camera and said he'd like to take some photos of me, for you. Nice of him, I thought.

I look back almost eight weeks and wish that I could have settled into this 2IC job better than I have. I've grumbled a lot and worried you too much. It's only a matter of wanting to play a more active role and be more closely involved with the diggers. I can't stand sitting around doing all these mundane jobs, it's far too inactive and boring. Now that sounds really selfish, doesn't it!

Still, I guess it's all part of being in an army and being in an operational setting. In the long run, there won't be too many young officers who can claim that they have served as a platoon commander and a company 2IC in a war zone, so I should be grateful for the experience and the opportunities it will present in the future.

Millions of kisses.

PS The song *Everything is Beautiful* is playing on the US Forces radio station (Goo ... oood Morning Vietnam). It's a lovely song, but seems a little out of place here.

PPS I've completed about one third of my tour. In another 23 weeks we'll be experiencing six days of R and R bliss.

29 May

What an easy time I'm having nowadays. Sleep in till 0630, three good meals a day at a table with a white tablecloth, cold drink on sale, films at night, sitting on chairs in the shade of a canvas tent, listening to the radio, hot showers anytime of the day (cold showers are more refreshing in the heat of the day).

There are only six soldiers under my direction in the base right now, as several of the others are on a small patrol just outside the wire. These short activities called 'TAOR' (Task Force Area of Responsibility) patrols are designed to keep the enemy from getting close to the task force perimeter. They also keep the local population out of our rubbish tip and from pinching our wire fencing for use in their own cattle yards.

We man a machine gun and a telephone picket all day and night, so there's little opportunity to get any of the badly needed maintenance jobs done, such as cleaning up the area, sandbagging, painting and repairing the tent lines. I spent a bit of time yesterday filling 50 sandbags, just because I had to do something physical and because there was just nobody else available to do it.

R and C begins on the fourth. I hope it's good weather because the swimming pool at the Badcoe Club is really first class and I intend spending all my time there with cans of coke and good books as my companions. The sun and water may help clear up some of the skin rashes I've had for a few weeks.

Do you know, my love, I think the reason for my discontent is because I'm so lonely. I'm longing for your company. How easy it would be to settle into this work if I had your love to come home to each day.

I received your photos today and added them to my collection. What a beaut history of the Winter family. The Con-Tact certainly protects them, as the others are becoming faded and a little tattered, although loved all the same.

This is terrible weather. Here I am at 8 pm and my shirt is soaked with perspiration.

I love you, I love you, I want you and I'm going to get you. Any plans on what we could do during R and R? Mum said in her last letter that we should spend our precious days in Sydney. Just you, M-J and me. 'Do what you and Ray want to do, without a thought of anyone else.' Good sport my Mum!

I've got a ringworm on my bum. This is probably from the mongoose that inhabits my tent. Last night he/she sat on the sandbags opposite my bed and noisily munched a packet of army biscuits. Poor thing it must be starved. I wonder if any of your dried caterpillars are still around? No, he/she would probably pass them by and go back to the army biscuits.

Yesterday I had to escort two American Red Cross girls from task force headquarters to the 7RAR lines. I arrived at TFHQ and went into the officers mess to ask of their whereabouts and was confronted by two lovely ladies, one black the other white: Vernan and Bobby from South Carolina and Colorado.

Hi! Great! Yeah! With huge pearly smiles and warm personalities. Round eyes too.

I knew as much about their country as they did about mine. 'Colorado, is that where the big canyon is?'

Vernan thought that our tent lines were 'just like the summer camp I use to go to, back home.'

'We're not sure what you ladies are here for so I told the diggers that you sing, tell jokes, do magic tricks and strip.'

Shriek. 'Oh, Peter, you mustn't tell them that, we're just here to spread a little joy.'

They were a refreshing change to the daily routine and spent an hour walking around and speaking to anyone we came across. Pity that 90 per cent of the battalion was out. However, the 60 or so fellows that keep the place running really enjoyed their company.

About 4.30 every afternoon a couple of the diggers and I get a soccer ball and spend an hour kicking it around between the rubber trees. It's very humid and we finish in a breathless, sweaty and muddy heap. The cold shower after, does wonders.

Last night at the open-air theatre I saw *If*, a film about several young students rebelling against the stuffiness and bastardisation at an English college. They turn on their fellow students and the system with machine guns and mortars and level the place.

In some ways, I was reminded of my first years at Roseworthy, where we were subjected to incredible personal harassment from the senior students and some staff. I'd like to return to that place some time in the future to see how it is changing/progressing.

I count my three years there as the best in my life because it took me from a young, immature student to a more confident, independent, young man. I also clearly remember that it was there that I had the great pleasure of meeting you.

I was thinking, after the film, that there have been a few times in my life when I've stood up to authority and the principles I believe in and while I didn't resort to violence, I certainly stated my case in the strongest verbal terms.

First, there was my final Roseworthy year confrontation with principal Herriot. I came off second best because he expelled me for a few weeks and you'll remember that we were banned from going to the Graduation Ball, as you had bought a new dress for the occasion. Then I had a run-in with the boss (Schrieber Bros) while working as a seeding labourer at Keith. That didn't do me much good either because at the end of the six weeks he only paid me half of what I was expecting. All he said when I confronted him about it was that I was lucky to get that much.

I remember feeling very angry too at the man in uniform at the Adelaide Railway Station when he abused the Aboriginal we were talking to and, when we stuck up for the lad, he started abusing us too.

These aren't major issues but they have given me an understanding about the injustice we sometimes have to face. I see the same occurring here too and perhaps that's why I'm not very comfortable when I'm around Major 'W'. The thing is though, I'm not able to respond and I'm certainly not able to show any objection.

I'm determined not to show the same arrogance to my soldiers. I make it a point to listen, even if the subject isn't the most stimulating. I try and look at the person and let him do the talking rather than interrupt. I stop what I'm doing, switch off the radio and give him all my attention. The diggers seem to like the idea of having a friendly ear because there's always someone dropping into my tent to give me some of the latest gossip or to just have a chat. For instance, Private Whatmore has just spent a half hour talking about photography and what to look for when buying a good quality stereo player. Apart from that he just dropped in 'to see how things are going'. On another occasion a corporal delivered a beaut cup of black coffee with a slice of lemon and two buttered biscuits.

'Why?' I asked. 'Well sir, you don't look too happy and the boys were having a cup anyway.'

We are in the middle of a military forces drug abuse prevention program with hard-hitting radio interviews and newspaper articles, as well as some US Army films. I haven't seen or heard of any drugs being used in the battalion. Those on operations are definitely free from any however, I wouldn't be surprised if one or two who spend their time at Nui Dat have had some exposure. This would come in via the truckies and logistics soldiers who travel regularly to and from Vung Tau. Anyone in the Vung Tau and Saigon units would have easy access and there's probably quite a bit floating around down there. All hell would break loose if anyone was found with any kind of drug substance. Apart from being returned to Australia, I wouldn't be surprised if they were discharged from the army altogether.

Remember Ian McNee? He's leaving us to go back to his civvy job. He was going to extend his National Service term to see out this tour, but is a bit tired of 'the System'. Lucky bastard, he'll be back in Australia within a week.

6 June

The photo I have just received makes me feel so very proud. I've showed it to everyone who comes by including 'the Major', sergeants and numerous diggers. Firstly M-J, how he has grown. He's so big, so good looking, so healthy. Then I study you. How lovely you are. You make a lovely couple. I wish I could make it a threesome. I will carry the photo with me where ever I go. Just like my dog tags, it'll be a compulsory part of my uniform. Whenever I feel low I'll prop it in front of me and remind myself what a fortunate person I am.

I received two letters and photos when I got back from Vung Tau. I think I broke some kind of record on this last R and C. I only spent 75 cents, all on Cokes. That must make me the cheapest Charlie in all of Vietnam. I spent all my time by the pool reading *Drum*, swimming and sleeping. I feel so refreshed that I almost can't wait for tomorrow when we start the crazy business all over again.

Major Barry Petersen is back in Vietnam, with 2RAR. I haven't caught up with him yet, but was speaking to one of his sergeants in Vung Tau. I'm surprised they allowed him back after his previous, spectacular involvement, but apparently as long as he stays in Phouc Tuy it's OK. I guess things have changed since those early days when the CIA had a price on his head. He's only been in country four weeks, so it's likely I'll come across him sometime soon.

Now, he is one officer I'd be proud to work under. When Guy and I were at the Infantry Centre, Ingleburn, as brand new National Service officers in 1966, he was a captain just back from Vietnam. He took us under his wing and gave us a lot of support when things didn't go our way, even though he was suffering trauma from his experiences. I'll never forget the way he verbally ripped into a major who was giving us a very hard time.

I had a prelude to our R and R while I was in Vung Tau. I was reading a scene in *Drum*:

> 'Calinda,' his voice was thick with impatience and desire, 'get out of that dress and come over here. There's just one thing I need to make me feel like a man again.'
>
> 'I know Drum.' Calinda closed the door with one hand and stripped the dress over her head with the other. She looked at the bright body lying on the bed and as always when she looked at it she marvelled at it. 'And I feel like a woman again.'
>
> One step took her to the bed and to the arms that were waiting for her.

Back to reality. We've just heard that C Company (Greg Lindsay's platoon I think) has just lost three blokes killed by a mine. No further details as yet. Even though we don't know the soldiers involved we all feel shaken by the news. I feel very angry. I'm angry at the army for being here, I'm angry at the Government for sending us here, I'm angry at the enemy, for being such worthy opposition and I'm angry at Vietnam for being so far away from home. All in all, it's just a feeling of hopelessness.

Well my love I'm sorry to have to sign off on such a terrible note, but we've got to prepare for our next operation, which starts tomorrow. We don't know how long it'll be, but would expect it'll go well into July.

We got a real taste of the wet yesterday evening with a huge downpour which lasted two hours together with thunder and lightning. Not as much as will come soon, but still a reminder that nature too has its wild side and we will soon be living out in the worst of it.

By the time you get this letter I'll be out in some flooded paddy struggling under the weight of saturated gear and clothing. But tucked carefully in my left breast pocket will be two photos. One of you and M-J on the beach and the second, the most recent, wonderful photo of the two I love.

8 June – from Raylene to Peter's mum

With the lunch dishes still in the sink, the washing to be brought in and M-J to keep an eye on, I'll endeavour to write to you all. I've been very neglectful, as it's been ages since I've written, but time simply runs away with me. Not that I appear to do much extra activity, but just ordinary chores and a letter to Peter each day, and time just whizzes by.

At present M-J is right into my saucepan cupboard . . . a round nappied bottom sticks out of it and all sorts of scrummaging noises are coming from within. He just loves my saucepan cupboard.

He loves outside too and even before he's had breakfast he's trying to open the bottom latch to gain access to the adventures of the backyard.

He's suffering from teething problems and I'm suffering from the resultant teething nappies.

In Peter's last tape he mentioned writing you a lengthy screed on infantry procedure and their latest activities, mainly to interest Rex and the boys. It's good to hear what he and the platoons do and although it's all very way-out as far as our sheltered minds and lives go, it does help you to feel nearer. I only hope that it didn't worry you Mum, as I know Peter can be very vivid in his descriptive writings.

This time next week Peter will have been away four months. One third of the time gone. Terribly slow, but at least the time is going.

M-J keeps me busy and without him I don't know what I would do. Whether it is Kleenex tissues all over the bathroom, or coals from last night's fire all over the lounge room. This morning it was rice bubbles on the kitchen floor, followed by sitting in mud under the dripping back-garden tap ... Well, my days are full to the brim. I haven't had time to even read a book or finish knitting my jumper ... and yet I love every minute.

Thank you Mum for being the dearest, most understanding mother-in-law any girl could want, regarding Peter's R and R in November ... I guess you must be in love too.

XXX Raylene and M-J.

Chapter Five

The Horseshoe

10 June–1 August 1970

10 June

My darling, three days ago B Company moved to grid reference 495 620, a defensive position and fire support base known as the Horseshoe. It's an extinct volcano standing only about 30 metres high, but overlooks almost the whole of the south-eastern part of the province. The Australian forces have had this position almost as long as they've been in Phouc Tuy (that is, since 1968). It's a well established, two-company size position with mortar, artillery and armoured placements as well. It's strongly fortified with bunkers and trenches, wire and mines, but it's run down and needs a lot of work to get it into first class condition.

The tents, bunkers and sandbagged positions are rotting and many need total replacement. The vegetation has entangled the defensive wire and much of the entrenched positions and will need to be cleared. Roads and tracks require grading, and stagnant pools of water and piles of rubbish eliminated. Rats and mosquitoes have owned this place for several months and it's a bit of a dump. However, it will be our home for a few months so we've been tasked to fix the place up and make it more hospitable. 7RAR will make it their permanent battalion operational position and when it gets up and running it'll to be home to about 300 troops.

Fixing this place up will be our daytime job because at night we move out into the surrounding paddy fields and set up ambushes around the nearby village of Dat Do. It has been a VC haven for many years and is known to be the major supply source for the

The Horseshoe

The market place in Dat Do village

enemy moving to and from the Long Hai mountains, a huge mountain range to the south.

Each night at about 6.30 pm the company moves out, mounted on APCs, to a position about 2000 metres from the village. Then immediately after dark we break into six patrols and each moves to a predetermined ambush position within sight of the village boundary. The place is usually very open paddy field, so we have to lie behind the bund (mound) for protection. It's also the only place that is dry so while our lower half is lying in putrid mud and water, our upper part, together with our grenades, ammo and weapons, are kept relatively clean and dry.

We try to keep watch over foot and animal tracks which criss-cross the paddy fields, as these are the likely entry/exit tracks that the VC use. We lay there in total discomfort until just before dawn, when we withdraw to the main highway (Route 23), which runs east/west across the province. Just after first light the APCs, which have spent the night in defence of the Horseshoe come and pick all of the patrols up and we return to our day home until dusk, when it all happens again.

As yet we've had no contact with the enemy; although last night torch lights were seen by two groups, but they were too far away to engage with fire. Each ambush patrol carries a device called a starlight scope, which with some light enhancement from the stars you can search the countryside and see anybody that may be out there. We also use binoculars which can be very effective on moonlit nights.

You've heard about the Long Hais, the highest and most formidable mountain range located on the coast, about 10 kilometres south of our new home. This is where the main body of the enemy is located, deep underground, in tunnels that were built in the 1940s when the Japanese were the threat. They were used in defence against the French in the 50s and are being used just as effectively against the Government forces, the Americans and us in the 60s and into the 70s. They say they have fully equipped 100-bed hospitals there. They also say and I believe them, that the Viet Cong also have their R and C in Vung Tau.

The mountains are protected by an incredible maze of minefields and booby traps. A very effective defence, which we have come to respect. However, the occupants have to replenish their stocks of food and supplies, so we concentrate on ambushing their access into nearby villages, in an attempt to starve them out. To date we have had some success, but we haven't yet been able to bring them to their knees. The support from the villagers is far too strong for us to eliminate all supply routes.

Our day routine commences the moment we get back from ambush. There's a lot of personal cleaning up to do as well as the work details required to get this place into shape. By midday we're all pretty tired so apart from the security duties (manning the machine guns and sentry positions) we try and get some rest until 4.30 pm. Then we receive orders for the night's ambush and start preparing gear for the activity. Once a week, if you're lucky, you get a night off and it's free from all duties. That's when you can let yourself relax, have a few beers, watch a film or catch up with the letter writing.

One consolation about being here is that we can wear nothing but shorts during the day, so we're starting to get some colour back into our bodies and many of the skin rashes that we were all suffering from are disappearing.

My darling, they say a change is as good as a holiday and I must admit that apart from being a little tired (I haven't been able to sleep much during the daylight hours), I'm a lot browner, cleaner and happier. The latter is due to the fact that I am given command of a patrol each night, so I feel like I'm doing something useful again. The mornings are still involved with paperwork, obtaining stores and equipment, establishing work details, seeing to the hygiene situation and generally keeping everyone as comfortable and as happy as possible.

I hope everything is going along fine at home. I'll be sending $200 to you soon. Let me know if you need any more. It's a lot easier to react to your requests now that we're behind the wire during the day and in personal contact with the pay office.

Rats. The Pied Piper would have a ball. We are infested with them. I've established a competition with a prize of a week's supply of beer and soft drinks to the platoon who kills the most in a seven-day period. Trouble is that the rats come out in force at night, when we've gone. I'm thinking of going back to the Dat and capturing my mongoose tent mate. He would think this was heaven and would soon clean out the vermin sharing my bunker.

I saw Owen Cairns yesterday. First time I've seen him since he left B Company. He's looking very fit and happy. He's down with the Mortar Platoon which is located about 150 metres from my bunker.

Throughout the day and night the mortars, artillery and sometimes the tanks, fire off salvos in support of someone in the field or just to harass the enemy positions (especially in the Long Hais). Helicopters are forever coming and going and convoys of trucks are delivering all the supplies and equipment we need to keep this place running. Noise, noise, noise, day and night. No wonder I've had trouble sleeping during my time off.

16 June

It's hot and humid now and will be raining shortly. We're all tired and need a bit of action to get us going again. This type of life is easier in some ways (three cooked meals, hot showers, a bed to sleep on and clean clothes) but tempers are becoming short as these night ambushes aren't getting any results and too few of us are getting a decent sleep during the day.

For the last 10 days we've been living to the following routine:

1700 – Evening meal
1830 – Move out of Horseshoe
2000 – Move into ambush positions
0530 – Pick up by APCs and return to the Horseshoe
0600 – Clean up equipment and self
0700 – Breakfast
0830 – Work details
1200 – Lunch

1300 – Orders and preparations for coming night activity
1500 – Rest

... and so it starts all over again. The only relief is when you get one night off a week. But then you have to do security duty and radio picket for a couple of hours. Time for a decent sleep is very hard to find and this causes all sorts of problems. However B Company is setting a high standard and morale remains pretty good.

I'm halfway through a letter to Beth and Auntie Doss. I received a beaut letter from them together with nine *Reader's Digests* the other day and I've caught up on all the latest about what's happening around seaside Semaphore.

Doug, Karl and George are all well and are doing a lot of excellent work with their platoons. Bill Foxall, our artillery officer from 106 Battery, also sends his love. He reckons he knows you very well because I'm forever reading your letters and telling him about all that is happening in your life. He's a good mate and helps a lot when I'm feeling a bit low.

There still seems to be a problem with the mail system and we've been told that the posties are working to new hours. The bulk of the mail is arriving each Wednesday and many letters are at least a week old.

The following day. The first really heavy downpour is in progress, turning the red dust to thick, sticky mud. Drains are overflowing, tents are leaking, clothes are soaked and even in the cosiest bunker you can feel the dampness seeping in.

The ambush patrols tonight will be terribly uncomfortable. We'll be laying in mud and water, in raincoats that aren't waterproof. The mud smells to high heaven and sticks to everything. Weapons rust and ammo gets all clogged up, which often causes stoppages (weapon doesn't fire). It's almost impossible to see into the darkness, even with our scopes and binoculars, as everything is pitch black and gloomy. The only benefit is that during the downpours there are fewer annoying mosquitoes.

Your photos are still in my shirt pocket and not a day goes by when I don't spent time studying them.

I had a haircut today, the first in about 10 weeks, courtesy of one of the diggers. I also trimmed my mo, which had drooped well below the regulation length. So I'm all respectable again. Has M-J had his hair cut yet? I'd love to see his long blonde hair so please keep it the length it is in the photo until I get to see him in November.

It's now 3 o'clock in the morning on the eighteenth. I'm on radio picket in the company command post, for the next two hours. Everything is very quiet. Only the hourly checks, and one or two general reports about lights from the village have been recorded tonight, so it doesn't look like it will be a busy night.

It's now the nineteenth. I came in at 0600 with my 14-man ambush patrol, after spending the night among four graves. It wasn't the local cemetery, just headstones and a shrine in the corner of a paddy field. We stayed there because, as we were moving towards our proposed location we were fired on. Actually 6 Platoon, who were about 500 metres away, were firing on a group of 10 enemy that were moving towards the village and their rounds were landing among us. It was quite strange at first because we could see these red tracer bullets zipping past and flying off in all directions. It was quite mesmerising. However, we hit the ground (well, actually it was eight inches of water) and crawled forward to the protection of a paddy bund, where we stayed for 20 minutes with our heads down. The bullets were zipping and cracking all about us, so we couldn't do much more. When it had all quietened down we moved to the graves area and set up our ambush in this rather strange location.

We've been informed that B Company will be going out on a three-day operation tomorrow, as part of a battalion sweep through a known bunker area (grid reference 630 600). Although we will only be out for a few days, the other companies will remain in the area for much longer.

I'll send this letter off now, with all my love (and I've been asked to add, with all Bill Foxall's love too).

22 June

It's teeming down and I'm afraid I'll be out in it in about two hours. What a way to spend a night. Why can't I be in front of a cosy fire with the person I love?

Nothing much happened during the battalion operation. We had word that 25 Viet Cong were in a bunker system in an area 13 kilometres to our east, so we set off on foot to get ourselves as close as we could under the cover of darkness. By morning we were in a mosquito infested patch of scrub waiting for news that the other companies had reached their locations, when a lone VC came along a path near us and was shot. This would have alerted anyone else in the area and by the time we swept through the bunker system there was no one in occupation. We spent the rest of the day searching the area but all to no avail, so we were pulled out at the end of the second day.

The other companies stayed in the area. C Company found 16 mines and some booby traps set up. Unfortunately they've received four casualties during this part of the operation. There was even a crossbow booby trap in location, which was very surprising, as these haven't been used for many years.

We're now back at the Horseshoe because the local elections are soon to be held and they want us to protect the polling booths, ambush, patrol and be seen as a show of strength in the area. The VC are sure to try and disrupt the Government attempts at democracy, so we may be in for a bit of excitement.

Two US Red Cross girls visited us today and it created an amazing reaction from the lads. They spent an hour with us chatting, joking and playing a card game. What a welcome break from our usual routine and everyone felt really happy to have them here. It's interesting to see how well behaved 80 tired, lonely men can be when they are in the company of two lovely ladies.

Karl had a bit of bad luck last night. His ambush patrol was just moving into position at 8.30 pm when eight VC fired on them, resulting in three lads receiving leg wounds. One was shot in the heel, another in the ankle and the third received a knee wound. All the enemy escaped. Two hours later, Doug's group spotted four Viet Cong, 150 metres away and initiated a contact, but they escaped too.

We have an Associated Press photographer with us and he's been spending some time obtaining information for an article he will be submitting at the end of the month.

He came with us on the battalion search and has spent some time at the Horseshoe. He's a Frenchman who has covered the war in these parts for 20 years and when he leaves us he's off to Cambodia to cover the US operations there. Colonel Grey respects this kind of international journalist and is happy to have him join our patrols. As for the Australian media, they're best left in the bars of Saigon.

Tomorrow night I'm taking 15 diggers to a nearby village called Phouc Loi, to protect a medical team who will be treating the population for illnesses and injuries. There's also going to be a Civil Aid team showing some propaganda films, which might stir up the opposition a bit. It's a change from laying in a muddy paddy for the night, so I'm actually looking forward to it.

In fact, I might line up with the villagers to get some treatment for my skin infections.

I've got a ring worm on my bum, prickly heat on my stomach and a blotch of some sort on my right hand and left leg.

25 June

I received two letters from you yesterday. One was a remarkable six pages about M-J's latest adventures. How I miss being there to watch his exploits; crawling under fences to go next door to play with his friends.

It's great to hear that you're keeping busy with all kinds of things. You sound very happy and content with life at 501 [Lighthorse Parade].

Will we ever be financially secure? To think I've been here for four months and we've got $60 in the bank. It's so difficult to build the amount when we've got loans to pay off and other commitments. I'll send you another cheque for $110 next payday. I wish it was $1100. I want you to be happy. I don't want you to go without, but I can't see us getting ahead unless I'm promoted in the next year or two. I guess as long as we're all in good health, we shouldn't complain. However, I feel helpless when I hear that you're struggling to make ends meet and there's nothing I can do about it.

I also can't do anything about your loneliness. All we can do is to dream of the times we've had together and long for the times soon to come, when we will hold each other so very tight. Unfortunately, the feelings you describe can only be satisfied when we're together again, forever. Till then my love, remember always that I love you with all my heart and soul. I need you too.

Last night I went with a group of diggers to protect a Civil Aid team in the village of Phouc Loi, which is about 1500 metres south of Dat Do. There were nine people in the team which showed films and treated the villages for various illnesses. After positioning my troops to protect the gathering, I joined the medical team as they went about their business. It was very interesting to see the range of problems, from grazed knees to terrible tropical ulcers. About 300 people attended the clinic and most of them stayed to watch the films about the courageous and loving Government, battling against the brutal Communists.

I enjoyed talking to the captain who led the team and learnt a lot about all the excellent work being done throughout the country by the Civil Aid organisation. I reckon I'd enjoy that kind of posting. It would be far better and in many ways simpler, to win the hearts and minds of the people than to win the war by trying to kill the opposition. I couldn't help but feel that some of the people who attended the clinic were probably VC or at least had members of their family involved. There's no doubt, the medicines being handed out to the old and infirm would probably end up helping some sick soldier fighting for the local VC unit.

Major 'W' has set me a few unexpected tasks lately and I'm starting to fear that he's up to his old tricks again. Twice today, without warning, he's asked for some unusual information at very short notice. For instance, he wanted me to collect all the company canteen bills and advise him of how much each platoon owed. He gave me one hour to do it, even though I was in the middle of another request he'd given me, not 30 minutes before.

Well he got what he was after, even though it created some heartache among those who have let their credit grow a little too much. All in all, the diggers owe $767.95 to the canteen so there won't be any more credit allowed until some of the biggest bills have been paid. Fair enough.

Even though the routine of this place has its advantages, there's an underlying tension that's been building up here for quite some time. Everyone is on edge and there's been some clashes among some of the lads, which brings to the surface some fairly deep seated issues. The problem is simply that we can't get a decent sleep during the day, as there is always a job that needs to be done. Tempers are short and everyone is trying to keep out of each other's way for fear of stirring up another clash. The past few days has seen a change in 'the Major', too, and we're all desperately keeping out of his way. I think we'd all prefer to be out in the bush.

I must admit I'm a little more assertive when I carry out my 2IC tasks nowadays. No funny business from officers, sergeants or diggers. After all, if I can get the detail that the OC wants, then it keeps him off all of our backs.

It's now 7.30 on the night of the twenty-sixth. I'm not going out tonight so I'll have a bit of time to catch up on some letter writing.

It's now 9.30 and I'm on radio picket in the company command post. 'The Major', Sergeant Henderson and Corporal Fischer are behind me, playing cards.

By the way, the three lads from Karl's platoon who were wounded, are being returned to Australia for treatment and rehabilitation. Karl reckons that the enemy mistook his group for some of their own and were walking into the position when his machine gunner opened up on them. Unfortunately the gun jammed after just three rounds and their reaction was to blast away as they quickly turned and ran. We've been having a lot of trouble with our machine guns, especially since the wet season has come.

Now it's the twenty-seventh and I'm going out on ambush in an hour, taking Karl's place as he is pretty crook with a stomach complaint. Our intended location will be near Hoi My, a small village south-east of Phouc Loi. It's spitting with rain now and the usual downpour is promised, just as we settle into our location for the night.

The next morning. I've just had a cold shower and am sitting in the sun letting nature dry me and at the same time, cool and tan me. Two letters from you today and one from Stephen [Raylene's younger brother]. It's made my day. Stephen wrote to me from Jamestown during his school's football trip. He's growing up very fast and from some of the exploits he wrote about, he seems to be quite a boy now and having lots of fun.

I'm shocked to realise that M-J is 15 months. He's growing up so very fast too. I'd love to be present when he calls to you from his cot in order to have an in-depth conversation about what he did during the day. Also, to see his expression when you scold him for destroying yet another plant in our garden, would be a real treat. I fear I'm missing too much of my son's early years. He won't know who the hell I am when I finally get back to you both.

Sorry to hear M-J has got the sniffles, I hope it's nothing more than the usual winter wogs.

Bill Foxall says it's been a real pleasure to get to know you in the letters you send to me and he's looking forward to the next lot I receive. By the way, yes, he does the same job as your Dad did at Tobruk – Forward Artillery Observer.

Tomorrow afternoon we go on a two-day operation in APCs, then on the afternoon of the first, we'll be heading back to the Dat. From there, R and C from the second to the fourth, then we'll be returning to this place until 23 July. After that, it's anyone's guess. We may be going to a place south of here, to operate in the coastal areas. There are place names being mentioned like fire support bases Isa and Brigid, the Long and the Light Green and a village called Lang Phouc Hai. I'm not too concerned. One place is as bad as the other, although these places have a bad reputation for mines, so we'll have to watch our step. All I need right now apart from your love, is a good night's sleep.

30 June

I've been swept back in time by the theme from *Romeo and Juliet*. I've been basking in the sunshine of the Gold Coast and remembering our little flat at Main Beach, just before M-J came along. There are many great memories of our walks along the beach, the purchase of our little car, the 'Websters', our lovely friends and neighbours and a very pregnant you. I remember we saw *The Graduate* as well as *Romeo and Juliet* at the Main Beach theatre in the weeks before you went to hospital. I don't suppose the confinement nor the following weeks were much fun for you, but it was a whole new, exciting experience for me, as it was the start of us as a family. It remains in my mind as something very special.

I've just signed the paperwork to send you $120 for the furniture you wrote about last week. I'm sure the desk/bookshelf/safe/storage cabinet or whatever it is, will help brighten up our home. Are you sure that a packing case wouldn't do just as well? No!

The days of using packing cases covered with cheesecloth for furniture are well and truly gone for the up and coming Winter family.

I'm feeling a little guilty about not having paid Dad back any of the $1000. His loan helped us out when we were desperate and I feel obliged to pay him back as soon as possible.

I'm in a real reflective mood. *Reflections of My Mind* is playing on the radio and again, the past floods back. So many of the songs they play remind me of the good times we have shared. I seem to spend a lot of time thinking of the past. It's too difficult to think of the future when you're in a place like this.

It's now the first day of July, and I've scratched another month off the calendar.

I received a letter from you today dated 25, 26, and 27 June and you report that M-J has gone down with the flu. I hope he comes through it alright. I also hope that you keep up your strength and don't catch anything.

I'm thinking of you always.

PS Our company sergeant major is off home on R and R today. His wife lives four houses away from our flat at Brighton Le Sands. I wouldn't be surprised if Ron and Gill know them … The Melzers.

1 July

Another letter arrived today and as usual it's made my day. I'm sorry to hear that our little lad is suffering from the measles, as well as the flu. I know it must be very hard for you at times, especially at night when he can't sleep. I do hope you are looking after yourself, too.

Have I told you lately that I love you? How can I write on paper the feelings I have for you. I long for the day when we can finally be together again.

'United we stand, divided we fall' is playing on the radio. How appropriate for you and me, for this country and for our own. It seems that everyone in my world is separated or in conflict, for some reason or other.

I've made it clear to 'the Major' that on return to Australia I'd like to stay at Holsworthy. All I want is to settle in one place for a while; a place we can call home, where our love will have a chance to make up for all this separation and loneliness.

The company has returned to Nui Dat for a couple of days. We came in this morning, will be going to Vung Tau on R and C tomorrow and then returning to the Horseshoe on the fifth. If you are planning to send any tapes, we will be back at the Dat again on the twenty-third for 10 days, while they work out the next major tactical movements. It looks like the company will be repositioned elsewhere in the province.

Perhaps it's wishful thinking, but I've heard that I'm in the running for a posting as liaision officer to a US brigade situated to the north of Phouc Tuy. It's a lieutenant's posting, so perhaps I'll get a promotion to go along with the posting. The job entails living and operating with the Yanks, whenever they work in conjunction with Australian forces. It sounds like an interesting position, but as it's only a rumour, I'm not giving it much attention.

While you are experiencing terribly cold weather, we continue to struggle in this oppressive heat and humidity. As I write, I'm bathed in perspiration and even a cold shower is no relief. It rained extremely hard last night and now it's very humid. These rubber trees help keep the sun out but they also stop any breeze and it becomes very uncomfortable.

It was Major 'W's birthday today so the cooks made a huge iced cake and we presented it to him after dinner. The canteen was allowed to stay open later than usual so everybody could celebrate the occasion. We still have our problems, he and I, but I think there's a better understanding between both of us, so it's not troubling me as it was. Perhaps it's because I'm feeling more confident. Either that, or he's refocused his attention on the 3 Platoon commanders, who at this stage aren't too happy with him. It's his unpredictability that causes the trouble.

It's now the third and I'm beside the pool at the Peter Badcoe Club in sunny, downtown Vungers [Vung Tau]. I spent all day yesterday by the pool so I thought I'd do something different. I went down to the beach and tried my hand at surfing, but as there were few good waves, I turned my talents to sail boarding. However the wind wasn't very strong, so here I am, back in my usual location, with a can of Coke.

All my rashes, ringworms and prickly heat have disappeared thanks to the sun and cleaner conditions we've experienced at the Horseshoe. I'm feeling pretty good right now. Last R and C, I spent 45 cents, but this time I've really lashed out and spent $2. Some of the diggers spend up to $200 each break and have very little to show for it. (Actually, some do have something to show for it, but the doctor knows how to treat it.)

I've bought a silver peace medallion which I intend getting our names engraved on the three arms, as a symbol of our love. The army, in their usual blinkered way, have banned the wearing of them by any soldier.

4 July

I've had breakfast, packed my gear and have about one and a half hours before I start gathering the bleary-eyed, broke, souvenir-carrying soldiers, load them onto the trucks and head back to Nui Dat.

I could spend a few more days here quite easily. I'm returning with sore shoulders from my attempts at surfing yesterday. It feels as if someone has driven three inch nails through my biceps. Even though I slept well last night, I remember the agony whenever I rolled over or changed position.

The weather is turning cool and windy which means it'll be raining soon. I have a feeling that the trip back will be a wet one. The convoy of 10 trucks, without canopies, will be depositing 150 drenched, untidy soldiers back at the Dat, but I don't know of anyone who will complain, as we're all in such good spirits.

Tomorrow at 9.30 am we head off to the Horseshoe again. As the company sergeant major is on R and R, it looks like I'll have to take out the HQ ambush patrols every night, whereas before, we used to take it in turns. I don't really mind except that I still have to do all the other jobs (setting up the place with stores, checking the hygiene of the kitchens, toilets and showers, and rostering the work details) and there's little time for resting before I have to prepare for the night's activities.

I'll sign off now and finish this letter tonight when I'm back at the Dat. I'll be fighting off the mosquitoes with one hand and trying to write something romantic with the other.

It's now 5.30 pm and I've just finished reading the four letters I received when I got back. Three from you and one from Mum. Mum sent a photo of you, M-J, Joan and Jackie that was taken when you were last in Adelaide. Another one for my scrapbook.

I'm getting worried about M-J's illness and how you are coping. It must be so tiring to have him needing constant care, day and night. 'The Major' told me that his wife wrote that mumps were doing the rounds in the Holsworthy area. I hope that they won't add to your worries.

Here am I enjoying R and C and you're running all over the place getting medical attention and spending sleepless nights, caring for our little lad. I feel quite guilty about writing of all the fun I've had while you've had such a hard time of it. I can understand how you blow your top now and then and it's only natural that M-J is on the receiving end. How wonderful it is to know that he is aware of your distress by cuddling up to you and speaking his little phrases of love.

With regard to filling out the taxation forms, I'd suggest that you seek some advice from Mr Podmore. As we're in the bush, we won't be getting our papers for some time yet, so I can't help you. Please let me know immediately, if this is a major worry to you and I'll write to Mr 'P' and seek his advice. I guess I'll ask around here to see if anyone can help sort it out. As we won't be receiving our payment details for a while yet, I suppose there isn't any great hurry to get your forms in. Once I get my details, you could send everything over to me and I could get it completed and then send it to the Taxation Department from here.

We've been given orders to go bush for a fortnight, so our days at the Horseshoe are numbered. Tomorrow we head out in APCs to a spot about eight kilometres away and then we will patrol the area for two weeks. Apparently, a fellow in the area is carrying two million piastre to pay the various provincial Viet Cong units. It'll be a huge blow to their morale if we can stop it reaching them.

I've just finished tea and am now checking my own gear, for our new adventure starts early tomorrow morning. I'll try and write but it'll be very difficult, so please be patient.

Goodnight and I pray that you and M-J are feeling much better.

6 July – from Raylene to Peter's mum

Dear Mum, Rex and boys, I'm sorry I haven't written for a while, I've just been too flat out with Mark-John with the measles and bronchitis. Never the less you have all been in my thoughts.

M-J is over the worst with the measles but his little chest is playing a brass band and his cough is awful, it often causes him to vomit. Now he has a sore bottom and is most uncomfortable, poor little dear.

At present he is asleep and because he played with Andrew from next door, this morning, I was able to get the house in order and the ironing done. While he continues to rest, I'll see if I can write a letter to you.

I received a long-awaited letter from Peter yesterday. He's quite well and seems a lot happier. He has spent a few days back at Nui Dat and a couple of days on R and C. I didn't know this and didn't have a tape and parcel there for him ... which is a bit upsetting. Anyway, I hope he was able to have a bit of a rest, as they are working very long and irregular hours when they're at the Horseshoe. As company 2IC he also has to do other jobs while the others are able to rest, even though he's been out with them on night-time patrols. There may be a change in his job soon, as the company will be leaving the Horseshoe later this month and working from a new location.

It's been frightfully cold here at night, but during the day the sun shines warmly. I bought M-J an electric blanket, in an effort to keep him sleeping in his own bed all night. It's beginning to work, but he's still out of sorts, so I'm letting him come in with me for the first part of the night.

He has been sick for a fortnight now and during this time I haven't been able to do anything exciting or interesting, so I'm stuck for anything to write to you.

Hoping everyone is well in the family. Give our love to Grandma and Grandpa and the other Winters: a long distance kiss from M-J to Jackie.

I'll finish now and start a letter to my darling.

7 July

Dear Pop, thanks for your letter and paper clippings. The former was received with great interest, but the latter disturbed me terribly. The papers are really ripping the heart out of our efforts by printing crap like that. It's pretty hard to understand why the journalists would write such stuff when the truth is that few of them ever get far from the comforts of Saigon. In fact, it's shameful that a report like that is even printed, as it is so far from the truth.

Our commanding officer has banned most reporters from our area (apart from a few reputable AAP journalists who have been covering the conflict for 20-odd years), as he believes they are not interested in us or how we are conducting our day-to-day activities. They're only looking for something sensational to make a headline.

Anyway, I've read your letter a second time and I've ripped up the news article, so I feel better.

We receive weekly editions of the Surfers Paradise paper; not just to perv on the bikinis, but to read the Rotarians page. This organisation has established a scheme where all soldiers wounded in South Vietnam, can spend two weeks with their families, all expenses paid, soaking up the friendly atmosphere of the Gold Coast. We like reading about our mates who have been sent back for treatment, enjoying themselves as best they can. So far, about 800 soldiers and their wives have been able to spend some time there. All units here send money to the Rotarians to help support the scheme. 7RAR recently sent $3600. It's good to know that there are organisations that are doing something for our diggers. Not like the RSL, who shamefully, have all but deserted us.

Charlie Tilmouth, B Company's first major casualty will be up at Surfers in a couple of weeks.

We are on a 14-day operation which is revisiting the areas we were last in, to see if anyone has been here since we left. So far it looks like no one has been through the area, but it's early days yet.

When we were here before, everything was dry and dusty. It was a very hot and thirsty looking country. Now that the wet season has broken, we are continually up to our ankles in mud and water. The smallest creek has become a torrent, and the major river that we use to bathe in and wade across, is impassable. The bush, bamboo and trees are lush and green and where it was bare before, tall waist-high grass covers the open spaces.

We're never dry. We get saturated as we push through the undergrowth, we get rained upon at least once a day and we've had to wade across swollen creeks. When we stop, we make ourselves as comfortable as we can in the mud and slush. We now have to keep a watch for leeches, which come out of nowhere to check us out. It's become a regular thing to pull them off our legs whenever we stop for a breather. Some have suggested that we wear condoms over our 'old fellas' to protect ourselves, but it seems such a stupid idea. Even so, some of our radio operators have tried covering their handsets with condoms to keep the water out of the electrical circuits. Let me tell you that it's moment like these, you can't help but laugh at the situation. What I mean is, have you ever held a really important conversation with your boss, talking through a prophylactic?

It's raining now and we've stopped for a while. We are sheltering in small scrapes we've dug in the ground and are just sitting in them with our sieve-like raincoats, trying to make the best of a very wet situation. We've all got our mugs out to catch the sweet tasting water (no need to chlorinate it, as we have to do with water from the creeks and rivers). The rain is coming down harder now, so I'll have to stop writing.

Later. I was quite well off compared to some because at least I wasn't sitting in any muddy water. That was until my cup overturned and spilt into my little scrape. The machine gunners pit is being bailed out as if it were a sinking boat and the activity from elsewhere indicates that others have had a bit of trouble too. Well, one good thing is that it isn't cold, so you don't really care how wet you get. The trouble is the mud. It sticks to everything and clogs up our ammo and weapons. It is very difficult to keep them dry and clean in this environment.

The weather hasn't dampened our spirits though and there is a lot of quiet laughter regarding the situation. The lad next to me is sitting on the side of his scrape with a piece of string tied to a stick, trying his hand at fishing.

Later still. The leaves are still dripping, although the afternoon sun is streaming through the tree canopy. It really is quite peaceful. Once again we've settled down to life in the slush. All pits were eventually totally flooded. Despite being bailed out time and time again, the water keeps on seeping in. I thought I'd missed the worst of the flood until I pulled at an annoying tree root that was digging into my back. This made a natural underground tunnel from which poured, like a sewer, a great quantity of watery mud until I was covered in about six inches of it. I've since bailed it out, plugged the hole and am now nestled in my pit again, just like a pig in a puddle.

We've just received orders that we're going to move from here to a place 2500 metres to the south.

It's now half past six. The sun will be down in half an hour, so I'll finish off.

Mark-John has been very ill lately (measles, bronchitis, skin infection) and Raylene has had a very hard time of it. She's sounding very tired and worried in her letters. There really isn't anyone she can call on to help because all friends in the area have young families and are suffering similar problems. It's at times like this that we wish we were living in Adelaide where I know there are any number of relatives that could help share the burden. No doubt, Raylene will draw on her extra reserves of strength and see it through. But I feel this has taken a lot out of her.

The next day. Possum will come in about 45 minutes so I'll finish the letter and get it off to you.

Colonel Grey had a chat to me the other day and said he was considering sending me to be a liaison officer to a US brigade that is operating to the north of us. It's only for a short time, before they head out to another province, but it would be a very interesting experience. There was also mention of a possible flight to the demilitarised zone (at the border of North and South Vietnam) just to have a look for a couple of days. It all adds up to experiences which may help, if I'm to make the army a lifetime career.

I was shocked to hear about the car accident you had. It just goes to show that I'm not the only one that has to be careful.

You know, I'm a real fatalist when it comes to that sort of thing. Over here, we seem to accept the fact that some will go through this war unscathed, while others will not. It's all down to being in the right or wrong place at a certain time. If it's the latter, there's not a lot you can do about it. My guardian angel continues to do her job really well.

We're all worried about mines and while we know how to look

for the signs that the enemy leave, saying that mines have been planted in the area, we're particularly careful when we're in a suspect area. Whether you hit one or not is really in the hands of your God.

One lad stepped on a mine recently, it jumped out of the ground and failed to explode. Another time, one jumped, exploded and killed three. If you worried too much about it you'd never walk another step outside the wire of Nui Dat. You can't dwell on what might be. You've just got to get on with your job. Even so, it gets you down after a while. One or two of the lads have let it get to them, so they have been given jobs behind the wire at Nui Dat.

I've been here for 138 days. Oh hell, there's such a long time yet to go. In that time we've spent all but 30 days, on operations.

7 July

Dear Mum, Rex and boys, it's been almost 24 hours since we swarmed aboard our APCs and began our long journey, which marked the start of our latest operation.

We all prefer to sit on top of the APCs rather than inside them, because it's fairly claustrophobic inside and you get a little nervous if you can't see where you are going. It's too much of a shock to the system to travel to your destination without having seen all the countryside along the way. To suddenly have the back ramp of the APC lower and expose you to a strange part of the country (hoping like hell that the tankies have reached the right spot), is an infantryman's nightmare. Navigation can only be done properly from the top of the vehicle; where you can see all the major features, watch the vehicles manoeuvring through the bush, listen to the tankies passing on information over their intercom and from where you can constantly check their position on your own map.

After about two and a half hours and a rain storm had passed, we scrambled off, 'saddled up' and began to head off on our predetermined bearing to our first check point. It's great to see how well everyone switches on the moment we get on our way. Whenever we stop, they quietly check out their areas, watching in alternate directions and if no vegetation is nearby to afford them protection, they go down on one knee to lower their profile and be ready for anything, should it happen. No words are spoken, as hand signals are used to communicate various meanings: 'You watch over there, I'm going forward to speak to the scouts, five minutes before we move off again.' If talking is necessary, it is in whispered tones and kept very brief.

It was terribly humid as we moved our way on a compass bearing toward the only feature of any note in this flat, saturated, dark green countryside. The paddies, once cultivated and productive have stood idle for almost 20 years and are overgrown with thick bamboo scrub. We came this way only several weeks ago and it was dry and desolate, but now it's waist high with grass and saplings.

The Civilian Access Area stretches only about a mile from each village and the same distance off each side of the major highways. This doesn't always keep locals from going further out, but it's well known that they are likely to be shot or arrested if one of our patrols come across them. This is what makes these types of patrols so difficult. You don't know whether the person you've spotted is a farmer gathering wood for his family, or a VC. While you don't want to kill an innocent civilian (you can't just go blasting away at anyone), you can't afford to wait until you're fired upon.

As we pushed waist-deep through the lush weed growth, the soggy ground beneath our feet gave us forewarning of a flooded creek line ahead.

How quickly the countryside changes. Only six weeks ago this creek, called Suoi Lo O Nho, was as dry as the parched animal bones we found on its sandy bed. Now we're chest deep in fast-flowing water, forcing our way to the other bank. The smaller members of the patrol all but submerged. We cursed at the thought of all our gear (bedding, clothing, rations and personal items) being sopping wet. We'd have to wait for some time before we could wring them out and possibly lay them out in the sun, if ever the tactical situation allowed.

Then it rained. Not a gentle, sweet smelling, country-refreshing type rain, but a forceful stormy downpour which even made it difficult to see the person ahead of you. It made absolutely no difference to anyone, because we were all saturated anyway. Ninety-seven men, wearing uncomfortable, ill-fitting clothes, carrying enormous loads, well-oiled weapons and unlimited quantities of ammo, trudged on through the undergrowth with one purpose in mind; to get to our destination as soon as possible so that we could have a bit of a rest and a quiet smoke.

Finally we reach 'the Bone', the small hill we've been aiming for. The lead scout props and scans the rocky clearing which stretches for almost 1000 metres ahead. The wet season has brought new life to this familiar feature, as knee-high shrubs and saplings now cover the once bare hill.

Two of the platoons head off on separate tasks, while another remains with company HQ and sets up an ambush position, which will be our home for a few days.

As we lie in the mud and commence setting up our individual positions, we think of the last time we were here: of 4 Platoon's 2000 metre chase after the enemy, eventually catching up with them and killing two; of Kavanagh, the lad who died strangely of dehydration only 500 metres from here; and, of the stand-off against a large enemy group caught in their bunkers, just to the east, which resulted in Hughes being killed and Tilmouth being seriously wounded.

Yes, we know this place well, even if the rejuvenated countryside gives the appearance of an entirely different landscape.

Last night after digging our grave-like holes (to protect ourselves from enemy mortar and small arms fire) and setting our hootchies low over them, we settled down to the loneliness of the night routine. The rain came again but this time we were prepared.

Then the fire-flies, cicadas, frogs and other strange night creatures took over the darkness. Their sounds made it all the more lonely.

So here we are, still in our holes, still damp and muddy, still waiting for *it* to happen. If it does, we will be straight in there with everything, but till it does we just lay here and wait.

They say we'll be here for 10 days. That will be hard to take. At least there will be one re-supply by chopper, which means a mail delivery (the only link with home and the only thing that keeps us sane).

The next day. It's just on 1800 hours, or it's 6 pm, or the big hand is on the '12' and the little hand is on the '6'. That means it'll be dark again in an hour. Another night of rain and insect and animal noises. At least it doesn't get cold, although it does get very dark. You can't see six paces ahead of you.

This is to our advantage because any enemy moving through this area at night would have to use the small foot tracks that we ambush and even then, he'd have to use torches. So we have warning of his approach. Sometimes however you can mistake the fire-flies for distant lights and have to stay very calm even though it seems, a battalion of VC are moving about you in all directions. During the night, one third of our group remains alert and on sentry picket, at any one time.

Looking around me it's hard to imagine that there are 40 of us here. From my position I can only see five. Although there is some noise, it doesn't carry very far in this dense, wet scrub and we have sentries well out from the position to give us early warning should any VC stray our way.

I must look a disgrace; not the cleancut, good living, neatly-dressed soldier that people at home picture. My boots are heavy with water and mud and my saturated, baggy trousers are also covered in mud and are torn at the knee. My shirt is open, exposing my sweaty, hairy, dirty chest as well as my dog tags and peace medallion. My hands are red/brown and my fingernails are black. My hair is long and uncombed and I haven't shaved. Looking about me, I see five blokes who mirror the above description and one of them is 'the Major', so who cares.

The next morning. I've cleaned my rifle, shaved and feasted on a strong brew of Australian coffee and a US pecan roll, with condensed milk on top. What luxury.

Sorry about the state of my last pages, but what can you expect after carrying them around for several days in a saturated pocket, sleeping with them, wading deep creeks (stuffed them under my hat) and laying on the jungle floor with the lizards, frogs and leeches. I've found some dry, nearly new paper, so I'll finish off before it deteriorates also.

We've only been out five days but things aren't looking promising. The platoons and patrols have nothing to report and it looks like 'Charlie' has moved elsewhere. I wouldn't be surprised if we move to another area soon.

I'd better sign off as this letter, like this operation, will go on and on about nothing.

11 July

I've been sent back to the Dat, my love, to look after a few things that need attention. I'm not sure what is intended in the future but after this current operation, which may finish early if they don't find anything, there will be a major change in the company's location, so I've been sent back to make sure everything is ready for the next phase.

I'm relieved to hear from your last letter that things are getting back to normal, health-wise. I have caught up with Brian Hicks several times and he tells me how you are and I tell him how Bev is. I'm glad you and Bev are seeing a lot of each other.

I've managed to bring forward my R and R to early October and while there are some final details to sort out, you can plan on the second week.

You thrill me by writing exciting things such as 'by having an electric blanket you won't need to wear a nightie'. Now that's the greatest advertisement for selling electric blankets that I've heard and I'm all for them.

13 July. Private Cornes has just returned from his R and R in Taipei and has given me the low down on his escapades. He's a beaut bloke and has settled into B Company without any problems. He use to be in Mortar Platoon but didn't like the idea of being in base for so long, so he played up a bit. Eventually they sent him to another company and he's been doing well since then.

Does M-J recognise my photos or has he forgotten his Dad? I guess it's a bit much to expect a little bloke to remember me after five months, but I was wondering how hard it'll be to gain his confidence after I return. It'll be fun playing with him and learning all his characteristics again. I hope he doesn't get jealous of all the attention I plan to shower you with. He'd better learn to sleep in his own bed too, otherwise it could get a bit crowded.

I've just been informed that B Company will return from the bush on the seventeenth and be going back to the Horseshoe until the twenty-third. After which they'll spend 10 days at Nui Dat undergoing 'retraining', before heading off again, to parts unknown.

I'm now having to organise for their early return, which means several vehicle loads of stores being sent to the Horseshoe.

Every night at about seven, and in the mornings at the same time, I listen to Radio Australia and catch up on all the latest news. It gives a good coverage of world and Australian events and even if it concentrates on strikes and demonstrations, it helps keep up with what is going on back home. Sometimes it makes me feel so very sad to hear how the country is being torn apart by the politicians and unions. It's a shame that so many honest, everyday-people are being drawn into the turmoil. In the meantime, we are doing what is expected of us, even though we are being made out to be the cause of all the country's problems.

Every night swarms of large flying ants, attracted by the lights, descend on our tents. Tonight I'm bombarded by thousands of them and when it becomes unbearable, I attack them with a can of the army's best fly spray. It works for a while (about two paragraphs worth) but in they come again for a repeat performance. They win in the end, as I have to get under my mosquito net to finish my letters or the book I'm reading. By evening's end, I'm left with a floor and desk covered with insect bodies and their wings, which become detached during their death throes. They usually precede the night's downpour which is a Godsend for it not only cools the place down, it also gets rid of the insects until the next evening.

I've just been served a large salad roll and a cup of coffee by the company cook. If he keeps looking after me like this I'll come home with a rotund figure. It's a great evening snack which I appreciate immensely.

It's a dark, windy night which promises rain. Wouldn't it be nice to snuggle up together on a night like this. Give M-J a special hug and kiss for me and thank him for his drawings.

15 July

Dear Mark-John, good day little fellow. How are you? I certainly hope you're feeling much better after suffering all those ailments. Mum says that you did give her a few miserable days and nights but after all, you weren't feeling very well were you? Now that you're better, please remember that poor Mum is very tired and try not to be so demanding.

I've been told that you can run around and play games now. How you have grown since I last saw you! You were only just beginning to stand up when I left home. It seems ages ago, but it's only been five months. Keep up the good progress and I'll look forward to playing football with you when I get home.

You'll have to write me a letter and tell me what it's like living at Holsworthy. I know it's very cold, but your new electric blanket must be very cosy at nights.

Do you know, I'll be coming home for a little while in a few months. Even though it will only be for a few days, we will have time for all kinds of games and good fun. Then I'll go away again for a bit longer. But, soon after, I'll be back home again and this time, I'll stay with you for ever and ever.

Now, when I come home you'll have to get used to me wanting to be with your Mum a lot. You may feel left out of things for a while, because I'll keep hugging and kissing her all the time. But you and I will also have time to ourselves too. We will go for walks and you can show me all your favourite things. The playground, the backyard, and your best friend's sandpit.

What do you do when it's so cold and wet that you can't go outside to play? Do you read all your books and play with your favourite inside toys?

Well son, I'm sorry I'm not at home to watch you grow during this wonderful stage of your life, but I'll try and make it up to you when I get home. The three of us will have some wonderful times together.

We will go driving into the country for picnics and to the beach too. We'll visit all of our friends and perhaps you will be spoilt again by your grandparents. Won't it be fun to see them again!

Please tell your mother that I love her very much and that I miss her every day. Also tell her to take care and especially watch out when she is driving.

I've heard that you had an accident with Mum the other day, on the front steps. It must have been a horrible fright to have fallen down all those steps. Poor Mum hurt her arm and you bumped your head on the hard ground. Was it scary when you had to go to the doctor for a checkup? He's a friendly bloke who will always try and help you and Mum, so you should always be good when you go to see him.

Well my little mate, I've got to go to work now so I'll say goodbye. Have fun, stay healthy and look after Mum for me. Give her a big hug and kiss and tell her not to worry about me.

All my love

Your Dad.

15 July

My love, there are times when I feel so very, very lonely. Times when only your presence can pull me from deep blackness and hopelessness. These feelings come more frequently nowadays, brought on by a tune or song, a photo or as occurred tonight, a film. My only reaction is to take myself away from whatever it is I'm doing and go to my tent, so that I can be alone with the memory of you.

Oh God, how I need you. I'm feeling utter despair knowing that it'll be months before we will be together again.

Some blokes sit and drink together, discussing all the latest news and chatting about anything and everything. I'm in such a state that I can't think of anything to say or add to their conversations. I find everything so stifling, so useless, that I have to go for a walk, alone with my thoughts.

Even writing letters becomes a burden because they are only words on paper, they get no response, they can't really express my deepest emotions. Yet they are my only contact with you, the one who means everything in the world to me. You have me so tied up that I'm sure you rule my soul as well as my heart.

My love, all I can think about is you. To hold you, love you and to be so very close to you. To do the simple things in life like sitting at the dinner table and sharing the meal that you have prepared, lounging in a chair in our comfortable home, listening to one of our favourite records, sitting in front of the fire with you, touching your hair and caressing your face.

Darling, darling, we've spent so much time apart that I'm scared we will never find each other again. This is a nightmare.

It's now morning and I'm trying to keep busy so that my feelings of last night don't come flooding back. I have to take the company's gear to the Horseshoe and get the place in running order before they get back from the operation.

I'm still feeling lost and alone, but with the sun has come a realisation that I have to beat this depression, otherwise I'll be little use to anyone. Even so, the heartache remains. See what you do to me.

Yesterday we had another mine incident in which three were seriously wounded. A sergeant from A Company (Ian Dunn's platoon I think) lost both feet so they'll get him and the others back to Australia immediately. I believe his brother, also a sergeant, was killed in action in 1965. What a terrible thing to happen. How must the family be feeling? I guess there are many families throughout Australia experiencing such devastation, having their lives shattered by this war.

I'm seeing the bullshit that goes with living in a base camp every day and although it seems petty and insignificant, it creates its own frustrations and hardship for those who have to bear the brunt of it. The soldiers here are keeping the administration running smoothly and their efforts help to sustain those in the bush. They're often criticised by others who know little of what they have to put up with and while they may not live it rough, or be exposed to danger as much as those in the bush, they do an important job, for little recognition.

A typical job that was given to the few soldiers who occupy B Company lines was to paint all permanent fixtures. They were given tins of pink, blue, yellow, green and red paint and told to finish the job before the company returns in a couple of weeks. Apart from the fact that only three soldiers can be released from their duties at any one time, the constant heavy rain is making the task almost impossible. However, in typical army fashion, the job is being done bit by bit and the colours that can be seen scattered through the rubber trees make you feel like the circus is in town. I'm not sure if the colour scheme will go down too well with 'the Major', as his tent was painted pink and yellow, until I suggested that he would probably prefer a simple green.

I won't be sad to see the end of this place, even though it has a few great amenities. The company as a whole, has been here for less than 10 days in the last 10 weeks and only about 30 days altogether since we've been in country.

The eighteenth. I'm at the Horseshoe now. The company has been delayed by 24 hours so I've got the luxury of another day to set up. Just as well because the weather has taken its toll on some of our tents, bunkers, roads and tracks. The vegetation is now chest high, so we've a lot of work in front of us to get this place back to how it was.

A US Mobile Artillery Battery (self-propelled eight inch guns) will be sharing our area for a while. They have just come in from Cambodia and need some time for repair and replenishment. The soldiers are a mix of white and black and an unruly mob they seem to be too. I don't think any one of them has a uniform. Some wear open shirts or flack jackets, others go bare chested. Their trousers and boots look like they've never been cleaned. The relationship between officers and soldiers seems very strained, almost hostile. Although they're friendly towards all of us, I know they have some drugs with them so we'll have to be careful how they influence our lads.

Their guns are huge; bigger than anything I've ever seen. When they fire, the whole place shakes. The projectile breaks the sound barrier as it leaves the muzzle and the shock waves send anything that is not nailed down, flying. We will have to rebuild our five-hole toilet, because the first time these guns fired, the floor caved in.

19 July

I've got an hour to go before I finish radio picket and as nothing much is happening, I thought I'd drop you a line.

Today the dirty, uncouth, motley, ragged, smelly and tired company returned to the Horseshoe. Yesterday, I had set up all the administration and stores for them and was feeling pretty good because, as our storeman was off on R and R, I had to do all the planning and ensure everything was correctly documented and stacked exactly where it was needed. Then, with only an hour and a half before the company was expected, I was told they would be taking over C Company's area and not going back to their previous area. So I commandeered a truck and with the help of anyone I could find, moved everything over to the new area. We were just sorting it all out again when the word came through that someone had got it wrong, they'd go into their old lines after all. You can imagine what I said to the messenger. So, I commandeered another truck and got the stuff back to where it was originally. We had only just stored the last of it in its place when the company appeared. I'm sure no one knew anything about the trouble we'd gone to and I haven't said anything about it to 'the Major', but if I find out who it was that caused the mix up, I'll make sure he knows he's taken three years off my life.

On their arrival I had to organise the following for each of the platoons:

- beer and cool drinks;
- change of clothing and the collection of dirty greens for dry cleaning;
- issue of luxury items (shaving cream, smokes, writing paper);
- collection of equipment that had been damaged and issue its replacement;
- redistribution of ammunition;
- packing of stores to be returned to Nui Dat;
- hand out all of the administration papers that had accumulated over the weeks;
- finalise the paperwork required for those wanting medical and dental treatment and for those who are about to go on R and R;
- work out the duty rosters for the next few days;
- work out the duty rosters for when we return to Nui Dat.

I was flat out for the rest of the day and missed out on lunch and dinner. It looks like tomorrow won't be any easier.

Back here, the night ambush routine will be our main focus. What do you know? Here I am on radio picket and I've just recorded that on the first night out, Karl's group contacted two VC entering the village of Dat Do. One was killed and a quantity of documents and two weapons were captured. There's more action around the villages than out in the bush!

Today I heard that I won't be going as liaision officer to the Yanks, nor will I be going to the demilitarised zone. Apparently 'the Major' has said to Colonel Grey that he wants 'Winter to continue as 2IC because he knows the blokes and does the job well'. That's the closest thing I'll get to a compliment from him. Anyway, I'm feeling that all the hard work over the last day has proven the point.

It's now 11 pm and I've got 15 minutes left on radio picket, so I'll close off my letter until tomorrow. Good night my love.

21 July. I've just had another run-in with 'the Major'. This time over the issue of income tax forms and group certificates. I had planned to sign them out to everyone when we get back to the Dat, in two days time, but all of a sudden he wants them issued now. I tried to explain that the diggers won't be able to do anything with them until they get back and those needing assistance will be in a better position to get information from their platoon commanders and the administration staff. Then there's the risk that some could be lost during the packing and unpacking. 'That's *their* problem', was his reply. 'Get them out by midday.' And that was that. So I did.

The weather has been a bit strange. Very hot and sunny for a couple of days, then two or three days of heavy rain. A couple of drizzly days follow and then the sun comes out in force again. We're all making the most of the sun to dry out our wet and mouldy gear.

23 July. We're back at the Dat now and I'm settling in with all the added administration requirements. I've had to arrange pay, ID card checks, weapon number checks, next of kin checks. Routine Orders have had to be read, platoon stores issued and duty rosters finalised. In one way it's good to get back here and enjoy the added comforts and facilities, but there's a lot of bullshit that goes along with it, so it won't be long before we are longing for the freedom of the bush again.

For the next 10 days however we'll be pretty busy. The commanding officer has listed all those areas that the companies require training such as, casualty evacuation, mine warfare, weapon firing by day and night. We've got a lot of sport arranged too.

It looks like my new job will keep me here for longer than I had expected. They've lined me up for a job in the battalion's administration command post, starting after this retraining period. I'll be working with the battalion 2IC (Major Smethurst) and the operations officer (Major Cole). They're both pretty hard task masters but I think, after my experiences with Major 'W', I'll find it a bit of a breeze.

You've certainly had a busy time of it yourself. I'm proud of your efforts in helping our neighbours. I'm pleased that we're living in an army village at this time, as everyone understands the situation and is willing to help others, regardless of rank.

Poor M-J. You tell me he seems to have come down with the mumps. Well, I guess if he's going to come down with all the wogs that little kids get, then it's best to get them in one hit, rather than have them spread out over several months.

I'm glad I'm missing out on winter at Holsworthy. How I hate being frozen. I can still remember those dreadful nights on ambush exercise in the Holsworthy Range when it was so cold that some of the soldiers couldn't move in the mornings and had to be helped to stand and then a lot of massaging to get their arms and fingers working again.

The only good Holsworthy winter nights are those spent with you, before our open fire place. Snuggling up together in bed was pretty special too. Now you've got an electric blanket. I don't suppose we'll be doing that sort of thing again ... like hell!

That bloody airline strike you've just had, disrupted mail and supplies and some lads even missed out on their R and R flights. I can't understand how just a handful of people can create such havoc throughout the whole country and get away with it.

The photos you sent have been added to my collection. I spend the last few minutes of every day studying them and longing for the time when we can have a photo taken with all three of us in it together.

Tonight I'm Orderly Officer. I check that the gun pickets and sentries are alert and that everyone beds down quietly after 'lights out'. I visit all the areas and spend a bit of time chatting to the diggers. They show me photos of home, play their tapes and read parts of their letters. I get to swap some of my books and magazines too. It's beaut to see them so relaxed, after the strain of the past operation. They're showing two movies tonight, so a lot of our lads are taking in the pictures.

I'll sign off now my love with a prayer that you and M-J are feeling better. Thank you for all the letters you write. They are a terrific help for me to keep going when things get a bit tough.

25 July

Dear Mum, Rex and boys, the long and winding road has led me to a plateau which is almost at the summit of one of the bleakest, loneliest and troublesome mountains I've ever climbed. The peak is lost in the dark clouds which foretell of even more sadness. But, we're told the sun is shining on the other side. Those who have completed this arduous task tell us that it's a little easier on the downward slope, that you can follow a cool stream of sparkling water through lush green paddocks, where right at the bottom, there's a gum tree. A huge old tree with massive grey branches and sweet smelling leaves, which stands there to welcome us. Carved into the tree trunk are thousands of names of those who have made it safely over the mountain.

This is the mountain that is testing us all and along the way some have dropped out. Looking back I can see thousands of tired soldiers, carrying huge burdens, struggling, slipping, falling, being hurt, but still struggling on. Mateship is strong and without it many would have given up. The loads vary, some are heavier than others, but all backs are bent to take the strain. Now and then a cheery voice of encouragement is heard and some backs straighten for a while.

How we long to be on the other side, in sight of the welcoming gum tree. How we long to be resting in the shade of its spreading canopy, finally at the end of our journey.

This is how I picture my tour. I'm almost halfway through. What lies ahead is unknown except that it contains many periods of loneliness and feelings of frustration, futility and pain. One day however, it'll all be over and I can settle down again to a life of peace and calm, surrounded by those I love.

Sometimes I feel that some of us will never be able to return, because the journey over the mountain has been too tough. They'll make it to the gum tree but they'll never get back to the place they came from.

There's a song on the radio that tells it all: 'Lord we don't need another mountain, we have mountains and hillsides enough to climb.' I'm sure that everyone here agrees. Perhaps there will be some good that comes from this journey but to many of us, it's a lost cause because no one back home cares. I don't mean our families, I mean the rest of the population, our leaders, our countrymen. They have steepened the mountain side and have added to the weight in our packs. They are making this journey unbearable.

So here I am, resting on a boulder, almost at the top, taking a breather, before one last attempt to reach the summit. Yet even I am wondering if it's really going to be worth the effort.

In the meantime, life goes on. I played my first game of football today. On a very hard, rough clearing, surrounded by bamboo and bananas, B Company defeated C Company: 9 goals, 4; to 2 goals, 3. The conditions were very hot and humid so everyone discarded their jumpers after the first 10 minutes and from then on it was 36 hot, sweaty, tanned bodies going all out. I wonder what the locals would have made of it?

Private Cornes, our Glenelg star, was in ruck and his talents, although a bit rusty, were the main reason for our success. I can still hold my own when it comes to a bit of a scrap and came away with three goals to my name. I might add that I will be feeling a bit sore tomorrow when my muscles finally remind me that I'm not as young and fit as I used to be.

My bush days are over for a while. That should please you Mum. In a week's time I'll be leaving B Company and going to Administration Company as a command post officer. I'll be where all the action is recorded. My job is to collate all the moves of the platoons and patrols from 2RAR, 8RAR, and 7RAR and all the other supporting units. I'll be on the radio all day and at nights too. I'll tell you more as time goes by.

There is a comic strip in one of the Sydney papers called *Pogo*. That's the word we use to describe a base soldier. It's a derogatory term for someone who doesn't go outside the wire and who lives in relative comfort (sleeps in a bed, eats at a table, showers daily with soap, dresses in clean greens). Well mother, your son is now a Pogo.

29 July

I'm very worried, my darling. The letter I received yesterday reminds me of the time, before we were married, when I was at the Infantry Centre, Ingleburn and you were in Adelaide. As I immersed myself in the wonders of a new career, I was unaware of the difficulties you were having and how your health was deteriorating. If it wasn't for your parents, I'd never have known that you were sinking into a world of despair. Now I get a letter that is scribbled, misspelt and not at all like anything I've ever received from you. I was totally unaware of how ill you were and the terrible time you've had, and here I am telling you about all the problems I'm having.

You must tell me everything that is happening, so that I know that the two most precious people in the world are not suffering, or so I can at least do something to help. I'm hoping that the next letter I receive will tell me that all is well. I know we have a lot of friends and neighbours that will help, but I won't feel easy until I know your back on your feet and handling the regular family routine, with your usual confidence.

Please let me know how M-J handled being with another family. What was his reaction to staying at Liz's place? I hope he doesn't go down with whatever you've got, especially since he's already struggling with other illnesses.

30 July. I received your welcomed letter this afternoon and am so relieved to hear that things have improved. I'll write to the Steens

and thank them for their help. I might have some trouble winning my son back, if he's so happy to be with other families.

You don't know how relieved I am to know that you're better. It's like a great weight has been lifted from my heart. But please, let me know what caused the illness.

It's now 20 past midnight and I've just come from running a range practice that lasted four and a half hours. I'm really buggered, but it was good to see that everything went well. I'll jump straight into bed, smelly clothes and all. There's time for a shower in the morning, because we've been told we don't have to front up till seven.

31 July. Another month is almost at an end and the good news is that we are almost halfway there.

Tonight we are having a formal Dining-In night, wearing polyesters and our Vietnam ribbons. We are celebrating six months in the country and the fact that this will be the last time the battalion as a whole, will be together until we embark for Sydney next year. It's great to catch up with all the others and hear how they've been getting on. It's surprising to see so many new faces, not just among the officers and NCOs, but also the diggers. Doug's platoon has had 19 changes. In a fortnight we'll lose another 11 soldiers who are from the fourteenth National Service intake. They'll pack their bags and leave us and then be out of the army just as soon as they reach Sydney. That's not going to be too easy for them because they'll be with their digger mates in a war zone one day, then back with their civvy friends the next. What a great adjustment they'll have to make to their lives.

6 Platoon remains the same because they're from the sixteenth intake, which means they'll see the whole tour out.

It's now 3.45 pm and we've just returned from mine training. It's rained all day and we are all feeling a little washed out, in more ways than one. These tropical downpours leave the place in such a shambles and yet in no time the place dries out and things are back to normal. Remember the tropical storms on Elcho?

I'll get this letter off to you because I'm not sure what the next few days will bring. This new job may distract me from my normal letter writing.

1 August

I've received your letter dated the twenty-ninth. That's the fastest the postman has ever delivered your mail. Just as well, because you've now been able to set my mind at ease about your illness and what you plan to do in the coming weeks.

I was pleased to hear that your Mum had arrived to give you a hand and even though she has suffered from the Holsworthy weather, I'm sure her presence will be of great comfort to you.

How has M-J survived these last few hectic days? Poor fellow, must wonder what the heck is going on. Please don't hesitate to call on extra help from our neighbours as they will be only too willing to lend a hand. Keep me in touch with how you pull through this difficult time.

I haven't heard anything official about my move, but I'm getting used to last minute changes. Major 'W' hasn't said a thing. You'd think after all the time I've spent in B Company he'd at least say thanks and good luck, or something.

I've received letters from Joan, Dad and Mum and one from *Reader's Digest* (how do *they* know where I am?). All the family is well and their letters tell of parties, dances and happy times. When I think of what you're missing out on I feel guilty, because I've dragged you away from all your friends, into a lonely life. I promise to make it up to you.

Yesterday I had a pleasant surprise, I was listening to the local armed forces radio when a program recorded in the studio of 5KA was played. It was specifically for all South Aussie soldiers and included interviews with wives and families and had a lot about what was happening in sport and news from around the State. It was really nice to have something unexpected come from home.

Next payday I'll have $204 in my book, so let me know if you would like me to get some over to you.

Remember when we moved from Canungra to Sydney and couldn't find a place to stay? You and M-J had to sleep on the kitchen floor at Ron and Gill's place, until I could find something suitable. I never want you to go through anything like that again, so I'll do anything to see that you and M-J live in decent surroundings.

If only we could spend some time together to plan and work at our future. It seems that the army keeps pulling us apart before we can establish anything worthwhile.

Have I told you lately that I love you? How else can I feel about a woman who has waited so many times for me, put up with my moods and never once said anything to make me doubt her love. Oh boy, how lucky I am. You are everything to me and I'll never let you down again. If ever I become difficult in years to come, remind me of what we've been through this year and I'm sure I'll soon snap out of it.

How does your garden grow, or should I say how is M-J's jungle training centre.

Darling I'll sign off now, give M-J a hug and a kiss from me. Show him my photo and see if he recognises me.

Chapter Six

Pogo

7 August–3 October 1970

7 August

My love, I'm sitting in the battalion's administration command post which is located five foot underground in the middle of 7RAR's Nui Dat location and this has been my second home since B Company returned to the Horseshoe four days ago. Although I'm still on the company's books, the intention is to post me to Administration Company so as far as I'm concerned, I'm no longer under the influence of 'the Major'. The problem is, that from now on I'll be classed as a Pogo. I'm not sure which is worse.

Here in my underground world, I'm surrounded by maps, charts, radios, telephones, log books, code books and operational procedure forms. On the wall behind me, in fact covering the whole wall, is a map of Phouc Tuy Province. This is covered by a clear plastic sheet on which is written, in coloured chinagraph pencil, the areas of responsibility each battalion has and some detail about their latest activities.

Another map shows in greater detail the area that surrounds the task force base. This is divided into sectors with names such as Somme, Messines and Buna which denote the areas that are regularly patrolled in order to keep the locals well back from our perimeter wire. Each battalion sends out two patrols every 24 hours, to search and clear an area 5000 metres around the base. All task force patrols are logged on this map and those from 7RAR are controlled and supported from this command post.

On my right, there is another map which details all the artillery

Battalion's administration command post

and mortar predetermined targets that would be used if Nui Dat or the Horseshoe were attacked. All patrol locations are also plotted, so that they can be supported by a fire plan which will immediately go into action, if they are attacked.

The wall to my left is covered with clue boards which hold special forms used when a unit requests assistance. I've just filled one out to provide helicopter support for C Company's next maintdem. There are others for every conceivable activity or request.

Then there are the radios. There's one for the base defence, which links us to all the companies in the 7RAR Nui Dat area. There's the battalion command net, which keeps us in touch with the operations command post, which is located at the Horseshoe. The task force command radio has us linked with all other units within Nui Dat. Our administration net is the way in which all companies within 7RAR are supported and re-supplied. Our fifth radio is to control the battalion's Nui Dat patrols.

The telephones link us to all our companies, including those at the Horseshoe and through special switchboards, to all other HQ within the Nui Dat base.

Almost every transmission that is sent or received is partly or wholly in code. That means we have to do a lot of encoding and decoding before messages are sent and received. Then, everything that is said over the radio or telephones has to be written down in the daily running log sheets (in triplicate). You can imagine that when there is a lot going on it can get pretty hectic.

I have to arrange the roster to make sure there is a sergeant or an officer on duty at all times, together with a private from the Signal Platoon to look after the equipment and another to act as a runner.

My routine is a lot different than in the past:

0630 – Reveille
0700 – Breakfast (in the officers mess)
0730–1230 – CP duty
1230 – Lunch (in the officers mess)
1315–1430 – Task force HQ conference
1430–1615 – Battalion duties and rest
1630 – Battalion conference
1800 – Dinner (guess where)
1830–2230 – CP duty

I'm enjoying being involved in the bigger picture. I'm able to follow the movements of every platoon, I hear the commanding officer brief his company commanders and I get to meet officers from other units that I didn't even know were over here. Everything that is happening in 7, 8 and 2RAR, and their supporting units, I get to hear about.

8 August. The days have been hotter lately, with little rain and the nights are slightly colder. I'm still settling into my new routine and am feeling that, by working in the command post, I'll get a wider perspective on what's happening within 7RAR. This may help me to understand some of the strange decisions which, as a platoon commander and 2IC, I couldn't see sense in.

How's the car going? I hope, with all your travelling about it remains reliable. You'd better get the garage to check out the clutch if it's giving you problems. Well my love, it's '62 and awakey' or in other words, 62 more sleeps until I'm heading back to you on R and R. I'd better start a fitness program so that I can last out all through those exciting days and nights. Come to think of it, so should you.

How's your Mum? I hope all your illness and M-J's sickness are well and truly over and she's survived the ordeal of looking after you both, even though not feeling so good herself.

I've been issued with four new sets of greens with my name printed across the shirt breast pockets. I wear silver pips, the gold 'Australia' on my shoulders and carry a pistol in a holster on my hip. It's almost if I were on special duty in some HQ in Australia, rather than in the middle of a war zone. I'm safe and sound.

17 August

The intelligence summary reads like a shopping list:

> 19 VC killed;
> 6 VC captured;
> 1 VC Hoi Chanh;
> 9 weapons of various make and model, together with ammo;
> 550 lbs rice, 72 lbs sugar, 20 lbs biscuits, 10 lbs salt, 10 lbs tobacco, 20 cartons of cigarettes, 12 tins of cooking oil, 30 lbs dried fish, 50 torch batteries, 40 large tins of condensed milk, 22 cakes of soap, 10 tins of baby food, 156 tins of fish in oil, large quantities of medical supplies and clothing, including children's clothes.

In the area of operation called Monkey, at 0315 on 12 August 1970, at grid reference 402 633 (which is 3500 metres south-west of where I sleep) a platoon from 8RAR, with the help of a section of APCs, ambushed 50–60 Viet Cong who were leaving Hoa Long. They had seen the enemy enter the village at about 10 o'clock but were not in a good position to make contact with them, so had crept closer to the track they had used and set up an ambush.

After a five-hour wait they saw the group coming from the village, loaded with supplies. The ambush was sprung and lasted almost half an hour, with artillery being used as cut-off along the likely western and southern escape routes. Many of the enemy raced back into the village, to seek shelter. After the initial action, an armoured force from Nui Dat descended on the scene and surrounded the area, blocking all tracks. A sweep was made at first light with the help of helicopters, to count the cost and flush others from their hiding places. Meanwhile, the local authorities began a search of the village, in an attempt to identify the VC who were being sheltered.

Many of the wounded left in the ambush area were women, some of them quite young. Some were found lying in the creeks, covered with reeds and trying to hide beneath the water level by breathing through hollow reeds. One young lad tried to bluff his way out by pretending to be a local farmer, tending his field. The area was a terrible scene of slaughter and mayhem.

Soldiers who had sprung the ambush and caused the carnage then had to tend the wounded and get them into choppers, which took them to Nui Dat and Vung Tau field hospitals for further treatment.

I wonder how they felt when they observed the results of their ambush. It would have been a pretty awful experience. It's one thing to attend to a dead body, but having to patch up their victims, especially women and young girls, would have caused all kinds of emotional turmoil. No wonder some of our lads are all mixed up about this war.

The ambush success has had a huge effect throughout the task force and everyone is talking about it. It has lifted morale and provides a classic example that we are succeeding with the military war, even if the political side may be heading for an embarrassing withdrawal.

Sorry this letter is all about horrible things. On a brighter note, I've got to tell you that I'm suffering from a rash which covers the tops of my legs and my scrotum. I've got an ointment to try and clear it up, but the itching is driving me crazy. I only hope I can get some sun and surf on my next R and C, because I know it's about the only treatment that will work. Don't worry, all will be well by R and R.

21 August

The weather has changed recently and it's becoming dark and drizzly. For the first time in six months I've felt a little cold. The rain and the wind has kept up for the past eight hours and there doesn't seem to be a break coming. I feel sorry for those in the bush.

Because I'm still on the books of B Company I was able to join them on a two-day R and C and it was beaut to catch up with them and still feel part of the company.

On the truck journey down to Vung Tau we passed the area where 8RAR ambushed a large number of Viet Cong, a week ago. They killed 19, and APCs, tanks and artillery were used in the very aggressive follow-up. The rice fields we passed showed a lot of damage, with armoured tracks criss-crossing a huge area. The bunds had been broken and it looked like most of the crop would have been destroyed, which no doubt wouldn't please the local farmers. I wondered if they are given any payment for their destroyed crops. Somehow, I don't think so. So much for winning their hearts and minds.

I'm afraid that the B Company officers are not a happy bunch. It's obvious that they are all feeling the way I did about Major 'W'. It's not very often that you get all the platoon commanders and the artillery forward observer speaking in one voice like this and I was somewhat surprised that they felt almost exactly the same as I had when I was in the thick of things. Bill reckons that now that 'the Major' doesn't have me to focus on, they're all copping it. Anyway, they've decided to put up with it for a while, but may have a quiet word with someone if it gets any worse. For once, I felt that all my problems of the past had been understood by my mates and while I was sorry for their difficulties, it made my departure from the company a little less harder to take.

Colonel Grey has suggested that when I finish my stint in the command post (as yet he can't say when), I'll be posted to another company as a platoon commander. He's considering that, on return to Australia, I should remain with the 7th Battalion and be promoted into a captain's position, as part of the rebuilding of the unit. It all sounds great, but I'll take it as it comes and not get carried away with any of these long-term possibilities.

When I returned from Vung Tau, I was surprised to see four letters and your tape waiting for me. The tape was wonderful. All the news about Mark-John, his latest sayings, tricks and tantrums. It was wonderful to hear his voice as he told you of all his latest adventures. He isn't the same little baby I held in my arms all those months ago, is he!

Please give Grandma Bowey a big kiss from me, for her eightieth. I hope it's a lovely day.

22 August (180 days to go, 185 days away). I received your latest letter yesterday, along with the monthly edition of *Reader's Digest*. In the past two days I've written six letters and am starting to find it hard to say anything interesting. You can relate the latest command post story only so many times before it becomes boring.

Fancy celebrating the halfway mark already. Apart from the first few days here, which remain very clear in my memory, the rest of the time is just a blur of bamboo, sweat, dust and mud. We've covered a lot of ground, had some never to be forgotten experiences and learned a lot. Even so, I wouldn't like to do it over again.

I can't fully understand your feelings about the home unit. While I know it is a drain on our income and takes money which you could use elsewhere, it is an important asset which will be worth something in the future. Remember also, it was my decision to purchase that unit, not Robyn and Guy's and without it you and M-J would have continued to sleep on kitchen floors and in terrible old caravans. The days before we moved into the unit were a nightmare. Surely you haven't forgotten how bad it was. OK, so now we are in an army home and we don't need the unit, but I'd prefer to wait until I get back, so we can check out the resale value. It also depends on whether I stay in the army and if so, where we'll be posted. So please darling, have a little patience. I'll try and send you extra money from my pay book to help clear some of those worrying debts.

You mentioned the wet picnic at Belair National Park. What wonderful memories that place has for me. When I was very young and Dad was involved with the Adelaide Cricket Club they would hold their Christmas party in one of the picnic areas. It would always finish off with a visit from Father Christmas, carrying a sack of presents.

I can picture Mark-John getting stuck into his barbecue sausage. Pretty soon he'll be racing around with all the other kids, in the creeks, up the trees and around the tracks. By the look of him, in those photos you sent, he's growing up into a healthy, happy young lad and why shouldn't he, with a Mum like you to take care of him. Your photo is absolutely beautiful. What a pity I'll have to send it back to you. You look so lovely. No wonder I'm content to be under your thumb. What a delightful position it is too.

PS Only about 40 days to R and R.

25 August

The days are passing fairly fast, although I must admit this job isn't as exciting as others I've had. I'm not complaining, as I don't yearn for the hard-hitting, exhausting life I had. It's just that this is so different.

I enjoy listening to all the activities going on throughout the province and get a special kick out of hearing familiar B Company voices. I'm getting a clearer picture of all the efforts going on. The problems, frustrations, humour and emergencies I hear every day have broadened my outlook towards the war and the way we are going about our task.

Last night I saw a beaut film called *Generation* starring two young people I didn't know and David Jansen. It was about a young married couple; modern types, with new ideas about life, including delivering their own child. Jansen played their father who was desperately trying to understand them and be a supportive parent. The girl was eight months pregnant and every night would go through her breathing exercises (memories of Main Beach).

The birth scene was fantastic and I remembered what you went through, my hospital visits and the waiting. I couldn't help but remember your pregnant months at Main Beach and even though I was away in Canungra for most of the time, what time we did spend together was really wonderful. I often think about you, your figure and how proud I was walking with you, because everyone could see that we were so happy and that the child you were carrying was the result of our love.

Karl and Owen came back from their R and R yesterday. They aren't feeling too flash because it was all over too quickly. Owen will be taking on the job of 2IC, B Company, so I wished him all the very best.

I'm feeling excited as the days to our R and R get closer. I guess I'll feel like Owen and Karl when it's all over, but we will at least have shared some time together and it will strengthen us for the final phase of the terrible journey we are on.

I've moved into the Administration Company lines as Owen has taken over my old tent. It was amazing what rubbish I got out of the place. Everything, including old letters, boots and clothing, was covered in mould. I came across all kinds of gear I had forgotten about.

I hope everything is OK in Adelaide and M-J isn't being spoilt too much.

I'm fine, my rash is slowly going away. I'm sure it was something I laid in when I was last in a Dat Do paddy.

26 August

A card arrived in the mail today and it jolted me. What a sexy thing to send a lonely soldier! Thank you my love for helping me through these worrying times.

I guess I haven't got a lot to worry about, although when I read the papers and hear the news on US and Australian radio, I just get fed up with all the things that are making our task here so much more difficult. Even your concern about our financial position and the doubt that we'll ever be able to make ends meet, makes me feel sometimes that we are living in different worlds.

You're in a world where everything you do is controlled by the mighty dollar. I know it's not easy, especially with having to care for M-J. Your friends are in more settled lifestyles and already appear to be building a secure future, with a house, stereo, TV and car. All the lovely things that I suppose you'd like us to have. Hopefully we'll have all of that one day, but right now the situation isn't as clear for us as I would like it to be. I feel trapped by what seems to be the never-ending demands on our life, the expectation that we must have a house and car, as symbols of success and security. Right now these thing are not as important to me as just staying healthy and having a loving family. Our financial state is something we can work on together, when we are at last together.

I look about me and I see people apparently happy, but it's all on the surface. Their only concern is for themselves. They care little for what's going on around them. In many ways they're as trapped as I am. My problem is that I know you are struggling, but there is little I can do about it from here. I wonder if it would be any different if my life had taken a different track. What if we had stayed on Elcho, or had taken that job with Australian Volunteers Abroad? I'm young enough to change direction when all this is over, but will it really take us where we want to go?

I wrote the following last night, in an attempt to sort out my confused mind:

> Soldier, prepare to return to the world and to face again the pressures of everyday living and to carry the burden of the world's problems; air and water pollution, an uncaring Government, uni student demonstrations, union strikes, violence, extortion and the mounting road toll. All of these will soon be your problems again. You'll have to adjust to a changing lifestyle, just as others back home are doing.
>
> The loads you've humped about the bush over here will seem light and comfortable compared to the burdens you will take on board back home. You've looked forward for so long to climb aboard the freedom bird, but what unfriendly jungle will it take you to?
>
> It is far worse than the steaming Vietnam jungle you've cursed for 12 months, for this new one is filled with dangers that you have never faced before and this time you won't have your mates with you, to lend a hand. You'll be in a community that won't care about where you've been, or what you've done. Your experiences will mean little in this uncaring and frightful place. You have wept when your mates died on the battlefield, but they do not weep when people are slaughtered on the roads.
>
> The foul smell of burning forests and vegetation will fill your lungs together with the smog from the cities and the waste from the industrial smoke stacks. Unlike the quietness of the jungle, there will be little silence where you are going. There will be little time to see the beauty that is left because you'll be caught up in the accelerating race for life and the fight for financial rewards.
>
> Living in painted boxes, row upon row, with a hallowed piece of ground that is fiercely protected, is all they aspire to. Their boundary fences keep outsiders from viewing the heaven that is theirs and keeps them from seeing how others live. They don't wish to see beyond their own world. They don't wish to hear what others are saying. They don't care.

Soldier, remember the simple joys in your life. Sitting under a tree beside a flowing stream in some isolated part of the jungle, a quiet joke with your mates at a time when the situation was so very difficult. Don't ever forget the sunrise or sunsets you witnessed from the bunkers at the Horseshoe.

You never knew the problems of money, or the pressures of constant payments and strangling debts, while doing all you did but, I'm afraid these will be your main focus from now on.

Why? Why is it that the one chance you have had to escape from the deadly rat-race society, you are throwing away with the foolish notion that things will be better when you get back home? You'll never get a chance like this again. You'll never have mates like this again. You'll never feel so wanted like this again. You'll never fit in like this again.

Why do you want to return to a place where the likelihood of you being killed is 500 times greater, where the everyday pressures are becoming too great for too many, where the moral standards are changing so rapidly that society is confused and angry?

You're not ready for all of this. You are going into a battle ill-prepared. You haven't been trained for this. Many of you will not survive unless you are prepared to surrender to the enemy and accept their selfishness. Will you make the necessary adjustments? Will you become like them?

I'm not sure that I fully believe all that I wrote, but I do feel strongly about the pressures that will be on a lot of us when we return. It won't be the same as when we left. Whether that's because of what we've experienced here or whether it's what has happened at home in our absence, I'll probably never know. Perhaps it's a bit of both.

Whatever my love, I'll need you more than ever.

27 August

It's impossible to explain to you how I'm feeling, because it's a mixture of emotions. It's nothing to do with my job, in fact I'm enjoying the new experience. It's more to do with what I see and hear around me. It's an uneasiness about the future that has me questioning: What direction am I – are we – heading? I don't just mean you and me, I'm including everyone.

I spend a lot of time talking to others and I must say I'm not the only one feeling uneasy. In the two evenings I have off, I get to thinking. During the lonely hours when I'm lying in bed or sitting at my table writing letters and even at the films, I realise that these are really lost hours. They should be hours spent with you and Mark-John. I read your letters over and over and try to picture how it would be if I were home. I longed for the experience of Vietnam, but now know that the benefits will never make up for what it is taking from us.

I remember writing to Mum and telling her how important it was for me to be in Vietnam. I needed to prove to myself that after years of training, I could handle the situation. Well, I got the answer to that after about four months and now that selfish quest has been satisfied. I also wanted to know what the basic instincts of warfare were like; the tension, the fear, the mateship. What was it like to be shot at and to shoot back in anger. Again, that was answered in the first few months and I now realise that words like pain, death, killing and mutilation all play a part. It becomes a very personal thing and I'm not interested in the subject any more. I may return a little richer, money-wise. I'll certainly be a lot more wealthy, experience-wise. But in the end, I'll be the poorer.

On to more pleasant things ... Thanks for the news that you're beginning the pill again, in preparation for R and R. I'll have to continue taking my pills too (paludrin and dapsone for malaria), so we will have to sit on the bed together and ensure that we both do the right thing.

I've just realised that I don't have many civvy clothes to wear when I get home. Apart from my 'about the house' wear, I don't think I've got anything suitable for a night out. Perhaps we'll have to go shopping, so that I can get something decent. I don't think my uniform will go down too well in the flashest restaurants.

31 August. I received your package containing almonds and dried apricots and got stuck into them straight away. I did offer one

or two to my neighbours, but it was pure luxury to sit back on my bed and devour them, as I flicked through the latest *Playboy*. I'd forgotten how apricots have a laxative effect, so paid for my greediness a couple of hours later. Please, no more apricots.

All my skin rashes and infections have finally gone and I'm feeling pretty healthy. I certainly can't complain about lack of sleep any more. I'm sleeping soundly and feel a little guilty when I think of my mates out at the Horseshoe.

Dear little M-J can now recite *Twinkle, Twinkle*. I can't wait to see him in action. I hope he doesn't go all shy on me, after all, I'll be just like a stranger to him. Then no sooner will he start getting used to me and I'll be off again. It'll be so confusing to him.

Every payday we get issued with a 'supplementary pack' which is a box of goodies such as toothpaste, shaving cream, and razor blades. I hardly needed any of mine when I was with B Company, so I've built up quite a store of bathroom essentials. By the time the year is up I'll have a crate full of stuff which should keep me going for a year or two, so that's one area we will be able to save money.

Wasn't the Federal Budget a total letdown. I'm blowed if I know how they can come up with something like that. It's as if they don't want to win the next election.

I feel happier now that you've had the car checked out. It sounds like it'll keep on going for many years to come. If your Dad gives it a cut and polish, it will seem like new. You just remember to drive safely, whether it be in the heaviest Sydney traffic or in Adelaide.

7 September

I'm writing from the Horseshoe where I've been for the past three days and will remain for another week. I'm running one of the 'Q' stores ['Q' for Quarter Master] while Steve Chamarette has returned to the Dat to fix up a few problems before he goes on two days R and C. Apart from the daily administration business, I also do a few hours in the battalion command post as Duty Officer. Every second night I take out an ambush patrol consisting of whoever can be scrounged up from the administration troops.

The 'Shoe has improved a lot since I was last here and it looks like a lot of work is being done to keep it in top shape. Life here is a bit more hectic than back at the Dat. Day and night there's always something happening in support of the units in the field. Tanks, APCs and vehicles of all sizes race to and fro. Guns and mortars fire away at some distant target and helicopters fly in and out with all kinds of cargo. Soldiers are either preparing to go out on a patrol or are just coming in from one. Others man the machine-gun posts and keep watch over the countryside. The battalion command post is always a buzz of radio traffic from the many patrols and activities in this part of the province.

C Company is to the north and has had two contacts in the last 24 hours. They have been acting on information that says two enemy groups were planning to meet at a certain place and it seems they may have disrupted those plans.

B Company will come into the 'Shoe tomorrow morning for three weeks, after their latest operation.

A Company is working out of fire base Brigid (grid reference 518 541) and has been there for two to three months. It's located near the sea, in sandhills and they've had several actions in the last few weeks. Two nights ago, while ambushing along the beach, they spotted a VC swimming about 100 yards out to sea, trying to get past their position and into the village of Lang Phouc Hai.

D Company will be moving out from the 'Shoe tomorrow to go into the Tan Ru area, which B Company has just left.

There have been several structural changes in the battalion lately. Mick O'Brien has changed places with Doug Gibbons. He's been doing a great job as Intelligence Officer, working with the local authorities, but is now being given the chance to command a platoon. I'm not sure if Doug likes the change. Owen is back as 2IC, B Company, and Terry Howard is Mortar Platoon commander. There's still no obvious place for me, so I keep floating, until a vacancy pops up.

The commanding officer celebrated the battalion's official birthday a few days ago by flying over the Long Hai mountains in his Sioux helicopter and placing the battalion's pennant at the highest point. I'm not sure how long it stayed there before being torn down by the resident VC, but everyone agreed that it was a great way to make a statement.

I've heard that Rex has had a bit of a turn and has been hospitalised with high blood pressure. I've written to him and wished him well. I've also suggested that one of the benefits from this war, should anybody consider that anything good would ever come from here, is the casualty evacuation procedure that is in place. We call the procedure 'Dust Off', but basically it gets our wounded from the battlefield to the hospital in Vung Tau, within minutes and from there they receive such wonderful treatment that the likelihood of recovery is enhanced enormously. It's all centred around helicopters and their capability to land almost anywhere, fly in the worst of weather conditions, recover the injured from the most difficult terrain, then fly by the most direct route to hospital, while the trained crew is treating their injuries.

There is no reason why this can't work throughout Australia, with regional council owned and operated choppers (just like St John Ambulance) landing on the roads to pick up the victims of road crashes, then flying to the nearest hospital, landing on their front lawns, roofs or car parks, and having them in the operating theatre within minutes of the accident being reported.

All chopper crews are first-aid trained, and carry what is needed to treat the worst battle injuries during the 15 to 20 minute flight to the hospital. From there, the professionals take over and everything is in the victims favour, because such a short time has elapsed since they were injured.

In a recent mine incident, three of our lads were seriously injured. The platoon medic did his best to handle the immediate issues of blood loss and shock. The Dust Off was on location within 10 minutes of the explosion to provide a higher level of first aid treatment. As they flew toward Vung Tau, they were able to radio ahead and advise the medical staff (who, by the way, include civilian doctors and nurses from Australia's leading hospitals, offering their expertise to gain some valuable experience) of the extent of the injuries. Everything at the hospital was ready for them as they landed and our lads were rushed into the operating theatre for treatment, all within 25 minutes of the mine exploding.

I guess it's the latest version of the Royal Flying Doctor Service. But I reckon there's huge potential for something similar being set up in all the capital cities and country areas. If there is one thing that gives us all the greatest comfort, it's knowing that, should anything happen to us, we will be in the hands of the greatest medical team that has ever served the army. From the platoon medic, to the Dust Off crews, through to the wonderful medical staff at the Vung Tau hospital, we've got a casualty evacuation system that is the best in the world.

How is Lesley [Raylene's younger sister] enjoying her stay with you? I hope the weather allows you to get about a bit. No doubt M-J is enjoying her company and that should give you some relief from his constant demands. I hope she's giving you a chance to have some time to yourself. That reminds me, please thank M-J for sending me a Father's Day card. I'd forgotten all about that (no breakfast in bed). What a lovely thing for my son to do.

R and R is the only thing that keeps me going these days. I keep making plans about what we'll do and where we'll go, because I want the time to be so special. We won't have a lot of time, so we've got to make the most of it.

I guess once R and R is over we'll then have to settle down to counting off the days until February. That's going to be the hardest part of this whole sorry saga.

I saw *Midnight Cowboy* last night and can't say it was the happiest film I've seen. Dustin Hoffman was great and I liked the theme song, but it left me with a rather hopeless feeling. Not the sort of feeling I need right now.

Have I told you lately that I love you? I miss you and I want you so much. I'm tired of thinking about it, I want to do it.

It's now 4.15 am and the command post is cold and quiet. There are three of us here, waiting for the dawn and hoping that nothing will happen in the next two hours to spoil another lovely Horseshoe sunrise.

I hope your day brings you peace and happiness.

8 September. I was ready to post my last letter when I received your very welcome one, written when you were on your way back from Adelaide. It was a real relief knowing you were enjoying the trip and that Lesley had already settled into her role as baby-sitter and was doing such a great job in sharing the load. I'm so relieved by your letter. It's made my day much brighter, knowing you're feeling so great.

This evening I saw Steve McQueen in *The Reivers* a film about a young boy's four-day experience, when he goes with two friends to a whore house. It seemed out of character for McQueen, but it was a lot of harmless fun, as this young 11-year-old learned all about the good and bad sides to life.

It looks like I'll stay here at the 'Shoe until the twenty-second, when the whole battalion will gather at Nui Dat for rest, retraining and belated unit birthday celebrations.

I'm making the most of the sun and the policy here that allows us to go about our tasks dressed only in shorts. Apart from a slight tan, all my skin ailments have gone and even my pimples are clearing up. What a pity that there's not a similar policy back at the Dat. It would lift morale enormously.

B Company returned yesterday and everyone looks very fit, although quite thin. Major Warland however has lost a lot of weight and in fact, looks a little ill. There is a weariness about all the blokes, so a break will do them good.

I look forward to your next letter as it will give me an idea of what you are planning for R and R. Being as sex-starved as me and as keen to get on with it, or rather, get it off, I'll be interested to hear what terrible things you have in mind.

Well, I'll post this now and hope that it will catch you soon after your arrival back at 501.

11 September

Yesterday we received a report that 80 enemy had been spotted in the Long Hais and in response, all the artillery began pounding the area. We sat on top of our bunkers with binoculars and watched the impact area and even though it was difficult to tell how effective it was, it was an exciting distraction from the daily chores.

I've just sent off a 13-page letter to Don and Marg Albert. It's a summary of everything that has happened in the first six months and gives them, I hope, a clear impression of what it's like over here. I'm sending it via you because I don't have their address, but also, I'd like you to add a few lines to give them an understanding what it's been like from your side.

You control my emotions. When I receive a cheerful letter, I feel on top of the world. When you're in the dumps, I am too. Thanks for writing so often and thanks for being truthful about your feelings and emotions. In many ways our letters are a record of the fluctuating emotions of all army families separated by this war. We express our fears and frustrations, our hopes and dreams. We describe our daily activities and our plans for the future, all with the realisation that everything could be shattered at any time. You and I are living on a prayer that the time will pass without incident and soon we will put this all behind us and live the rest of our lives in love and peace.

I know that you are going through the same emotional turmoil that I struggle with and therefore I want you to tell me all of the difficulties you are having, in the same way that I pour out my emotions to you. In this way we'll share this burden and be able to comfort each other when it gets too much for one person to bear.

I'm relieved that your last letter was cheerful, as the previous one was quite worrying. Thanks for writing so often, I get about three letters a week and your handwriting alone is enough to get my heart pounding. It seems to me that as R and R gets closer, your letters become more suggestive. Can it be that you feel the same excitement as I do, that you have the same sexy dreams as I do, and you think the same loving thoughts during the day, as I do? Have you planned in intimate detail the hours we will spend together too? Well my darling, I've made love to you so often in the past few weeks that I'm almost exhausted.

You ask whether I might have forgotten your charms and expect a *Playboy*-type woman waiting for me on my return … Well I do have one waiting for me. You are all I desire and you have every charm that I could ever desire. I'll have to examine your navel to see if it has a staple through it, as all good centrefolds have.

My R and R has been officially set as 8 October. Which means I'll be leaving on that date and arriving in Sydney at 6 am on the ninth. Let me know what arrangements you have made. As far as I'm concerned, as long as I can spend every hour in your company, I don't care what we do or where we go.

How is Lesley enjoying her time at Holsworthy? You seem to be getting around a bit. If you give me the names of her friends who she saw off to Vietnam, I may be able to catch up with them. Perhaps they may even be destined to be reinforcements for 7RAR. We've had a lot of new blokes lately and as I'm usually involved with their march-in administration, I could be one of the first people they meet when they get to Nui Dat. How come Lesley knows so many soldiers?

I'm going back to the Dat in three days time and have been given the job to organise the battalion's sports, during a 10-day rest period, beginning on the twenty-second.

12 September. The day started out to be a bad one, with all kinds of disasters coming my way. Firstly a truck slammed into the front gate, twisting the frame and reducing our security by 50 per cent. I called on a tank recovery team to pull the frame out of its foundations, load it onto a vehicle and take it to the Engineers so that we could get it fixed and back in position before nightfall. The tank was halfway through the job when its hydraulics blew and I had to get a bulldozer to complete the task. Shortly thereafter, a problem arose in our sewage pit and another emergency was adverted by calling on the Engineers to sort it out. No sooner had I settled down, when the message came through that D Company hadn't received certain documents they were needing, so I had to arrange a chopper to get out to them, quick smart.

The days are hot and humid and everyone is bathed in sweat, even when we're sitting around doing general office work. It remains hot until about two o'clock in the morning, then starts to cool down to a comfortable temperature. There is no need for any bed clothes during the night, apart from a mosquito net.

Is the weather in Sydney good for naked night manoeuvres?

I prefer cool evenings for love because two, hot, perspiring bodies can certainly generate some heat which becomes uncomfortable, in a lovely sort of way. Then you need to take a cool shower together, which is a wonderful consolation for all the exertion and a marvellous way to save water.

Do you remember the old 'Elephant Jokes' of a few years back? Well they've started up again because a few weeks ago the commanding officer, while flying over a jungle clearing, saw what he thought were some very strange tracks. He sent a patrol to investigate and they reported that they were made by elephants. These were the first of their kind found in the province for decades, so few local people believed the report. Since then he has seen the tracks several times, but no one has been able to back him up with any sightings. Now some drawings are beginning to appear on the noticeboards showing Viet Cong riding on the backs of armoured elephants which are trampling all over our tanks and APCs. There have also been poems written about the colonel seeing pink elephants. Now, he's not too pleased about all of this, so he has asked for research to be done to see if it's possible that the VC could be using the animals to carry supplies and heavy weapons into the area. It's all been a bit of a laugh, but in the back of our minds is the possibility that he could be right.

Well, the day is coming to an end and all the problems that began earlier are now over, so I can turn in feeling that I've completed another successful day. What problems await me with the dawn?

Another day over, one closer to our meeting.

PS You don't have to change a thing. You have always been my *Playboy* bunny, my centrefold, my pin-up.

13 September

Once again I'm on command post duty and as usual, at this time of the morning (1 am) it's very quiet. The active hours seem to be between 7 pm and 10 pm (as the Viet Cong are trying to get into the villages) and 4 am and 6 am (when they're trying to get out).

I go back to the Dat in two days, which doesn't thrill me too much, because compared to being here, there's not much excitement and far too much bullshit.

In two days time there is a period the villagers call the Children's Tet or the Children's New Year. This is the third Tet holiday of the year. The first being the thirteenth lunar month Tet, or the Chinese New Year, the main national holiday. The other is the normal calendar NewYear.

Throughout the province a competition has been organised by the Government to see who can make the best display of lanterns out of local materials such as bamboo, rice paper, and string. The decorations that we see throughout all of the villages are glorious. The people obviously enjoy their celebrations and are putting in a lot of effort to make the biggest and brightest lantern. One I've seen is about seven metres in diameter with decorations showing all of the countries in South-East Asia. It was nice to see that they included Australia. Many of the other lanterns are designed as stars which apparently denotes the future and their longing for peace and happiness.

I'm reading a book called *Minister* by Charles Mercer who I think wrote *The Cardinal* and *Rabbi*. It's a good story and I try to pick it up whenever I have a few spare minutes. I've read more books since being here, than in my whole lifetime. It's a great way to pass the time. Then again, there's not much else to do.

In every letter I receive, you describe Mark-John's latest escapade. What a busy boy he is. He's certainly winning the hearts and minds of all our friends and neighbours with his good looks, blonde hair and happy nature. I'm really looking forward to getting to know him again.

I'll be leaving Vietnam on the ninth and arriving in Sydney at 6 am on the tenth.

We have 27 days until our meeting. That's only six more letters to you. What I wouldn't give to speed up these next few weeks and then slow the following six magic days to a snail's pace.

I was interested in the descriptions of your yoga exercises and wonder if I'll be coming home to a hippie and a house full of incense. I just had to write down my feelings about it in 'strine':

Toomee Wyvoose Sorl Keedup
Yer god derbeege owken
Wodden thweld yadoen yogat fer rens
Plashin goorl lonyaf ace
Sit jus fermi
Makenyers elfup fermy redurn
Musay yime onnered
Buddone ged garry daway
Oryle neva noya
Done miss sunner stanmi
Wod dever yad doofer beudys saken doot
Bud dive forlway sed
Foney wicked beer lone
Juz fera dia died
Proofyerd dowen eedit
Owl lonken yerstan onyer reddin derkorna
Ord ya jusit ten thin kabowd dit.
Orlmiluv

To My Wife Who Is All Keyed Up
You have got to be joking,
What in the world are you doing yoga for and
Splashing goo all on your face.
Is it just for me?
Making yourself up for my return?
Must say, I'm honoured.
But don't get carried away
Or I'll never know you.
Don't misunderstand me,
Whatever you do for beauty's sake, do it
But I've always said,
If only we could be alone
Just for a day, I'd
Prove you don't need it.
How long can you stand on your head in the corner?
Or do you just sit and think about it?'
All my love

17 September

I'm back at Nui Dat and am already bored. It's raining very heavily and the wind is blowing it inside my tent. My floor is flooded and I'm feeling quite cool.

The only big thing on my agenda is to organise the sports for the battalion's 10-day break. The last time I took charge of a sports day was on Elcho Island. That was a great experience. Those days seem a million years ago.

Do you know we've been apart for 234 days?

The nineteenth. You said in your last letter that you've forwarded my letter to Don and Marg Albert, but there were things in it that I hadn't told you of. Well, I'm not sure what parts of the letter you refer to but if they were new, it was because I had either forgotten to tell you about them or else I didn't think they were of any great importance. Why should I not tell you about everything I do? There's no benefit in keeping any of my life here a secret. Anyway, remember that I'd originally planned that the letter would go to my brother John, but thought halfway through that he'd probably be hearing about my exploits from Mum, so it would be better to send it on to someone who didn't know anything about the place. Anyway, I'm sure you have received more information from me than anyone else, so I'm surprised that there was something new in Don's letter.

By the time I got to the end of your letter you were sounding more worried and anxious than ever before. You mentioned again the state of your finances and as I've said before, please let me know whenever you need extra and I'll send you everything I've got in my pay book. Then you informed me that our tenant was planning to leave. Well surely that's not any real problem. It's not as if we couldn't find someone else. It's an excellent area and ideal for a newly married couple, so it certainly wouldn't be vacant for long. It's an ideal time also, to increase the rent.

Darling, I know it's difficult enough looking after M-J, and having to exist like this for another five months, but we're over the worst of it and I need to feel that you are able to handle the remaining time without these periods of depression. I need to have confidence that you are strong enough to last till I can get home and help sort things out. I need you to be my rock, the one I can confide in and rely on to see things through. In most of your letters that's the message I get. But every now and then I see you collapse, I feel that it's getting too much for you to handle. All I can say is please, please keep strong. We will have to talk about this when I'm home and we'll have to sort it out one way or the other.

Lesley wrote to me about her soldier friend, Kevin. Seems she is very much in love this time. I went looking for him and located him at the Horseshoe, where he's with 2 Troop, B Squadron, 3 Cavalry Regiment (armoured personnel carriers), which is closely affiliated with 7RAR. I told Lesley that I wouldn't be able to 'look after him' but encouraged her to keep in touch with him and help make his tour go as quickly as possible. I said that whenever I returned to the 'Shoe, I'd get in touch with him.

Since starting this letter, I'm relieved to say that I've received your latest letter and you seem to have picked up a lot. Even your handwriting is back to its familiar neat and tidy style. What a relief for me to know that you're feeling a lot better.

Here's an official letter from the army in preparation for my return to you:

> Dear Mr/Mrs/Miss ... this is to inform you that your husband/son/relative/friend, having completed an arduous tour of duty in the Republic of South Vietnam, will be returning to Australia on ... 197 ...
>
> You should appreciate that he is no longer the person who left home, fired with patriotic fervour and zest for adventure. He is now older, leaner, wiser in the ways of the world and probably suffering from skin complaints, nerves and a short temper.
>
> One of the early indications of his change in character will be his periodic hot and cold flushes accompanied by shortness of breath and trembling knees. This could be due to malaria, the Australian climate or the close proximity of a young woman in a mini skirt.
>
> He will gaze in awe and fascination at blonde hair, blue eyes, round eyes, clean bedding, trains and tight sweaters.

Be careful not to say to him 'lets go for a walk' or 'I wish it would rain' as his reaction may be unpleasant. If he enters your house by climbing through the window, humour him. If he walks into the back-yard with a shovel in his hand, don't abuse him. Gently take the shovel from him and direct him to the toilet and demonstrate how to operate the flush system. If he is reluctant to rise at a suitable hour simply whisper 'lights on the wire' and stand clear.

Encourage him to eat at the table and drink from a glass.

Habit may cause him to:

sleep with his boots on;
grind his cigarette into the carpet;
pee beside any tree;
rub coals from your lounge room fire onto his face and arms;
light up his hexamine stove whenever he wants a cup of tea.

Don't rush with your rehabilitation. These things will take time to change.

If a litterbug throws something from a passing car he will possibly scream loudly and dive into the gutter. This will humour and endear him to passers-by, but is not an action to be encouraged.

Never question him about rice paddies, rubber trees, mud, chlorinated water, or Saigon Tea. If your family is to have a meal of corned beef or vienna sausages, wait until he has gone out to a friend's place.

If you have any Asian friends, it may be prudent not to invite them over for a while as he may greet them with well known phrases: *Doong Loy* (halt), *Dura Tay Lin* (put your hands up) and *Chieu Hoi* (give up).

Above all humour him. The war couldn't shatter his composure, but civilisation might.

So my darling, even the army is asking you to be extra nice to me when I get home.

22 September

This countdown we're carrying on with is more exciting than an Apollo mission's final minutes before launch. Each time I cross off another day from my calendar and count the remaining days, I start dreaming about all the wonderful things we will soon be sharing. Your letters don't help me concentrate on the work I should be doing either. Now you tell me you've bought us matching towelling dressing-gowns so that we can laze about the house and spend some quiet nights in front of the fire. It's enough to make me go AWOL.

Is M-J caught up in this excitement, or does he take it all in his stride? Travelling back and forward to Adelaide, settling into different houses, meeting his relatives and friends and then leaving them for lengthy periods, is becoming common place. Now he's being told that someone called Daddy is coming to stay for a little while. I wonder what his little mind makes of it all. As long as you are there, he must feel secure and happy. Everyone else is just a distraction.

It's likely that I will get a new job after I return from R and R. With the whole battalion coming in for a 10-day rest, it's likely that a few changes will be made. We've also received a new lieutenant last week, so if he goes into a company, there will have to be a bit of a reshuffle and I'm hoping I'll be given a platoon to finish off my tour.

I've had my spell and it's time to get back to the bush. I've learnt a lot from my time as 2IC and in the command post.

Yesterday, as I was being driven to the task force HQ conference, the driver and I were discussing what we were going to do when we got back to Australia. He was a National Serviceman who would finish his two years soon after getting back. He wasn't sure if he'd go back to his old job. He just wanted to take some time off to think about things. I said that it was likely that I'd stay in the army for a few more years to see what came my way in the form of postings and promotions. I said that I'd really like to write a book about the time we'd spent here, from a soldier's point of view. He was real keen on that, saying: 'As long as you describe it like it really is, no bullshit stuff.' As we pulled up at the HQ he finished by saying: 'Someone's got to tell them the real story.'

He wasn't there to take me back to the battalion lines so I couldn't follow up the conversation, but I felt that he, like a lot of us, want the Australian public to know the facts about what we are doing. That we are proud to be here and are doing a fine job.

Our country's knowledge of this war is being clouded by what is seen on TV and read in the papers and is being influenced by the Moratorium marches, which hail the enemy as heroes. I can understand why he, as a National Serviceman, felt reluctant to go straight back to the society he once knew. He wants a bit of time to come to grips with his own feelings and check out what his civvy workmates and friends think of his involvement in the war. He seemed to be apprehensive about going back to his old routines.

25 September. I've found myself a copy of *Romeo and Juliet* and as I've been reading through the passages I've been thinking of our time together soon. Our meeting will be like the two lovers:

If I profane with my unworthiest hand
This holy shrine, the gentler sin is this:
My lips, two blushing pilgrims, ready stand
To smooth that rough touch with a tender kiss.
Good pilgrim, you do wrong your hand too much,
Which mannerly devotion shows in this.
For saints have hands that pilgrims' hands do touch,
And palm to palm in holy palmers' kiss.
Have not saints lips, and holy palmers' too?
Ay, pilgrim, lips that they must use in prayer.
O then, dear saint, let lips do what hands do:
They pray; grant thou, lest faith turn to despair.
Saints do not move, though grant for prayers' sake.
Then move not while my prayer's effect I take.
Thus from my lips, by thine my sin is purged.
Then have my lips the sin that they have took.
Sin from my lips? O trespass sweetly urged! Give me my sin again.

Being with you is all I need to refresh my mind and body. I need you so much and I am living these empty days only because I know we will be together again shortly.

Even now I know that the last day on R and R will be too hard to bear. But, we will have wonderful memories of the few previous days to keep with us, as we go our separate ways again.

Remember the film, when Juliet and Romeo wake after their first night together? With all her heart she wished the night would be eternal. So it is my lover, maybe if we wish hard enough, time will stand still and we will remain together forever.

> Wilt thou be gone? It is not yet near day.
> It was the nightingale, and not the lark,
> That pierced the fear-ful hollow of thine ear.
> Nightly she sings on yon pom'granate tree.
> Believe me, love, it was the nightingale.

Till we meet darling, I will continue to read this love story and picture you as my Juliet.

30 September

It's 5.45 am and I've got until 8.00 before I dismount CP duty. Nothing has been happening at all this past week, so the days and nights have tended to drag a little. My main job therefore has been setting up for the sports day. Having everyone back here has been good but it has caused its share of problems. Meal times are a crush, and take a lot longer to get everyone through. The canteens are crowded and there's a lot of effort required just to get a cool beer at the end of the day.

I've caught up with all the blokes again ... Greg, Karl, Doug, George, Mike, Owen ... and they're all fine. It's surprising how many new faces there are. I didn't know five officers and several sergeants were strangers too.

We had an open-air concert last night with rock bands, comedians, singers and a whole range of talent, found from within the ranks of the battalion. It held us all captive through two rainstorms and lasted from 7.00 to 10.30. The master of ceremonies was a corporal who does that sort of thing in Civvy Street. Two band members were also professional musicians, one from Billy Thorpe's

Aztecs and another from a Western Australian band. A couple of Aboriginal lads sang *My Boomerang Won't Come Back* and brought the house down. The finale was a soldier dressed up as a priest and he announced that he would close the show with a prayer. When all was quiet he began:

> Our father, who art in Possum,
> Zero Niner be thy name . . .

This had us all in stitches because the commanding officer flies around in a chopper called Possum and his radio call sign is Zero Niner. He went on . . .

> Lead us not into bamboo thickets
> And deliver us from Charlie . . .

When he got to the end, everybody yelled '*Amen*'.

All in all, it was a lot of good fun and gave us a feeling that the battalion is in fine spirits.

I'll be lucky enough to see another concert soon. This one has been organised by the ABC and stars Gordon Boyd, Buster Fiddess and some Aussie dancing and singing talent. They do a great job and it's a bit of fun, even if it only lasts a few hours. This is the first visiting concert that the battalion has seen since it arrived.

The battalion deploys again on the third and it'll be a relief to get back to familiar routines. The break has given everyone a real boost and we're ready for action again. We won't get back together again until early February, as we're preparing to return home.

B Company will be going to Brigid, a company-size defensive position near the beach and close to the dreaded Long Hai mountains. Three other companies are going to the Horseshoe and one other will go out bush. It seems that most of the future action will be around the villages, so it will be mainly night ambush routines that will rule our lives for a while.

By the time you get this letter it will be the fourth, which means you may not have time to reply. The army has confirmed, I leave here on the ninth, arrive in Sydney on the morning of the tenth and will be returning here on the morning of the sixteenth. When you write it like that it doesn't seem to be very long, does it.

My route will take me from Nui Dat to Saigon, flying by luxury RAAF *Caribou*. Then after sorting out my travel arrangements, changing money and getting Customs clearance, I'll board an international airliner with several Australians and 150 Yanks, to travel to Sydney, via Singapore.

I'll be bringing all the money I have in my pay book, so will be able to pay for any of our R and R expenses and also leave you with some extra for the weeks that follow. Everything seems to be prepared, so all we have to do now is wait calmly for the next few days.

I'm glad to hear that Guy and Robyn will be helping you out on the morning of my arrival. That will take some of the strain from your preparations.

This tension is almost as bad as the days before our wedding when everyone was rushing about to ensure all of the arrangements were finalised. No matter how calm we tried to be, as the days slowly went by, the more tense we became. What a relief when the day finally arrived and our nervousness changed to relief and happiness.

1 October. Once again I was extremely pleased to receive your letter (dated Sunday) and read all the latest news. You keep me in touch with the world and although I don't always like what I hear, it helps me to understand the way things are developing. I'm not too happy with the way our society is going and I would love to escape from it when I return. There must be places away from the rat-race, where we could settle down and feel at peace. You and M-J mean everything to me and I want you both to be safe and happy.

I'd give anything to know what kind of society M-J will grow up into and what the future holds for him. If only I knew that he'll be happy. I guess it's up to you and me to give him love and present him with opportunities, so he can make the most of what comes his way.

Tonight, several of us were talking about the turmoil in Australia and where it was leading. Some of the blokes see really big problems ahead and even suggest some kind of political revolution could be created by the division that is happening in our society. I said that I thought the average person (and the silent majority), would not let a few ratbags, hippie types and their union friends destroy what had been built up over the past 70 years. We may have some trouble and it may lead to all kinds of changes in our thinking, but in the end, commonsense will win through. We would never go down the road that America has gone, with riots and shootings.

What a time to bring up a family. No wonder most of us feel that we've been let down.

Once again, the weather in Sydney is lousy. But never mind because we're not going to spend a lot of time outdoors anyway. It's very wet and humid here. As a matter of fact, we haven't even seen the sun for two days running. The clouds just keep rolling in and bringing with it floods of rain. No wonder everything is so damp and mouldy.

Poor little M-J, he must realise something is going to happen soon because he's beginning to want to sleep with you. He must be so confused about where his home is and who his Dad is and I suppose he's now hearing all about me coming home for a while. Who the hell is this man called Peter that everyone is talking about?

I'm not sure if I'll get time to write again before I start my journey to you. I'm very excited and a little bit scared, as if it was my first date with you.

I've enclosed a clipping I've taken from a magazine, which I'd like you to add to your letter collection. Perhaps one day, if I have time, I'll try and write a few pages, not really a book. It'll be good to read these letters some day in the future, to get an idea of how we managed.

Two hundred and twenty-five days have passed, so that leaves 150 to go. I pray that the time flies by without any more hardship for you.

1 October

Dear Pop, It's 2300 hours and I'm again on duty in the battalion CP. It has been two hours since the last message came through and apart from my hourly telephone checks to the perimeter gun positions, I've done little else.

One of our ambushes, led by Sergeant Bourke, killed the 2IC of the main force enemy battalion (D445) last week. Actually, he was acting as the commanding officer, so with his demise they'll have a few leadership problems on their hands. For the last month we've stopped them coming south and meeting with local groups, so I guess this loss will put their plans on the back-burner for a while. The VC have lost a lot of their punch because we've kept them constantly on the move and away from their areas of influence, so we suspect the D445 battalion, who have been strengthened by many North Vietnamese, were coming down here to rejuvenate the local efforts. I think they must have also been a little concerned that the population is starting to believe we are controlling the situation, so a show of force was needed to regain some of the initiative. Whichever way you look at it, the enemy has had a difficult time in the last few months.

Have you seen the film called *M*A*S*H*. It's an hilarious story about a US Army Hospital in the Korean war. What made it so good was that we could all relate to the personalities and to the typical army situations which occurred. Despite its anti-war message and being a bit gruesome in parts (it deals with wounded soldiers being treated just behind the forward lines), we felt it had such a similarity with our own situation, that we asked that it be kept and re-run the following evening.

My R and R starts on the ninth and I'll be in Sydney on the morning of the tenth. I'll fly back here on the morning of the sixteenth in a state of utter exhaustion and with a strange smile on my face. Then, there will only be 140 days to go until I bid my bunker a fond farewell.

I'll be in a new job when I get back from R and R. I've finished my stint as a Pogo and will take command of Reconnaissance Platoon which is a sub unit of Support Company. I'm really looking forward to it as it will get me off my arse and back in the bush again. The platoon, which had been led by a very capable sergeant, received a few casualties in a recent action. From what I hear they're a pretty good team, so I'm looking forward to working with them.

I read my annual confidential report yesterday. It was written by the commanding officer (Lieutenant Colonel Ron Grey) and I was very pleasantly surprised and a little embarrassed that he held me in such high regard. I've known him for about two years and have come to respect and admire him. He never minces words and expects everyone to give 100 per cent. To have him say 'well done' is a great compliment.

Joke: A Jewish Father Christmas came down the chimney one cold winter's night. He was dressed in his big red suit with matching hat and gloves. He tip-toed over to the little boy's bed and went up to the sleeping child. Waking him up gently, the jolly old man said: '*Ho, Ho, Ho.* Hey kid, you want to buy some toys?'

Our intelligence section is preparing our yearbook which will be a pictorial history of our time here. They have asked me to carry the draft back to Sydney and deliver it to the printers. I'd better not lose this package otherwise there will be 800 angry soldiers after me. It'll be a marvellous memento and I'm sure we will all treasure our copy for the rest of our lives. Our medals too will be special reminders of what we have been through and I hope I'll be able to wear them with pride in the years to come.

I'll try and ring you from Sydney.

3 October – from Raylene to Peter's mum

I'm sorry I haven't written sooner but I've been terribly busy helping a sick friend and actually living with her. Now I have her youngest child with me and while both M-J and Vanessa sleep, I can put down a few lines.

My days are full of 'peacemaking' efforts between the two, who vie for my attention and are very jealous of each other. Vanessa is a year older but M-J is bigger and bullies her. Last night, sitting on his horse, he kept ramming into her, yet today she was pulling his hair for no apparent reason. So one is as bad as the other.

I received a letter from my darling today and I'm unable to reply as he will be home before my letter gets to him. We are both very excited. We will be staying the first night at the Gazebo, one of the most glamorous hotels in Kings Cross. They have a big floor show on the Saturday night, so we'll probably spend the evening involved with some first class entertainment. We will also stay a couple of days at a friend's holiday house at Saratoga, near Gosford before returning to our little home for the last few precious days.

On our way home on Sunday we'll call into the Bankstown shops and hope that the 'special phone' is working, so we can give you a call. If we can't use it, we'll telephone from our neighbours.

We hope that Rex is still improving. You wouldn't want to go through that sort of thing again, would you.

I can hear sounds of waking. I'd better go and change some nappies.

The next week of waiting will be impossible to bear, then we'll spend five glorious days together, before steeling ourselves for another extended period alone. What a life we lead.

Chapter Seven

Back in the Bush

17 October–15 December 1970

17 October – from Raylene to Peter's mum

A very lonely, sad girl writes this to you today. After six truly wonderful days I had practically convinced myself that it would go on forever, so when it ended, I did not like the feeling of being on my own again.

Mark-John and Peter got on marvellously, except when Peter and I came in contact. Whether it was holding hands or an arm on a shoulder, we would be greeted by a frown and an angry sound. During the days at Saratoga we accepted this and made a special effort to make him realise he wasn't being left out. So just as he was

accepting our being together as a family, it's all over and poor thing, he's more confused as ever.

The following morning, after we had said our goodbyes at the R and R centre at Kings Cross, M-J said, while eyeing the empty side of the bed: 'Daddy Home?' I tried to explain, but he trotted off throughout the house calling: 'Daddy, Daddy.' He finally went into the bathroom, probably hoping Peter was having a shave so that he could have his face lathered too. When it finally dawned on him that his Daddy wasn't around anymore he came back to me, crawled up on the bed and we both had a cry together.

On one occasion while at Gosford, they went for a long walk while I had a rest. I sat on the balcony and watched them making their way up the hill towards the house. I felt so happy, as they were obviously at home in each other's company. Peter had taught M-J to make cricket sounds by clicking his tongue and showed him the wonders of nature, like tiny grubs under rocks. They had a competition on how far they could throw rocks and watched silently a bird sitting in a nearby bush. Then they stopped and studied a lizard making its way across the driveway. They had picked a posy of weeds for me and M-J put them in a glass of water which was then carefully placed on the mantlepiece. When it was time for him to have his nap, he was just so excited about everything they had done, that he kept chatting away to himself for 15 minutes before he drifted off to sleep.

They look so much alike too. You can tell that they are father and son.

Peter has been through a great deal more than he has revealed in his eloquent letters. In our short time together he was a mixture of emotions; deep thinking, light hearted, funny, loving, and at times, sad and withdrawn. He tried so hard to be happy all of the time but every now and then he became quiet and M-J and I knew that he needed some time to himself. Even so, it was a wonderful R and R. I'll treasure the memories forever.

I now wait for his first letter. I know I mustn't expect the same amount of letters I got when he was 2IC and in the command post, but this first one is most important to me.

Peter was very pleased with how I'd improved our home with this and that. I'm proud of it too. If only we could show it off to you all.

I hope this letter finds you well. If I'm in Bankstown in the next few days I'll give you another call and tell you all about our wonderful few days.

I must now do some cleaning up, even though I feel very lethargic and disinterested.

17 October

My love, it is impossible to describe the feelings I had as I stumbled through the R and R return procedures, the loneliness that flooded my body as I sat silently in the bus watching the world pass by, the hopelessness that filled me as our plane took off and the beautiful countryside slipped away beneath me and finally the despair that is within me now, knowing I must wait four long, lonely, desperate months before I can hold you again.

I'm ashamed for leaving you as I did, but it would have been too hard for me to stay with you any longer. I didn't mean to shrug you off with just one kiss, it was just too much for me to stay with you any longer, saying our goodbyes and not wanting to go. I want you to know that kiss meant the world to me.

The trip back lasted an eternity and I slept a lot just to escape from the loneliness. I talked a little to my American neighbours, who were so excited about their Aussie experiences, but the last thing I wanted to do was share in their memories, so I just looked out the window at the clouds and thought of you, till I drifted off to sleep. I would have done anything to have the plane turn around and return me to you.

Even now I am locked up with such a helpless feeling that unless something happens to break me out of this, I'll go crazy. I guess it's for the best that I'll be going out to the Horseshoe tomorrow to join Support Company and get back into the swing of bush work again.

I've relived every glorious moment with you. You made them all so wonderful that they will stay vividly in my mind until the time we are together again. Thank you for spoiling me as you did and thank you also for understanding that there were some moments that I felt a strange uneasiness, so much so that I couldn't relax and had to go off for a couple of hours by myself.

I'm a little scared about getting back into patrolling. I'll have to get a lot fitter than I am if I'm to keep up with the physical demands of the job. But I'm worried that with only four months to go something may happen to me that will ruin all our plans for the future. Luck is needed in this game and I certainly hope that I get my fair share during these last few months. I'll be doing everything in my power to get back to your arms safely.

Nui Dat is still the same. I'm sweating again as I sit in my musty smelling tent and the familiar noises of artillery, choppers and soldiers fill my ears. It's not the best environment for someone who is feeling that his whole world has caved in around him.

Why must our lives be filled with all this loneliness? Why can't we live ordinary lives? Darling I love you so much it hurts. I need you to be near me, not another lifetime away. I've made a calendar and have coloured in the first day closer to you. As each of the next 134 days pass I'll colour in the little squares and watch the gap between us get smaller and smaller.

I'll sign off now and hope that your promised letter will be in the next mail. I desperately need to know how you are feeling and how little M-J is getting on.

As I sign off, we've been apart 32 hours. It seems so much longer than that.

God bless you and look after you.

PS

My money is spent and my spell is now over
Fond memories sing with the sounds of the plane
It's time to return to the life of a soldier
Back with my mates in the bush once again.
Adapted from *Queensland Drover*

20 October

I've been very busy since arriving at the Horseshoe. My first night was spent in ambush, my second patrolling 8000 metres about the neighbourhood and at 0900 tomorrow Recce Platoon will go out for a 10-day operation south-east of Xuyen Moc.

It's good to have all the worries of a platoon commander again and although for your sake, I'd rather be safe and sound at the Dat, all this activity is giving me a new lease of life. My R and R hang-over has just about gone, although you are never out of my heart.

It'll be some time before I will write again as we'll get no re-supply during this operation. We're taking 10 days rations, which is a terrible load, but will establish a firm base where we will stash most of our gear and patrol out from there each day. Ten days! It's been a long time since I've spent such a long time in the bush. Even with the little bit of work we've done in the last few days, my shoulders are stiff and sore and my legs are aching.

My new boss is Captain Thompson and what a refreshing change he is from my last one.

My new home is an underground bunker measuring five paces square and about seven feet from floor to ceiling. It's cool in the heat of the day but as yet I haven't had a night at home to see what it's like to sleep in.

The weather is extremely humid and we get the odd thunderstorm now and then. It rained all night on my first night out and I felt cold for the third time since being here. Perhaps I'm just getting too soft.

I've played your tape so many times and sing along with you and M-J. It was a wonderful idea to record the tape the day after I left and give me an idea of how well you both are coping. To hear him chatting to you about all the things we did and to sing all his favourite songs, just for me, made me realise how lucky I am to have such a beautiful family.

As I look about this bunker I am brought back to reality. I feel so distant from you and fear that we will never be together again. How stupid it is of me to feel like this. I can't do anything about our separation. No matter how hard I wish and pray, we will remain apart for another four months. I love you so much but all I can do, if I'm to survive these last terrible months, is to get stuck into the job and do everything in my power to see it through safely. Your continued love and support will be essential, because I can't do it without you.

I must go and prepare orders for my patrol, then pack my gear.

29 October

I'm sitting on the top of my bunker which is on the western side of the Horseshoe and which overlooks almost all of the battalion's area of responsibility that stretches west to Highway One (the main sealed road which runs north-south through the province and leads into Long Khanh Province, to our north).

The two signal flares fired at 6 pm each day by our Mortar Platoon, to warn the population that curfew begins in one hour, have just lit up and are drifting on their little parachutes across the village of Dat Do.

It's a very pleasant setting with golden sunlight shining through gaps in the grey clouds. The hills on the western horizon are the Nui Thi Vai and the Nui Dinhs (nicknamed 'The Warbies', adapted from the song 'They say don't go to Warberton [Wolverton]

Mountain, if your looking for a fight'). The countryside between is a carpet of different shades of green; bright green paddy fields, dark green scrub and the lush grass and weeds which outlines the roads and tracks.

It's such a clear afternoon that I can even see the radar station at Vung Tau and the white sandhills near Lang Phouc Hai, to the south. To the east there is the dark green area, from which I've just returned.

What a peaceful setting it would be if it weren't for the sound of armoured personnel carriers moving out through our gate taking the ambush patrols to their drop off points; the beginning of another deadly night's activities.

Support Company returned from its little outing at 11 this morning, having spent nine days searching the area east of Xuyen Moc (almost to the border). Recce Platoon moved separately from the main body and covered a lot of ground. We carried an extra burden of 10 days rations and believe me, it was almost the limit of our capacity. The intention was to form a small base and operate from there, but after only two days we had to move with everything to a new area. It was exhausting, especially for an unfit administration command post officer. We got off the APCs at grid reference 700 671 and moved south to the area of Lang Ca Thi (no village there any more), then operated for three days in the area of the Nui Tam Bo, which is on the extreme eastern border of the province. Finally, we spent seven days in an area which I don't think is on your map because it is further east still. It was very thick jungle, with lantana so thick that we were unable to cut or slash our way through. To make matters worse, the creeks and rivers were flooded, so we had to rope ourselves across.

We found two new bunker systems and followed tracks made by at least a section of enemy, but they were about a day or two ahead of us. I believe that we're going back in about two weeks in a hope that we will surprise them; they wouldn't expect us back in the area so soon. Also, I'm told we'll be walking in from the south rather than taking the APCs, which aren't the most silent form of transport. The bush telegraph soon gets word to the VC that an armoured column is moving toward their area and, as happened on this occasion, they moved out as we were moving in.

It rained almost every day and poured every night. We were wet for the whole time ... and I thoroughly enjoyed it. There are a lot of advantages when patrolling in the rain. You never go thirsty, the noise you make is muffled and you can more easily identify whether someone else is moving around the area by the tracks they leave in the muddy ground. We've also caught the odd enemy group sheltering from the rain, never believing that anyone would be out patrolling in such terrible conditions.

Overall, I was happy with our efforts, and pleased that I could keep up with my blokes, who must have been checking me out as much as I was assessing them. I feel I've been accepted into their team, and am pleased to be part of this tried and tested group of professionals.

What a surprise to get eight letters on my return. Seven (including a tape) from you and one from Mum. What a pity I wasn't able to answer each letter as it arrived. By the time I respond, all the issues you discussed are well behind you, all your problems have been worked through and all the feelings you expressed have faded or been replaced by the latest emotions. Again, I feel that I'm living about a week behind you. I'm unable to keep up with you, or support you at the times you need it most.

I can understand exactly how you felt for the first week after R and R. How lucky I was to be dragged out of my depression by the demands of the new job, whereas you had to struggle alone with constant reminders of our brief time together. Each of your letters recalled moments we had together and explained how difficult it was for you to break free of the heartache and pain that you were feeling. Seven unanswered letters, makes me realise just how hard it has been for you. I'm sorry that I wasn't able to ease your pain and help wipe away your tears. Our greatest dream will be that we will soon be together, spending everyday as if it were our R and R.

It's now two weeks since we were together and my calendar is slowly being coloured in. Even so, there are so many gaps yet to be filled in. Will it ever be completed?

It's nice to know that M-J asks about me. Tell him I think of him often and am looking forward to spending a lot of time together, exploring the wonders of the garden; the ants, the spiders, the lizards, the snails. All the amazing things we found when we went for our walks.

I miss you both very much and although I'm very busy I always make it a very special time just before going to sleep, no matter where I am, to think of you both.

I'm now seated on my stretcher inside my bunker and it's 10 to 7. The scenery is very different from the vast, beautiful countryside. Four rusty corrugated iron walls, steel pickets and heavy timber beams make up my 'home'. There are no windows, just two small vents that allow some air to circulate. Grenades, shovels, knives, bullets, webbing, weapons, maps and other essentials hang from the walls and line the shelves. I can't help but compare it to the lovely rooms of our home and the delightful atmosphere you have created. I wonder what you could do to improve my current living conditions? I think it would take exceptional talent to turn this hole in the ground into anything else but a hole in the ground.

8RAR left for home today and it won't be long before we'll have finished our duty and be packing for our own Return To Australia. Perhaps if we pray hard enough, we'll wake up tomorrow and find this hardship behind us.

Good night my love and thank you for your wonderful welcome back from my first operation.

30 October. It's been a shocking day, weatherwise. Since 8.00 this morning it has teamed down and the prospects for tonight's ambush aren't very pleasant. The ground is so saturated that all the water is now running off which means even the roads, paths and foot tracks are being eroded and resemble small creeks. The actual creeks and rivers are torrents and the paddy fields are swamps. My bunker is leaking and pools of water are forming on the floor. I haven't got any dry clothes and an assortment of shirts, trousers and socks hang from the rafters, trying to dry out. Everything I'm wearing feels damp and I wouldn't be surprised if I've got mould growing under my armpits.

I'm suffering from pimples again, mainly on my shoulders and back, where the webbing causes irritation. Could you send over a couple of tubes of Phorac cream to see if I can keep it under control.

31 October. What a shocking night it was to be out. Saturated with rain, caked with mud and at times shivering with cold. It's still raining and I'm down to my last pair of dry socks. My boots are soft and soggy and so am I. While we were out on ambush last night we couldn't help think that even the VC would have stayed at home and got some satisfaction that he was causing a lot of discomfort to a lot of Aussies.

I'm going out again tonight, into a better area I hope, but the prospects look pretty glum. Rain, mud and cold does little to lift the morale, especially when there are no enemy about to liven things up.

Another letter arrived today. It's a week old, so it looks like the posties are still dragging their feet. However, the letters do wonders and I must be the luckiest bloke in the province to have received nine letters in the last two and a half days.

I still haven't been able to play your tape because no one has a machine that is working properly. It's like a Christmas present that I'm not allowed to open until the twenty-fifth. I know it's going to be beaut and the suspense adds to the excitement.

The days are passing quite quickly. Tomorrow is the beginning of November and that means a new colour for our calendar. Isn't it strange how such little things become so important.

2 November

Dear Mum, sorry that it's been such a long time between letters. I'm beginning to settle into this new job. It takes a fair bit of effort to get to know everyone, earn their respect and start to have an influence on the way they work in and out of the bush. I'm enjoying the challenge, although I was tested to my physical limit on the first operation. I didn't realise how unfit I had become as a command post officer. Too much of the good life I'm afraid.

R and R was too good and it was extremely difficult to say goodbye to the two most precious people in my life. Raylene, being the well-trained army wife that she is, made my departure a little easier, but deep down we were just torn apart. There is no doubt in my mind that she is the strength I need to see this through. Without her it would be an impossible task. The hardships that we have to put up with, the conditions we must live in and the strain that we are constantly under would have got to me by now, but for her love and support.

Being here for another four months will be very difficult for us both and I have this fear that something will happen to stop us from being together again. Mum, please understand that the next few months will be very hard for me and I'll be living on the edge of my nerves, until I'm back home with all those I love.

My new job is great and it keeps me from feeling too sorry for myself. I've come to realise that there are a lot of people relying on me. Not just my family, but all these soldiers and their families expect me to do my job well and keep us all safe. It's a real dilemma in that I must lead them into all kinds of difficult situations and yet everyone is expecting to come out unscathed. I only hope that if the shit hits the fan I can do what is expected of me.

My new platoon are great. Much like the 6 Platoon blokes and I guess any other platoon over here. They've had their share of the action and are well tested in the art of warfare. They are a lot older than their years. I guess I am too.

I've been in Support Company for two weeks now and spent most of that time wandering the scrub, laying in ambush and searching for 'Charlie'. The war has quietened down a lot, especially around the villages. Even when we go deep into the bush there are few signs of activity. Our next operation begins in about a week, so in-between time we keep ourselves busy during the day by cleaning up the area and at night, ambushing around Dat Do.

8RAR left for home yesterday and through binoculars we could see HMAS *Sydney* pull out of Vung Tau. All of us wished we were with them. What a glorious feeling it must have been.

We've been told that our Return To Australia is being planned already. We'll be in Sydney on 8 March 1971 and will receive about four weeks leave. That doesn't seem much after what we've been through, however I won't be complaining as I walk down the gangplank and place my feet on Aussie soil again. They have also told us that we will remain in the bush on operations until the last day or so. You'd think that as our tour drew to a close we could be taken back to the safety of Nui Dat to wind down a bit, get all our gear sorted out and to celebrate our coming through the campaign safely. Perhaps they think we'll wind down too much and create some problems. Well, all I can say is that as the days get closer and closer to our RTA, we won't be too pleased about going out into the bush.

My R and R was glorious and the biggest surprise was M-J. What an amazing little fellow he is; constantly on the go and always up to something. We had a good time together and I'm sorry that I've missed out on so much of his growing up. Raylene has made our home a lovely, warm and comfortable place with a lovely, peaceful atmosphere. Despite all our financial worries, she has done wonders.

Since arriving here, I had become quite alarmed at the issues facing Australia. Pollution, strikes, Moratorium marches and a general decline in law and order. Newspaper reports and information from the radio had me convinced that we were all 'on the eve of destruction'. After spending 24 hours back home I realised that I was not getting the whole story, that while some disruptive elements are causing trouble, generally it's still the peaceful, lovely, friendly place I've always known. There are many changes happening in our lives right now and perhaps some things will never be the same again, but basically the everyday Aussie is a caring, friendly and hardworking person who appreciates the qualities of life that they have. I must admit, I was very relieved to see that everything was not the doom and gloom that the media makes it out to be.

The weather is very wet and it's becoming a little uncomfortable, what with all the mud and slush. There is little way of escaping from it. We lie in it at night while on ambush, we work in it during the day and even when we retire to our bunkers, we have to contend with water seeping in, damp clothing and mouldy bedding. No wonder that we are all suffering from various skin conditions.

My particular problems are pimples and foot tinea and I'm sure I'm in the early stages of crutch rot.

Keeping our gear maintained in good order is very difficult and we have to spend a lot of time stripping and oiling our weapons. The machine guns (GPMG M60) are proving to be a real problem. They are always jamming after just a few rounds being fired. That becomes serious when in the thick of a fire-fight, so all kinds of ideas are being tried to keep the ammunition dry and the gun working properly.

The battalion is setting new standards in all that we do, thanks to the leadership of our CO and his staff officers. I'm proud to be in the battalion and it's a real comfort to me to know that I've got a great group of mates sharing all this with me.

I'd better sign off now as I've got to prepare for another long night in some smelly paddy.

PS Raylene should be in Adelaide in December. I'm sure you'll see a big difference in M-J by then. Do you know, he's even showing a certain stubborn streak that you may be familiar with. I didn't know those sorts of things were passed down from father to son. He's got a great smile and sense of humour and loves to sing, dance and hold meaningful conversations about the latest adventure he has had in the garden. What a wonderful little kid.

3 November

It seems that the powers that be have decided to rest us, my darling, as they reckon that Charlie has pulled right out of the province. They've cut back our nightly ambushes from five-per-company, to three. That means we can roster the blokes to have a couple of nights off each week. A welcome reward after months of slog.

The days are just as busy. The work we've been doing on our position is showing results. We've re-sandbagged all bunkers and the trenches, cut back weed and bush growth from our defensive wire and even got around to painting our command post and the company commander's bunker. We keep the afternoons as free as possible to attend to personal issues like letter writing and preparing our gear for planned night activities.

Support Company has 16 bunkers along the western side of the Horseshoe and that takes up about one quarter of the feature. That means a lot of maintenance is necessary to keep the place in good order. The commanding officer is coming to inspect our area in four days, so we're hoping he'll be pleased with our efforts. Overall, the platoon has been working well. Sergeant Williams and the three corporals keep things going pretty well. I've got some first-class diggers that I can rely on to get jobs done without too much supervision. So, I'm pretty pleased with how it's all shaping up.

I received your letter about M-J's toilet training sessions and feel terrible that I'm missing out on such wonderful experiences.

We've only got 16 weeks to go before I'll be on my way home to you. That doesn't sound too bad does it.

4 November. Today was much like yesterday and the days before. We continue to work on cleaning up the area and it's all looking pretty good. The amount of rubbish we've taken away is amazing, as is the amount of vegetation we've slashed and burned.

Sergeant Williams went bush with some of the diggers today on a 'ready reaction' task which will last four days. I'm left with only 11 others to carry out the usual ambush routines. When he gets back the whole company will be going into our last area of operations to check whether the VC has returned to some of their old bunker systems.

You've probably heard about the 7RAR officer who was killed recently. I hadn't met him as he had only been with us for a month and it was his first operation. I'm not sure of all the details but we were told that he wandered off his route and walked straight into another platoon's ambush. It was a shock to us all but now that the official investigation is in progress, all the news about the incident has dried up. It's no use saying 'What if?' or 'Why?'. It happened and a lot of people are now suffering. But as far as we are concerned, it's over and we've closed our minds to it. We go on with the next part of the job. Even so, we're all feel pretty bad about it. You can imagine how the diggers who opened fire on him feel.

I haven't seen many of my old mates lately. B Company have been on their own at a place called Brigid, just east of the Long Hai mountains. Karl had a successful ambush two days ago. A Company are working away from the Horseshoe too and will take over Brigid in a week's time. C Company are here, but we see little of them. D Company have been bush for a couple of weeks and will be returning here in a few weeks time.

While all of our activities have been coordinated and commanded from the battalion command post, it doesn't feel as if we've been operating as a battalion. At times it's almost as if we're here on our own. It's been a platoon war, a real personal experience that has involved a few close mates. That's why it's so hard when you lose someone. You've lived every day with them, shared all the hardships, had a lot of laughs and relied upon them for all kinds of things. It's like losing a member of the family.

We've received information about the planning for our RTA, including things such as our march through Sydney, awards and decorations, leave and future postings. It's nice to know that we're beginning our final stages and can think of much nicer things.

We've even been told that, on 8 December, a TV crew will be here to interview soldiers for Christmas cheerios. I'm not sure where we will be at that time, but as only a few from each State will be involved, it's unlikely that I'll get my great chance to star in a TV show. I guess I had my opportunity during my time at Ingleburn when I was an extra with the show 'You Can't See Around Corners'. What acting! Then of course there was my centre page spread in the national magazine *Australian Life*. All of this talent, lost to the world.

I guess with all this thinking of home, we should start planning where we can go for a few weeks, once all this is over. I'd like to spend some time in Queensland where we could call in on Marg and Ian Bidstrup and our Main Beach friends. Then again, perhaps it would be best if we went straight home to South Australia first, to see all the relatives.

I think of you and M-J constantly and wish we could be together again. It won't be too long before that wish will come true.

PS Colonel Grey called me into his bunker this evening and we talked about some issues that had occurred earlier in the tour. He is in the process of working out who will get awards and commendations and was checking on some recommendations that had been given to him by his company commanders. I find it really easy to talk to him and once again, I am full of admiration. I feel that he really cares for us all.

6 November

Last night as the APCs rumbled along the dirt road that leads from the Horseshoe into Dat Do, I couldn't help but think what a lovely country this is.

It was about half past six and the farmers were returning from their fields with their little hoes and tools of trade slung over their stooped shoulders. The herds of cattle, with many new born calves, wandered slowly back to their village, oblivious to the great armoured vehicles nudging and bumping their way through. Old women preparing dinner, young children waving and giving the thumbs up sign and yelling for 'chop chop'. Other family members just watching in sullen silence.

Soldiers, civilians, women, children, armoured personnel carriers, bicycles, motor scooters and cattle. Smoke, fumes, dust and odours of animals, rotting rubbish and sewage. Rumbles, bellows, engines revving, horns blowing, yells and laughter. What a conglomeration of sights, smells and sounds.

The dimly lit houses made of tin, wood, concrete and thatch seemed so warm and homely. Young boys and girls were gathered in small groups, making the most of their time before curfew. So many similarities with our own lives and yet what future lies ahead for these people? They're making the most of their present days, because their future is unknown. The boys will be drafted into the Government forces or will go the way of the Viet Cong. The girls will live a life full of heavy labour, long hours, many children and little happiness. No wonder it is only the very young that smile. I'll be happy to leave this place, but I will never forget these people and their struggle. What a remarkable experience.

At the same time I'll never forget the Aussie soldier that has been my constant companion during these times. He's young; around 22 years. He's about 5 feet 10 and weighs 11–12 stone. He's not really well built, but is quite strong, fit and healthy.

He stands there smoking and joking with his mates, slouching, with his feet apart, shoulders hunched and looking quite untidy with his ill-fitting greens, muddy boots and grubby bush hat. His webbing is a little ragged but it's well cared for and fits snugly. His weapon, also showing signs of wear, is spotlessly clean and well oiled. The stock is tucked casually under an arm and the magazine rests on one of the ammo pouches of his webbing, holding it in a 'ready for action' position.

His expression appears to be one of boredom but his eyes are ever alert and he'll snap into action in a split second, if need be. He rarely shows any sign of emotion and will remain hard faced, even in the most terrible of circumstances. He will only laugh and joke in the company of his closest mates, but may give a wave to a little kid who gives him the thumbs up. He distrusts Vietnamese, politicians and military police.

His hands are stained, scratched and calloused and never far from a cigarette and his weapon. His face too, shows the scars of patrolling and an expression of weariness which comes from the constant physical and emotional strain. This makes him look a lot older than he really is. Who would recognise this digger as being the same young soldier who marched so proudly at the battalion's Farewell Parade last February?

I can't really describe the typical Australian soldier because they're all different, they all have their own hopes and dreams, they are all individuals. All I know is that they are decent Australians, they are good soldiers and they are proud of the job they are doing. I only wish that everyone back home could understand this.

Thank you for the photos of our R and R. What a glorious time that was. You mentioned that M-J has become attached to the photos. I wonder what he thinks when he talks to them and carries them around in his little trolley. I'm comforted knowing that he thinks of me.

You are certainly getting about. I'm pleased to hear about your gambling, barbecue and church activities and I hope we can do these kinds of things together one day. It'll be a welcomed change to do things as a family and to forget this whole lonely mess that has been our life for so long. May I add that without your constant love and comfort these last months would have been unbearable.

The magazine clipping you sent, in which you calculate what 'Your Man' is like, was interesting, but a little pathetic. They didn't include a green baggy uniform in the 'clothes' section, nor did they add an interest in guns and explosives in the 'hobbies'. Short back and sides didn't rate much of a score in the 'grooming' and I was disappointed that rape, pillage and plunder didn't get a mention in 'career interests'. I'm afraid you're stuck with a bloke that doesn't quite meet the ideal standards of the *Women's Weekly* ideal male.

16 November

It's a red sunset tonight and as it slowly settles below the cloudy, blue, misty, horizon, I settle down in the grass on top of my bunker to write to you, so many thousands of miles away.

We were choppered out from Binh Tuy (the province to the east) today after six days and 28,000 metres of chasing, ambushing and stalking the elusive enemy. It was the hardest, most nerve wracking operation I've been on.

Firstly, we were dropped by choppers on a beach at grid reference 710 614; an area known as Tam Bo. From 0930 to 1830 my platoon headed as fast as we could go, in a north-east direction for 17,000 metres, into the area of operation, which was in the vicinity of the May Tau mountains. No sooner had we reached the area, when the main body of Support Company contacted 20–30 enemy, heavily camouflaged and carrying large packs. The fire-fight lasted 30 minutes and from their aggressive, disciplined reaction it was thought that they could be North Vietnamese. From then on we chased them north for four days.

Every night we had to dig in, as an attack was considered most likely. As each day dawned we were warned to prepare for a bunker attack, as it was thought that if he couldn't break contact with us, he would sit and wait for us to come into one of his prepared positions. This really put pressure on everyone, as the only way to keep the initiative was to remain as close to the enemy as possible and yet we knew that he could easily draw us into a situation which favoured him, at any time.

We finally found their main bunker system and it was lucky for us that he had left that morning, as we found signs that their strength was closer to 50. The system was one of the best I've seen and we would have had quite a problem on our hands had they decided to stay. I guess he wasn't sure of our strength, so felt it was best to get right out of the area and live to fight another day.

Every night I thought of you and prayed that nothing would happen. I made a pact with my guardian angel too, just in case my prayers weren't heard. As it turned out, both helped, as the enemy retreated well to the north and beyond the line we had clearance to pursue them, so we had to give up the chase.

So, we are now back at the Horseshoe and apart from the usual night activities, it will be about two weeks before we do anything like that again.

We've had a couple of mine incidents lately. About two weeks ago a digger from 6 Platoon stepped on a mine which jumped out of the ground but failed to explode and yesterday another group (A Company) did the same thing. They say that the wet weather probably stopped the mines from exploding. What luck. With less than 100 days to go, you begin to wonder how long this luck will last.

The wet has gone and it's now becoming quite hot, although the creeks and rivers are still flooded. From now on we needn't take our hootchies out because we won't need protection from tropical downpours. I slept with only a silk over me on the last operation and that was only required to keep the mosquitoes from biting through my greens.

The rice harvest is in full swing and farmers and their families, dressed in their black 'pyjamas' and wearing their huge conical sun hats, are in the paddies from dawn to curfew, reaping their crops by hand. The roads are chock-a-block with ox carts carrying the harvest to the threshing areas, where again, by hand, the grain is threshed and gathered. Everyone is working very hard and it'll be weeks before they'll have the job finished. In the villages you can see the haystacks and heaps of rice growing daily and it seems to have been a good season.

The Viet Cong will expect their cut and I guess the Government will get a share too, so I hope the farmers and their families are left with enough to make all their labour worthwhile.

I have just finished reading the four letters that were waiting for me and once again, the news makes me realise that even in Australia some horrible things can occur.

The news of Don's accident was a terrible shock and while I'm relieved to know he's in good hands, it's going to be a long, hard road to recovery. I'll try and get a letter off to his family, but in the meantime please extend my best wishes to Marg. Poor Don, what was he still doing on Elcho? I thought he was going elsewhere.

Your second letter brought me news of the 'peeping Tom' episode, so I'm particularly worried about your safety and security. I'm so angry that the military system has stuffed up again and the Provos (military police) have failed to support you. They know who he is and that he's done this before and yet they aren't willing to do anything about it. I'm so proud of what you've done to settle the issue once and for all. I'm very interested to know that the secretary of the Liverpool RSL is offering to help, because the League hasn't done much to help anyone returning from Vietnam. Let me know what comes of it as soon as possible because if it's not settled soon, I'll have a few words to someone here and see if Colonel Grey can get some appropriate action taken to get the bastard discharged.

Please give my special thanks to the neighbours and to Bev particularly, she's been a great friend. I reckon that all the families should get together and have a meeting with the Holsworthy family support unit to get this kind of thing sorted out, once and for all.

It's their job to help you while we're away. I tell you what, there'll be a few angry soldiers coming to visit them in the new year, if they don't start assisting their families more.

Have you heard how Guy went in his exams? It'll be good to spend some time with them, just like before, and hear of their future plans.

Brigadier Henderson is the task force commander you saw on 'Four Corners' and yes, he's a beaut bloke. He and our commanding officer get on very well and that's a sure sign that the brigadier is a very capable soldier and leader.

How come Mick O'Brien is returning home in January? I haven't seen him much and right now B Company is out bush and will be for some time, so I can't check him out. Perhaps he's in line for a promotion and a posting.

You'll have to send me the details of your plans to return to South Australia.

Thank you for the card . . . a lovely thought. Thank you also for praying for me. I've been doing a bit of it myself lately.

I'm feeling pretty tired right now, so I'll sign off and get to bed.

17 November

My love, R and C will be coming up shortly. I'm certainly looking forward to getting away from this place for a little while. The bunkers, sounds of artillery, the briefings for ambush and the familiar doings of a soldier, all get a bit tiring. Nothing that a few days at the Peter Badcoe Club can't fix. I haven't been there for almost four months, so it'll be a pleasant break.

In years to come I'd like to settle in a place with rolling hills and valleys, trees and open spaces. Just like I have before me now, as I look across wide open fields to the distant mountains. The colours are changing now that the rains have gone. The paddies are turning to yellow and brown and the deep green freshness of the vegetation of a few weeks ago, has a slightly dusty appearance. Each afternoon, when I escape to this favourite spot of mine, I leave behind the sights and sounds of war and for a brief moment gain a sense of peace and relaxation.

I wonder what the future holds for us. I hope it will include a place where we can sit back and look out at natural bushland, where we can share peaceful evenings, just sitting quietly and admiring the scenery. I reckon we deserve something like that.

The curfew flares have just been fired and the clouds over the hills diffuse their light, making it appear as if there is a bushfire in the area. Now they have gone out and another lonely night begins.

I've finished a letter to Don, but it's difficult not knowing how bad he is. Is he fully alert, or in a coma? Is he able to get about, or is he bedridden? I've enclosed his letter with yours, so please read it and see whether you think it is appropriate.

Freddy's pal [Freddy was Mark-John's toy frog] is living in my bunker. He's yellow and brown and about the size of a saucer. He hops around the floor chomping on insects that have been attracted by my small lamp and others which suddenly appear from who knows where. Right now he's eyeing off a very large worm. Now this worm is eight inches long and I'm wondering just how he's going to get it down. I'm not sure whether frogs can suck. If so, he'll probably slurp the worm, just like we eat spaghetti. If not, he's going to have to devour it in stages and hop around with half the worm hanging out his mouth for quite some time. Nature study in Vietnam is a very interesting subject.

18 November. Once again I'm in my favourite spot, soaking up the sun and the atmosphere that Phouc Tuy hands out recklessly today. It's only 12.45 and after a lunch of lamb chops, I thought I'd take a few minutes to let you know how things are progressing here.

It's very windy today so I've taken shelter behind one wall of the bunker, but I can still see the marvellous view. I can't stay long because in a few short hours my thoughts will turn towards tonight's ambush.

The TV camera crew have already taken their interviews for their Christmas show. They weren't here long and not many diggers got the chance to send their greetings. If you see the show you should get some good views of the 'Shoe but alas, I missed my chance at stardom.

I'm certainly looking forward to the Christmas cake you made. I hope I can handle all that brandy. Brings back memories of the cake you and Margy Bruce cooked for Ian Bidstrup and me, when we were working at the Royal Show.

How is our lovely son? Is he still mischievous and adorable? He'll be a real little man by the time I get home, so I'm looking forward to having long discussions with him about all the important things that happen in his busy life. Do you know, it's been 33 days since we were last together.

I'm covered in pimples again. I'm not too worried because everyone seems to have problems with them. The sun is helping to clear them up, but who cares, my appearance is the last thing I have to worry about. There's no one here that I have to impress, so I'll just let nature do its work.

I've enclosed my latest poem. I'm having trouble with a couple of lines, but I'll send it anyway.

You've married a soldier and now live a life
Full of worry and trouble, separation and strife
You know the feeling of being left all alone
To weather the storm till your soldier comes home
Loving a soldier is really no fun
But it's sure worth the price when the battle is won.
Loving a soldier is, goodbye to the plane
Wondering if you will see him again
Reluctantly, painfully letting him go
While inside you're crying, for wanting him so
It's being quite young, yet feeling so old
It's mostly to have, but never to hold.
Your friends all marvel at your quiet and calm
Not knowing each doorknock sets off an alarm
They don't know the hate that you feel for the war
They don't see the tears that can't flow anymore
The nights all alone that are so hard to bear
With the memories that only two lovers can share.
Loving a soldier is learning to pray
And meaning every single word that you say
You married a soldier, now your fight has begun
A fight that's a battle which has to be won
Though he is the soldier, who'll fight where he must
Your war is as hard and your cause is as just.
So shoulder your burden, as he does his pack
And struggle as he does, with the load on your back
It's your fight as well, you're a soldier's wife now
So do what you must, see it through, somehow
Together you'll struggle against all kinds of foe
Knowing that somehow, your love will grow.
Remember, though you are oceans apart
You'll always be the one in his heart.

28 November

I'm in the process of replying to a nurse from Armidale who wrote to me asking for names of blokes who'd like pen friends. I initially felt that seeing she'd gone to the effort of writing, I should do the same, however I'm struggling. It's not appropriate to write a formal letter and I'm not in the mood to write a chatty letter, especially to someone who would know little of our conditions and experiences. So I'm stuck in the middle of the second paragraph and have put it to one side for a while.

Being in Support Company has it's drawbacks, as we are on constant call as 'Ready Reaction Company'. This means we have to be on 30 minutes notice at any time of the day or night, to react to any call for assistance, or to go anywhere in the province for any purpose whatsoever. I've just come back from one such action, which was in the area of Long Tan, 5000 metres to the north of the 'Shoe.

As a matter of fact, I'd just got back from a night ambush and was going to breakfast, when the company commander said I'd have to go out on one of these special jobs. In this case it was to investigate some reports that an enemy patrol was moving through the area and possibly reconnoitring positions from which to set up mortar base plates, which would be used to fire on the Horseshoe or Nui Dat.

It was an uneventful patrol which had us out until the twenty-fifth and as soon as we got back, we packed up all our gear and went back to Nui Dat in preparation for our R and C. Now it's the last night in Vung Tau and tomorrow we'll head back to the grind.

The weather has been lousy with high winds and rain, so most of us have stayed indoors reading, playing cards and sleeping. I guess any rest from the usual routine is better than none, however some reckon we could have just as well been in our bunkers at the 'Shoe.

I read George Johnston's book *My Brother Jack* and was amazed at the similarities with my early years. I thoroughly enjoyed it and as the inclement weather stopped me from doing my usual swimming pool regime, I completed it in only two sittings.

The rest of the time I spent writing Christmas cards to our relatives and friends. I'll post them from Nui Dat.

I received your rude card and the cake you baked for me, when we got in from the Long Tan patrol and I've already devoured several slices. Some of the diggers have mentioned their liking for home-made cake and it looks like I'll have to share it around before too long. I can't work out how they knew I'd received some goodies from home, unless the digger who receives all Support Company's mail smelt the alcohol coming from the parcel and spread the word. Aunt Ethel sent me a large tin of salted mixed nuts and a Christmas card. I'll send her a card and a thank you from the dozen or so who helped devour them.

I also got a five page letter from your Dad, which was a wonderful surprise. I know he doesn't like writing, so this must have been a special effort for him. It was great to get some everyday news about the family and his words of encouragement were very much appreciated. I guess, having been through the Tobruk campaign he, better than anyone, knows what I'm experiencing.

29 November. I went for a walk tonight along the dark stony paths that lead between the tent lines and rubber trees in our Nui Dat base. It's a depressing area with musty smelling canvas, rotting sandbags, rusty corrugated iron and red clay earth. The stars, although bright and sparkling did nothing to ease my loneliness, as the vastness of the night sky seemed to emphasise just how far apart we are.

There are many more lonely nights ahead for both of us and too many patrols and operations to go before I can at last start to relax and learn how to share things with you again. I have a horrible feeling at times, that something will stop us from being together again. I've even had one or two nightmares recently, which have me returning to Australia, but you aren't there to meet me. I keep telling myself that it will soon be over and it won't be long before we are holding one another so very tight. But still, these future delights seem so distant. We must cling to the slender threads of love we share through letters and pray that nothing happens to destroy our future.

30 November – from Raylene to Peter's mum

Sorry about the late reply regarding what to send Peter for Christmas, but as all mail seems to be going to Vietnam via the RAAF base at Richmond, I didn't feel it was necessary to reply at once. Parcels have only been taking about six days, so there's no extra hurry for Christmas parcels.

I haven't got any marvellous suggestions about what he might need. I have sent him a highly potent Christmas cake. He'll have to go easy with it or he's likely to get drunk!! My Mum sent him a parcel of Avon deodorant and a couple of paperbacks. My one and only suggestion is a tin of fancy biscuits or some magazines. They get a little extra in their rations for Christmas and their cooks prepare a special meal for those lucky enough not to be out on operations. So, if the VC decide to have the day off, Peter should have a good meal. It will be an odd sort of Christmas for him, that's for sure.

One reason I haven't been very quick with my answering is that M-J has had tonsillitis again and sinusitis too. Now I've caught the bug and am having to fill myself with antibiotics so that I will be well enough to come home, as planned on 6 December. I think I will be catching the morning flight, direct to Adelaide.

I've got so much to do next week. I've got to get a few things fixed up with the car, get it tested for re-registration and have it serviced, ready for its two month rest up in our garage. I've got the info from the NRMA as how to look after it.

I've also got to book the plane, clean the house, get the garden (especially the lawn) in some sort of order, change my address at the military post office, so they will send on my mail to Adelaide, inform the family liaision group of my going away and ask them to keep an eye on the place. Then there are a few parties. One is for all the 7RAR children, being given by the neighbouring battalion (5RAR) at Holsworthy, on the fourth.

M-J is still awake (9 pm) singing to himself in his cot. Every now and then he calls out 'dink peeze, Mummy'.

I think it's about 90-odd days till Peter comes sailing home. It doesn't seem that long after all these long months but there's still a lot of worrying to do and I won't feel relaxed until I know he's on the *Sydney* and it's heading south, out of that terrible part of the world. Have you heard from Peter lately? He's been on an operation in the neighbouring province. It's been so quiet in Phouc Tuy that they are chasing them elsewhere. I don't like the idea at all.

I've decided that I haven't liked this year one bit; what with extra worry, loneliness, continuing financial burdens, illness, prowlers, gossip, weather and above all, the endless feeling of insecurity, I'll be mighty glad to say goodbye to 1970.

Peter is starting to feel very apprehensive. His letters aren't telling the whole story, but I sense he's not the same young man we knew at the beginning. He will need some special love when he gets home. Come to think of it, won't we all. Must say good night, hoping everyone is well.

30 November

My lovely wife, Xuyen Moc was attacked last night by a large VC force. Rocket propelled grenades and mortars ripped into the military posts north and south of the village for half an hour before the ground attack overran both positions. Five local soldiers were killed, including the commander of the southern post. Four civilians were wounded and 27 local soldiers are missing, believed captured. The enemy has also taken a heavy machine gun, two radio sets, numerous M16 rifles and a 60 mm mortar.

None of us are too pleased at what has happened because, apart from all the captured weapons and equipment, the local military are supposed to be taking over from us as our Government reduces our commitment. If this is the best they can do, then what hope is there for the future? You can't help but feel that this attack was a show of strength by the enemy, to prove to the rest of the province that they are still a viable force. We'll have to do something pretty big, in retaliation, to win back the local population's respect and support.

Our recent area of operations, as you know, was east of Xuyen Moc and the enemy we've been chasing lately have had something to do with it. I guess we'll be sent back into the area to try and sort things out, as I doubt whether the local military will be up to it.

Some of our officers and NCOs are smiling again as they see this attack as a sign that things will brighten up a bit. They reckon we were all getting it too easy and we've been caught napping. Others say it's an act of a desperate enemy that needed to do something spectacular, to win back some support. Either way, it means we're in for some increased activity for the next few months.

I shared your cake and your Mum's cake and goodies with the platoon soon after we got back to the Horseshoe and they reckon it was great. I'm now munching on the cashews and sultanas that your grandparents sent. Would you send me their address so that I can include them on my Christmas card list.

In your parents parcel they included a book called *Are Pigs People?*. I was wondering whether they knew that the 7th Battalion unofficial mascot is a pig. As soon as I'm finished with it I'll get it circulating around the officers mess and I'm sure it will be appreciated.

A very strong westerly has been blowing for the past 48 hours and it's whipping up a real dust storm. Even so, we've continued to work on our bunkers and trenches as this latest incident has given an increased urgency to what was becoming a mundane, meaningless task.

It's not likely that the VC could do anything but fire a few mortar rounds at us, as we are too heavily defended and even then, our reaction would be immediate and devastating. Mortars, artillery of every calibre and tanks from both the 'Shoe and Nui Dat would engage with counter bombardment fire and patrols would be sent out to sweep the areas. An attack would only be possible if they were able to come within range and that means keeping clear of all of our patrols and ambushes. It would be a very heroic thing to try. Still they tried it once (Long Tan) and if they're desperate enough, who knows what they would be willing to do?

Ian Dunn is returning to Australia in a couple of weeks and will leave the army to join the Police Force. Chris Johnson leaves 7RAR when we finish our tour and is returning to England to rejoin his old regiment. Greg Lindsay has been having bad trouble with a knee injury and will probably miss out on his SAS selection, so he is likely to take discharge when we RTA. I haven't seen Karl

Metcalf for about two months but he's still the same tenacious little fellow that we have all come to admire. He always seem to be where the action is.

My promotion to lieutenant has been confirmed for 1 January.

I hope all is well at home. Should I send this letter to Lighthorse Parade, Holsworthy or to Balmoral Road, Brighton? I'm not sure when you decided to head off again. Either way, please take good care of the two most precious people in my world.

5 December

To my Birthday Girl

Happy Birthday for the eighth,
Happy Birthday for the eighth,
I'm sorry I'm so late,
But Happy Birthday for the eighth.

Are you at the age where you start to get younger every year? I hope your birthday is a happy event, with lots of ice cream, cake, lollies and presents. Wish I could be there. This is the third one I've missed. It's becoming a bit of a habit.

It's been fairly hectic for the platoon lately, especially in the night ambush roles which leave us tired and a bit on edge. Some of us have been out every night for the last nine nights. We've been going out at 1800 and coming in at 0630. Then it's straight into our daily routine of strengthening our defensive area and when that's finished, preparing for the coming night's activity. When we're not ambushing we're also required to go out for a few days to check familiar track and bunker systems, to see if there are any signs of the enemy returning.

The constant effort that is needed to keep ourselves alert and ready for any kind of action is really tiring. The physical effort of carrying all our gear and travelling long distances or laying in some stinking paddy for 10 hours, isn't too much of a worry anymore, it's the need to be always on the lookout. That can be for any kind of a sign that indicates an enemy presence, or the possibility of a mine. Then there's the ever present threat from an enemy ambush or worse still, stumbling into a bunker system.

Even the routine of night ambushes brings with it a heightened feeling that you're always being watched. The villagers see us entering an area and even though we don't move into the final position until after dark, they notify the enemy of our presence by keeping lights on in their houses. VC trying to enter a village for re-supply, know to keep well away from areas where these lights are shining.

Every day I've been trying to write, but lately have had no time for personal business and so by the time you receive this letter your birthday will have passed. At least you'll know that I've been thinking of you. However what a disappointment that once again, I'm not able to be with you for your special day. If anyone asks: 'What did your husband give you for your birthday?' – tell them that he gave you all his love.

I received three letters today. There must have been a hold up in the post, because one is eight days old.

I'm pleased to know that the Alberts are fighting on and apparently winning the battle. I hope we can call in on them during my leave. Don should be well and truly on the road to recovery by then. Their strong religious faith has a lot to do with how well they are coping. I admire them for that.

You'll have to tell me of M-J's reaction to the plane trip. He's certainly a well-travelled little bloke, so probably takes it all in his stride.

Your cake has been devoured, your Mum's too. Aunt Ethel's salted nuts are all gone as have your grandparents. All I'm left with is four empty tins and a lot of compliments. I guess I got my share and no doubt, I'll get to share someone else's Christmas goodies. In one sense it's like being invited by the soldier's families to share their food with them, so we won't really be having a lonely Christmas this year.

Well, it's now 82 days to go. It's getting closer, but there's still a lot of patrolling and ambushing to do. We are all hoping that our part of the war remains quiet. The attack on Xuyen Moc hasn't led to many changes to our routines as yet.

D Company hit a mine yesterday and received four injured. Most of our casualties have been from mines and I guess that's what all of us fear. There's one thing to be shot at; at least you can retaliate. With a mine it's all a matter of chance. An inch either way and you won't step on it. You'll probably never even know it was there. But if you hit one, it creates a terrible feeling of loss and frustration, because there's nothing you can do to get back at the bastards who put it there. Then there's the feeling of: 'Why him and not me? I walked over that place just minutes before'; or 'Why did I take that route? I could have led them another way.' I guess there's a fair bit of blame that is felt by many, after being involved in a mine incident.

The platoon is doing really well. They're a good bunch that get stuck into any task asked of them. They bitch a bit, but who doesn't when you have to live like this. Everyone is fit and well. We're all counting down the days to RTA.

Well, I'd better get this off otherwise you'll get it even later. Sorry for not timing this to reach home on the morning of the eighth.

I've also been trying to finish a letter to Mum which has now been in the closing stages for the past week. I hope you will meet up with her soon and fill her in on all my doings. I'm finding it difficult to keep her up with all my news, without worrying her too much. I'm not sure whether she fully understands what I've got myself into.

I guess it's hard for her to imagine what we do and how we live over here. I've been as descriptive as I could in some letters but I'm sure, like most parents or friends living their daily lives in the comfort of Australia, their perceptions of what is happening and what we are doing are far from reality. For instance Mum asked in her last letter, why was I always 'wet and mucky?' I'm sure she felt that in this day and age, even a soldier should have one hot shower a day and a change of underwear. She also described the Horseshoe as 'a camp centre you go out from'. If only she could see and hear all of the sights and sounds that are before me right at this moment, it would be a horrible shock to her.

I suppose it's best that she (and other soldier's parents) continues to picture it all in the simplest of details and knows little of the experiences we face. I'm hoping that even in their protected, peaceful and sheltered lives, the people of Australia realise what we are going through and appreciate our efforts. Wouldn't it be a shame if all of this was for nothing?

8 December

There is a lot of colour in this strange country, my darling wife. Yellow and red are the national colours of South Vietnam and their flag is yellow backing with three red horizontal stripes. The pagodas and shrines are ablaze with rich colours, but predominantly red and yellow. These people love to decorate their houses with all kinds of colours. During festive seasons the villages are decked out with streamers, flags and lanterns.

There is also a lot of beauty. Not just the magnificent countryside, but the people too. On special occasions the women dress in all their finery which includes the *au dai*; a white silk trouser covered by a colourful, full length silken dress which is split to the waist on both sides. It is very sexy. Most of the young women wear this style of clothing for every day wear too, but not in the colourful material that is kept for special occasions.

I'm sitting in my usual evening position, having at last been awarded a night off. I've just seen my platoon head out on another night ambush and felt a little tinge of guilt as I waved to them from the comfort of my camp chair. I can now turn to peaceful thoughts of home as their thoughts turn to the problems of one more mosquito ridden night in a smelly Dat Do paddy.

The sunset is a golden yellow with tinges of red. The countryside is a deep green and the sky is a darkening blue. The whole province is a blaze of natural colour and it really is a beautiful sight.

Our 24-hour operation into the Phouc Buu area was uneventful. We found some old, destroyed bunkers but there were no signs of recent habitation. The APCs picked us up at 0730 and raced us into an area halfway between Xuyen Moc and the 'Shoe. It's a very low lying area and we had to check out some old village ruins, the surrounding paddy and jungle.

The jungle is mainly swamp with waist-deep mud, head high elephant grass, vines and thick, tangled, thorn bushes. The going was very tough and exhausting. Picture a scene from some scary movie with steaming swamps and dark, mystic forests with strange twisted shaped trees. Add to this the thick, quicksand-like mud which sucks your legs deeper and deeper the more you struggle, until you are hopelessly stuck, waist-deep in black smelly ooze. Then the dense, above head height, elephant grass which hides all other features from your sight and makes you feel claustrophobic and hopelessly lost. You have to rely solely on your compass bearing to lead you out of the area, to the objective you are hoping to reach before nightfall.

Happiness is leaving the swamps, finding your objective and setting a perfect ambush. It's not very often that you hope an enemy patrol will come through during the night, but I was so sure of our position, I felt that we could have hit any number and come out on top. However, the next day dawned and we moved on to another task.

I've been working on a new philosophy – only dread one day at a time. As I've said before, there are only three days in Vietnam – yesterday, today and tomorrow. To tell you the truth, I don't even know what day it is. I think I know the date, even though I made a mistake in the month when dating this letter. Yesterdays are happy days because they allow our mistakes, inadequacies and embarrassments to be things of the past and we can look back and always find something to laugh about. For example, when our forward scout disappeared into an overgrown, flooded bomb crater. He emerged covered in mud and slush, with water pouring out of his pockets, webbing and rifle. He couldn't understand why we were all laughing at him.

Todays aren't too bad because the work program often fills in the long hours and there's a chance you won't get selected for the night's ambush or patrol. Even when you are required to go out, you've got the activity to concentrate on and you're with a lot of others, so you don't ever feel alone or scared. It's only when you are by yourself that those feelings sometimes come to haunt you.

Tomorrows are the worst. Anything can happen and in your dreams and imagination it always does. It's the fear of the worst, that tomorrows bring.

But soon, tomorrows become todays, and todays become yesterdays and we find ourselves another day closer to RTA.

After arriving back from the bush, I called my corporals together with the idea of giving them a blast for some problems we have been having. It's been brewing for a while, so I thought it was time to get things sorted out once and for all. I was fairly angry so had noted several points to make and where I wanted things to change.

However, when they came into my bunker and I realised that they were as tired and worn out as me, I decided that it would be best if I just aired my concerns and let them see what they could offer to fix them. We spent a good hour discussing a number of points and it seemed to ease the situation. It certainly gave us all a good chance to get a lot of things off our chests. I felt afterwards that had I continued with my intended approach, things would have worsened. We are all feeling the strain and the corporals realise that some of their diggers too, are nearing their limit. In many ways they are trying to protect them from seemingly meaningless tasks and give them as much time to rest as they can.

Recce Platoon is a good team and they've worked hard in the bush and around the 'Shoe. They don't have to prove anything to anyone but themselves. If everyone carries out their jobs thoroughly then we should finish this tour on a successful note. I'm confident that everyone is doing their very best in these trying circumstances.

Once again my darling, I sign off with all my love.

Thinking of you on your birthday.

9 December

I was sitting in the small tent, known as the Officers/Sergeants Annex, reading a magazine article about Lieutenant Calley and the Mai Lay massacre, when the news came through that 'Callsign

21' was in contact, was being mortared and the enemy were attacking them from three sides. It was about 0730 and I remember thinking as I was running back to my bunker to get my gear ... 'good old Karl, always where the action is'.

At 0800 we were given the five minutes call, to get down to the chopper pad because the action was continuing and we were to be inserted to try and block off the enemy's withdrawal. While my sergeant was inspecting and checking the platoon, I ran down to the company CP to receive orders. 4 Platoon, B Company (Callsign 21) were under heavy attack from about 20 enemy. They had received nine mortar rounds from a 60 mm mortar and the gunships they had called in to help, had been fired upon by heavy machine guns and one had gone down and another had been badly holed (the one shot down had made its way out of the battle area to crash land on Highway 23). Karl had been one of two wounded. He had been hit in the leg and the other was a slight head wound.

While we were waiting on the landing zone for pick up, additional information was being sent to us from the CP, so that we were kept informed of developments and knew what we were flying into. They thought this could be the same group that hit Xuyen Moc, which meant they could be part of a force that numbered as many as 200. There were a lot of jokes being told while we waited. A sure sign that the diggers were feeling pretty anxious.

At that time the padre came down to the landing zone to give us some support, but his presence made me very uncomfortable. I felt that he was giving us the 'last rights'. Still, as we clambered onto the choppers, I hoped he was saying a few prayers for us.

As we were flying in we saw the downed chopper being lifted back to Vung Tau, beneath a Chinook helicopter.

Support Company flew into an area 3000 metres north of Karl's position and as soon as we hit the ground we scrambled for cover, expecting at any time to receive some incoming fire from a well-armed enemy. The choppers certainly didn't wait around, some barely touched down while we jumped out onto the soggy, grass covered ground. I could swear I saw one of the chopper's crew

At 0800 we were given the five minutes call . . .

. . . as soon as we hit the ground we scrambled for cover, expecting at any time to receive some incoming fire from a well-armed enemy.

literally pushing some of our diggers out. They get a bit shaky when one of their own has been shot down.

We immediately split into two groups and raced for designated cut-off positions. By this time, the enemy had broken contact and the whole of B Company were following up their withdrawal route, so if we were to expect anything it would be in the next hour or so.

By 1300 we were still ambushing the main tracks out of the area without any sign of the enemy. B Company had come across a huge bunker system involving 50 well-constructed bunkers, two heavy machine-gun pits, and two rifle ranges. It covered 300 square metres and had been the training camp for a large force of well-trained enemy. They also found one dead enemy soldier, numerous bloody bandages and documents which told us that the complete D445 battalion had been occupying the place for quite some time.

So that evening, as we ambushed a track/creek junction on one of the likely routes out of the area, we were kept alert by the fact that we could confront a force of about 200 very determined enemy soldiers any time in the next 12 hours.

The following day we moved west about 5000 metres trying to cut any tracks they may have used. It's now the third day and although we've covered another 5000 metres, we've found absolutely nothing.

B Company have followed their withdrawal route which went west but it looks like that once again, he's given everybody the slip. You can't help but admire them. They are carrying their wounded as well as their heavy weapons and going like mad to get some distance between them and us. They probably went west because they saw our choppers flying into the north. They must know the area like it's their own backyard.

It's now 1800 on the third day since being reacted. B Company are still following up their escape route but we are being lifted out tomorrow, about midday. I'm covering a large track east of the contact area tonight and we're a little more relaxed now than we were two days ago.

My dinner consisted of a cold tin of meat balls and beans, a packet of biscuits with jam and cheese and a strong cup of lukewarm coffee. With 30 minutes before stand to, I'm thinking of what you might be doing at this time. It will be about 8 pm at your place and you are probably washing the meal dishes with your Mum, chatting about all that's been happening around the neighbourhood. Your Dad and Stephen are playing some game with M-J in the lounge room and soon you'll all be settling down to another peaceful night's sleep. What a contrast there is in our lives.

Personally, I'm pretty fit and seem to be holding up to all this running about. I still suffer from pimples. They are all over my shoulders, chest and back. My crutch rot remains (I've had it for about four months now) and my toes and feet break out into rashes and tinea after a few days slogging through all this undergrowth. None of these things are getting any worse, so I guess I've got nothing really to complain about.

Well it's time to sign off so, from my little position between a fairly large tree and a clump of bamboo, I'll say goodnight and sweet dreams. Give M-J a kiss for me.

PS Just for the records; The bunker system was at grid reference 742 699 and Karl's contact was at 736 693.

PPS I've been told Karl will be RTA'd for treatment on his wound. He's a lucky bloke, a real character and I will miss him.

PPPS I'm now back at the 'shoe and I've received a half a dozen South Australian beers from Rex, for Christmas. I hope he doesn't mind, but I think I'll share them with my sergeant and corporals tonight, as a toast for us getting through this last little episode unscathed. After all, it could have ended so very differently.

15 December

I've finally finished reading the letters from Gill's class (they wrote to me for the second time) and I must say, I'm pleased with how they have set to and written such interesting and rather funny letters. There were two, especially, who asked questions that I guess are universal. One asked: 'Why do we have wars?' and the other asked: 'When will the war be over?' How do you answer kids when they ask such questions? It's like the song by Johnny Cash where his child asks ... 'Daddy, what is war?' – 'That's when men fight and die.' ... 'Daddy, why?'

I wonder what I'd say to Mark-John if he asked me such a question.

I'm sick and tired of the whole thing now and feel that what we're doing is a waste of time. I'm convinced that most of the

Vietnamese don't care who wins or who is in Government, just as long as they can get some kind of normality back in their lives. The younger generations need some kind of security for their future. If that is under the Communists, so be it. For most, it would be more stable than what they have now. As one local soldier said to me when I asked him what he thought of the VC. 'Vietnamese, same, same.'

B Company had a mine incident yesterday; D Company, a little while before; A Company, just before that; and Support Company just before that too. Maiming, killing, destroying hopes and dreams ... It's so sad, yet who cares?

Support Company is going to Brigid, the defensive base near the Long Hais (grid reference 518 541), for five weeks. We'll be taking over from A Company who are going on R and C and then into the bush for the remainder of their tour. The position, which is constructed in the sand dunes near the village of Lang Phouc Hai, consists of a section of three mortars, two 105 mm guns and a company of infantry. Our role will be to carry out night ambushes of the tracks which lead from the Long Hais into a number of fishing villages, along the coast. We'll also do a bit of patrolling through areas known as the Long Green and the Light Green.

I'm pleased that we're going to have a change of scenery. The 'Shoe was starting to get us all down. The constant night ambushing and patrolling, the ready reaction duty and the never-ending work we were doing on the defences. Brigid will require as much work, but I feel that the sun, sand and sea will give us a new lease of life. I'm not too pleased to be operating so close to the Long Hais, as it's the main base for the local enemy battalion and there has been a lot of activity around the area for quite a long time (it's well known that all the villages are pro-VC).

Darling, I miss you terribly and I feel a real pain in my insides when I think of all the love, companionship and family activities that we are missing. I guess I'm getting to the stage I was before R and R, although this time I can only think of getting back to you for good. I've been relying on all your photos to remind me of what I am missing and what I have to look forward too. At times

I feel they are the only real contact I have with you because they give me the physical presence that I need so much. I feel so sad that the only link we have to keep our love alive are several fading photos and some hopes that we'll have a happy future together.

Raylene, I love you so very much. More than I ever have before and I know our love will continue to grow as time passes. What I need is to be with you and some time to get to know you again. I think we have both changed over these past months. Perhaps we're more mature than we were and we accept that life comes with its share of sadness. We've been through a lot of emotional strain and I'd like to think that it's made our love stronger. Time will tell whether everything we've gone through will lead to better things. I know I'll never be the same. I'm not the same person I was when I left.

I'm not sure how I've changed, but with your love I'll be able to put all of this behind me and get on with my life with you.

How are all the relatives treating M-J, or more to the point, how is M-J treating all his relatives. I bet he's won their hearts. I miss him too ... terribly.

We've packed up all our extra personal gear and sent it back to Nui Dat for storage. All we're taking to Brigid are the bare essentials.

There are many Cambodian refugees living in the area west of Brigid and from what I've seen they're far more friendly than the locals. We'll get to know some of the local soldiers a bit better too, because we'll take a few of them out with us each time we go on night ambush. I hope they have been checked by the security people, because I wouldn't like to be going out with VC sympathisers, or who knows, VC soldiers wanting to know more about our tactics.

We thought, about two months ago, that the Viet Cong had ended their offensive, but lately things have been hotting up. Intelligence say that this will keep building up till 21 December, after which it will slow down until March 1971.

Please look after yourself and dear little M-J.

PS I received Christmas cards from Dad, Aunty Doss and Mum, Rex and the boys.

Chapter Eight

The Final Phase

19 December 1970–23 February 1971

19 December

Darling, today is the foundation day for the National Liberation Front and tomorrow is the foundation day of the Viet Minh (the Vietnamese who defeated the French back in the early 50s). So tonight should bring about a few activities. We are within mortar range from the Long Hais, we are surrounded by high sand dunes and are pretty close to a number of small hamlets, so we are in a location tailor made for something to happen. We'll have the usual four ambush patrols out and there will be some local Vietnamese Army ambushes set too, but it won't stop them, if they want to make some real trouble for us. A bad time to spend my first night in this place.

Brigid

Brigid is about 200 metres square, consisting of about 20 sand-bagged bunkers, reinforced with steel pickets and corrugated iron. The area is surrounded by barbwire which is seeded with trip flares and claymore mines. Three mortars and a 105 mm artillery gun are located in the centre and a section of armoured personnel carriers gives us added fire power from their 50 and 30 calibre machine guns. It's not a bad defensive position, but really it's just a secure place to stay during the day and from where we can move out into ambush positions at night. Periodically we send out area patrols which spend a few days further out: in the Long and Light Green, along the beach line and in the shadows of the Long Hais.

7RAR has occupied this place for the past eight months, so it's well developed, although there is a lot of maintenance required, because any strong wind causes the sand dunes to shift and this covers the flares and mines and erodes the bunkers.

I received your letter reporting that you arrived safely in Adelaide and that M-J has already established himself as head of the household at No. 33. What a wonderful Christmas he's going to have, surrounded by all his doting relatives.

There is still some talk about a Christmas cease fire. Even so, we will continue with our usual patrolling and ambushing activities around Brigid, because we don't trust anyone, especially in this area.

I've received a card and letter from Marg and Don Albert. Don is walking with the aid of a stick and is amazing all the specialists with his recovery.

The card from your parents was great. The gum leaves hang above my stretcher and the eucalyptus scent is wonderful.

Grandma and Grandpa Pollard have sent me a card and I got a real rude one from Joan.

What were the flowers I sent you for your birthday like? Interflora did all of the arrangements and were very helpful when they knew of our special situation.

I have to go now because we have to plan for the defence of this place, should anything eventuate tonight. If the night passes without incident, I'll send this letter off with the early morning mail. If something does occur, it may be delayed somewhat.

21 December

Another month is drawing to a close, my darling, and with it, another year. I won't be sad to see the last of it and when January dawns we'll have only 55 days to go.

We'll be going on a six-day operation along the Song Rai on 9 January and will return to Brigid until the twentieth, after which we'll go to the 'Shoe until 12 February. Our last operation will be from 12 to 20 February and that leaves only four days left before RTA. Of course whether any of this comes about depends on the situation at the time. The important thing to keep in mind is that they intend having us out on operations right up until the last minute.

The VC didn't do much to celebrate the NLF (National Liberation Front) foundation day. Only 20 attacks were reported in the whole of Vietnam and nothing occurred in any of our areas. They must have had the night off, celebrating.

Life at Brigid is very relaxed. We go around in shorts only, soaking up the hot sun and getting very tanned. We sleep and rest as best we can in our bunkers and play a few games of volleyball during the day before we begin our preparations for the night's ambushes. We eat our ration pack meals for morning and lunch, but get a hot box delivered from the 'Shoe each evening, which provides a good three-course meal. We ambush every night and these are sometimes extended to three days and nights.

We've been out with some Vietnamese soldiers. This is quite an experience as they can't speak English and we can't speak Vietnamese. The messages usually get through with hand gestures and a lot of goodwill from both parties. I went out with seven of them the other night and was quite impressed with their skills. I'm glad nothing happened because I'm not sure how I would have commanded the group, when only half knew what I was saying.

Every day we get a front seat view of jet fighters bombing the Long Hais and artillery firing at the craggy features. Through our binoculars, you can study every square foot of this infamous mountain and see the devastation that has been caused over the years, by thousands and thousands of tons of explosives. Yet, as you peer up and search each boulder, crack and crevice, you can't help but feel that someone is peering back down at you.

The only thing I can find to bitch about right now is the ever present wind which blows from the east. It throws sand, with quite some force, into everything; clothes, hair, eyes, weapons, and food. It shifts the sand dunes causing our bunkers to cave in, unless we keep sandbagging and reinforcing them. It's a never-ending job to keep our underground homes from filling with sand.

Well I'll sign off and see what goodies have just arrived in a parcel from Mum, Rex and the boys.

22 December

My darling, We were seated atop 22B [an armoured personnel carrier], nicknamed 'Paula Mary' by its crew and were moving in rhythm to the bumps and swerves in much the same way as a rider seems to be part of his horse when at full gallop. The dust thrown up from the tracks covered us, clogging our nostrils and filling our mouths. We looked more like dirty, scruffy scarecrows, with beady, bloodshot eyes, than alert infantrymen on the daily APC patrol through the scrub that surrounds Brigid.

The three APCs cut this way and that, swerved here and there and raced with high revving engines through the low scrubland, searching for freshly made tracks, or any sign at all, that would indicate that someone had been through the area overnight.

The area is known to have been mined. Not a mine field as such, but more a place where individual, anti-personnel or anti-tank mines are placed by VC to catch unwary patrols. We passed the remains of an APC that hit a 100 pound mine early in our tour (Bob Pothoff was killed) and our minds flashed to the news received this morning that a truck carrying 10 Vietnamese soldiers, just two and a half miles from here, hit a mine of such explosive force that they can't find the remains of many of the soldiers. Also, an anti-tank mine, large enough to destroy an APC, was found on Route 326 this morning. It was made safe by a team of Engineers.

With these thoughts in mind we sat on our bucking APC as we went about our routine patrol duties. When our machine stopped, the corporal with me began talking again (you can't talk while the APC is moving without getting a mouthful of dirt). 'Wouldn't it be a bastard to hit a bloody mine', he said. I didn't answer, so he continued: 'Mum would get the telegram and she'd probably think it was a Christmas wish from me.' 'Just like in *Catch-22*', I said, 'Dear Sir/Madam/Miss. We hereby notify you that your Son/Husband/Brother has been killed on active service in Vietnam.' Then they'd probably add: 'May we extend our deepest sympathy and take this opportunity to wish you a Merry Christmas.'

The APC moved on again so we couldn't continue our conversation, although we kept praying that the tankies, particularly our driver, were experienced and kept off the well-worn routes and away from track junctions and other likely mined areas.

Well, we got back OK, but it seems that everyone's thoughts are of home and their families. As we were cleaning up, one of the diggers who was sitting at the entrance to his bunker, stripping and oiling his rifle, said in a rather dejected tone: 'I guess even

Father Christmas will have to get air and ground clearance to get in here.'

We'll probably receive a good meal and an extra beer on Christmas day but there won't be much joy to go with it. Most of us will probably spend the day alone in our bunkers with our thoughts of home. They'll play Christmas carols over the loudspeaker and read out news articles about what is happening in various cities back home, but it won't make any difference to our depression. After all, even if you place Christmas decorations on the barbwire or hang your socks at the front of your bunker, hoping to find a present in them in the morning, you can't get away from the fact that you are in some arsehole of the world, rather than being where you should be, at home with your family.

It's now 1800 and as I've got a night off from ambushing, I'll try to catch up with some letters to family and friends. If I had the time I'd try and send them a present. For example:

You: A beautiful crown of jewels, because you are my Queen of Hearts.

M-J: A book in which I had written all of my mistakes, so that when he grows up he can learn from my experiences and be happier with his life.

My Mum: A single yellow rose because right now it seems to be the most gentle and peaceful thing I can think of.

My Dad: Something made of rich leather. He's a hard working, generous man who has had to battle a lot throughout his life but he has always stuck to his principles. I admire and respect him a lot.

Your Mum and Dad: I combine them because they are such a close, loving couple. It would be expensive and beautiful because I owe them so much.

Your letter of the eighteenth was magnificent. It's the best letter I have ever received and I can't get the smile off my face. I've read it so many times that the pages are wearing thin. You expressed your love in such a wonderful way. I'd go AWOL right now and come straight home to you, if there was anyway I could get out of this place. Thank you my love for such a wonderful Christmas letter.

Good night. I'll dream of you too.

Merry Christmas, my love.

25 December

We had moved into the position (a graveyard very close to a group of houses that are suspected to be supplying rice to the VC) after darkness had fallen and quickly set up the ambush, placing the nine claymores to cover the likely enemy approach.

We found that the only way to get a clear view of the approach was to lay on top of the graves and use the headstone as some kind of protection.

The stars were very bright, the night was warm and the mosquitoes were making their presence felt as we settled into the ambush sentry routine. Then, around 9.30 pm Judith Durham of the Seekers started to sing Christmas Carols to us. *Merry Christmas* followed *Silent Night* and then four or five other traditional songs of peace and goodwill to all men. Her lovely voice drifted out of the darkness and took us thousands of miles away, to be with our families and friends. Low voices from all about me joined with her in the chorus of one song and our spirits were lifted. (Now that's a strange thing to say considering we were lying on gravestones in a cemetery.)

As the Voice Aircraft made its way back to Nui Dat and Judith's songs faded into the distance we again began to concentrate back on our task. Around 10 o'clock, the quiet was disrupted by a nearby ambush patrol firing upon a group of VC who were coming out of the Long Hai foothills. Nothing came of that incident and for the rest of the night we were left alone to make the best of our Christmas night.

When the dawn sky began to show its brilliant colours my patrol returned to Brigid to go about another days work. Christmas was nothing special. Oh, we had a church service sitting on top of the CP and the task force commander came in for a while, but otherwise it was just like any other day.

In my bunker around midday, I toasted your health with a cold can of beer and ate some biscuits Mum had sent me. I have pinned M-J's card to my wall. The little ceremonial soldier in his red jacket, blue trousers and white gloves is the only bit of colour in this drab place and I will treasure it for the rest of my stay here.

So tonight as I seal the envelope, my thoughts will be with you again. With only 60 days to go (72 till we will be together) I'm praying that the time will go fast and we will all keep safe and well.

27 December

Darling, if I owned a farm in Vietnam and my home was in hell, I'd sell that bloody farm and go home.

It seems that as the 'days to go' become less and less, I'm becoming more and more impatient. I get stirred up over many little things that, at other times, I was able to shrug off. I'm not at ease among others and I'd much prefer to spend my time writing to you or resting in the privacy of my bunker. I don't think I'm the only one that feels this way, however I'm supposed to be a leader, I'm expected to be able to control my feelings and set an example for others. But I tell you, it's becoming more and more difficult.

I'm filled with mixed emotions and feelings about what I've seen and done. At one moment I'm proud to be part of it all, the next I feel I could walk away from everything, without any regrets. I admire and respect many of the senior officers and yet I see them as part of a system which is failing to support us effectively. Do you know, we've been told by some Defence Department boffins in Canberra that we've been cut back on the number of sets of greens and pairs of boots we can be issued with. They have even reduced the quantity of spares for some of our weapons. Even before we came over here, our Quarter Master, Captain Cliff Nord, took a sandbag of worn out weapon pieces (we've always had a lot trouble with our machine guns), to the HQ responsible for supplies. He tipped them out on someone's desk, in an effort to get them to understand that their cost-cutting decisions may cost lives. Good old

Cliff, he wouldn't have minced his words either. It didn't make any difference however, and now they're at it again, as part of the gradual reduction of support for the war.

My feelings towards the politicians and their Government departments are unchanged. They are all a pack of bastards for being too weak to sustain our efforts. It doesn't matter what side of politics they come from, they lack strength and leadership to see this difficult task through. They are more interested in their own future, than ours.

The media too has failed in its duty to give a balanced view of this war. They have turned their backs on us and would rather get some graphic footage on the evening's TV news or photo and headline for their morning paper, than present their stories in an informed and fair way. All we get is a paragraph or two on the latest casualties.

I want to get home to you as fast as I can and yet I despise that part of the community that is discrediting all that we have done and all we stand for. I and a lot of others, feel let down and betrayed. If it weren't for my diggers and their mateship this would be a terribly lonely place.

With such a heart full of negative feelings, it's no wonder that I rely so much on your letters to reassure me. You are the only stable thing in my life.

28 December. I went to sleep at 7 pm last night and slept without stirring for 12 hours. I guess I have reached a low point in my physical and emotional reserves and need something special to give me a boost. I know I can't let these feelings get on top of me, because I've got too much to do and too many people are relying on me. I'll just have to see it through as best I can.

When reading what I have written, I realise that it's not the hard slog that we're doing that is causing my depression. It's not the patrolling, ambushing, fighting, (although I must say the fear of mines is never far from the surface) because all of that is within our own control. We are trained for that and we are confident whenever we are in the bush. No, it's the disappointment of being let down by those who involved us in this war in the first place and by those in opposition, who are doing everything in their power to discredit us and make personal gain from the events. These things are beyond our control and we are being used. If our political leaders won't support us, if our own media aren't willing to understand us and if our own communities don't want to know us, then what the hell are we here for? Why am I being denied a safe and secure life with my family? Why do I have to live in a hole in the ground, put up with all of these bloody sores and rashes, eat partly cold food out of tins, squat over a hole in the ground whenever I need to relieve myself, always feel dirty and uncomfortable and always feel lonely like this? We may wear a green uniform, but that doesn't mean we don't have feelings, like other Australians.

It may just be that the year has almost come to an end and I feel it has been such a waste. A waste of lives as well as a waste of our life.

With all of that I'd better sign off before I get deeper into this subject and end up bursting into tears, because I'm feeling so sorry for myself. What a way to spend Christmas and the new year.

1 January

The first day of this new year has almost ended and I can't say that I was very impressed. At midnight, it seemed that everyone in Phouc Tuy fired their flares of red, white and green into the still, starless sky and, for about 10 minutes, a million man-made stars lit up the sky. Then they faded, one-by-one until once again the night was black and lonely.

On return from ambush I had to prepare the platoon for our two-day patrol into the swamp area along the Song Rai and its delta area. We leave tomorrow morning by armoured personnel carrier and our job is to search some old bunker systems and a network of tracks that wind their way through this mud, mosquito and crocodile infested area. We'll be wading waist-deep in water for quite a bit and will have to watch out for the changing tides, as the water depth changes dramatically in a very short time.

In the last days of 1970, a 6 Platoon contact and a follow-up

B Company HQ ambush resulted in 21 enemy being killed and a huge quantity of weapons and documents being captured. Unfortunately, in the initial contact led by George Wenhlowskyj, a lad was killed (Private Lloyd, a scout when I was with them), and three others were wounded. They attacked a large force of enemy who were in a bunker system and engaged them with everything that was available. As is the usual tactic, the enemy held them off all afternoon, then withdrew under the cover of darkness. However, about 10 hours later a large group of them walked straight into an ambush set up by four APCs and the B Company HQ. Right through the night the ambushed force kept returning to the scene, in an effort to retrieve their dead and wounded, so that action lasted for quite some time.

Those killed included the 2IC of D445 (the Provincial VC Battalion), political officers, platoon and squad commanders. The documents recovered included nominal rolls, tactical procedures and a lot of personal letters, which will probably lead to a number of local civilian arrests. It's been a major blow to the enemy, one that will take him months to recover from. It's all the talk of 7RAR and has lifted morale throughout the task force, because this is the enemy unit that has been causing so much trouble in the Xuyen Moc area, in past months.

They think that a few who escaped may be sheltering in the swamps, so we'll be looking out for some very recent signs.

Thanks for letting me know about your Christmas celebrations and all that M-J got up to. I was pleased to hear of the compliments you received from all those admiring men. You're a beautiful woman, you attract a lot of attention and you should be proud of that. I am.

The first sunset for 1971 isn't at all pretty. The sky is grey and there's a strong westerly blowing which is making it very uncomfortable. I'll always remember the beautiful sunsets that I witnessed from my Horseshoe bunker.

Well, my gear is packed and I'm about to settle down to study my maps. I always spend about an hour or so checking my orders and the maps of the area we are going into. I try to predict all the different things that may occur and have plans ready in case we run into anything unexpected. We know the area fairly well, so it's not as if we are going into the unknown.

News has just come through that one of George's diggers has died of wounds. He was Private Meyes, who I knew as one of the riflemen.

I'm absolutely amazed at how this army works. Here am I very unsure of myself and constantly battling with my feelings about whether we should or shouldn't be here, when someone hands me a large brown envelope, shakes my hand and says: 'Well done.' I'm still not sure what to make of it, but I've enclosed the envelope with this letter for you to have a look at.

There have been so many personnel changes within the battalion over the past year that there are few originals left. Even within Support Company, there are so many unfamiliar faces. When we march through Sydney, the company will only be 50 strong (that's about one third of its correct strength) and I'll only have a platoon of 18.

Well my darling, I've got some studying to do so I'll sign off.

4 January

The APCs had taken two and a half hours to bash their way through the dense scrub, wade the disused paddies and scream along at speed through the clearings, so it was with mixed feelings that we scrambled off, collected our packs and moved into the quietness of the jungle. It was great not to have had to walk the whole way into the area, but APCs are very noisy, where we prefer to operate in silence. They crash their way through at top revs, leaving great track marks all over the place whereas, we take one quiet step at a time, moving with the vegetation, being part of the environment and trying to leave no sign of our presence.

We waited until they had left the area and the silence of the jungle had returned before we headed off on our predetermined bearing, which would take us to the river and the swamps of the delta region.

From that moment on we waded ankle deep in muddy water, then knee deep in thick ooze and soon were waist and chest deep in the tidal reaches of the river. Whenever we found a small island of dry ground we rested and did what we could to protect our gear from the next onslaught. For two days we waded, swam, and pushed through some extremely difficult terrain. We even had to build rafts of bamboo to ferry some of our gear across the deepest parts of the swamp. We bashed and crashed our way through thick secondary jungle, thrashed through lantana and 'wait a while' thickets and slipped and tripped across the mangroves, all the time struggling to keep ourselves upright in the thick, black slush.

Eventually we arrived at our destination and found ... nothing. The only way out was the way we got in, so we tripped and slipped, thrashed, crashed and bashed our way back. While we didn't encounter any VC, we had our share of ants, crabs, snakes and mosquitoes. We were also wary in the swampy areas and especially careful when wading chest deep across the rivers, because of the crocodiles and sharks I had seen on my air reconnaissance, a few days before.

When we got out of the swamps we were covered in mud from head to toe. As we made our way through the more open country the mud began to dry and our clothes became stiff, smelly and very uncomfortable. I harboured in a thick forest of bamboo so that we could clean our weapons, prepare a hot brew and get our heavy, wet and muddy gear off. In the end, I decided to extend our rest for a couple of hours, as it had been a hard slog through the swamp and some of us were feeling pretty whacked.

Just before I signalled that it was time to saddle-up and move on once again, one of the diggers called me over and showed me a 'memorial' he had made. 'I'm leaving a memento of my time here in country', he said. 'This is what I think about this place.' There in the middle of our protective bamboo forest, in all its glory, stood a flush toilet carved out of a large anthill. It was a life size copy of the luxury piece of porcelain that we had all known in our past lifetime. He had lovingly hollowed out the bowl, given it a seat and a raised cover. The square reservoir even had a button on top and in the place you would normally expect to see the maker's symbol, he had carved a large number '7'. Finally, he had placed toilet paper from his ration pack on a stick beside it.

As we both stood before his masterpiece, I wondered what the first Vietnamese who came across this sculpture would make of it. Perhaps he would think it was a shrine of some kind, or even a throne (nearly right there, mate). It wouldn't occur to the finder that this was one Aussie soldier's expression of his feelings of the war.

I got the platoon together and as we pulled out of the position, I had them file past this memorial. There wouldn't have been one digger who didn't fully agree with the sentiments expressed by our sculptor.

We eventually married up with the APCs which took us all the way back to Nui Dat. We must have looked a real sight and been a bit on the nose because Captain Thompson offered to put off his debriefing for an hour, while 'I freshened up'. Many of the platoon had to receive treatment for the scratches and splinters received in our battle with the lantana and thorny thickets. Others, like me, had old rashes return in some embarrassing places and needed to smother themselves with tinea powder to gain some kind of relief.

As soon as the formal briefings were over we got ourselves ready for our last R and C.

What strange memories I have of this war to tell my children.

5 January

Here I am on R and C, my last in-country holiday by the sea. Karl is here, limping around with a swollen, black and blue left foot. He'll stay with the battalion until our tour ends and will be given a desk job somewhere, which he's already finding very hard to accept.

I've caught up with George too and we chatted about the big contact he had been involved in recently. It was a pretty hairy time for 6 Platoon, but they handled it really well. Both Karl and George are still angry at the report submitted after the APC/B Company HQ ambush, which followed George's contact. They reckon it barely mentioned the fact that the APCs were there, let alone that it was the 50 and 30 calibre machine gun that kept up such fire power that the enemy weren't able to counter attack. The armoured personnel carriers, too, had laid out a huge number of claymore mines as part of the ambush and it was these that created all of the devastation when they were fired at point blank range into the enemy.

Karl will be posted to Adelaide on his RTA. He doesn't know anyone in South Australia, so I'll give him some addresses to help him settle in.

That Letter Of Commendation was a complete surprise to me and I'm not sure whether I have really earned it. I feel I've done very little, compared to many others and when I look back, I must admit I'm not proud of everything I've done. I've said some pretty stupid things at times and could have handled situations a little better. I've had excellent NCOs that have kept the platoon operating in spite of my inadequacies. However, I've learnt a lot from all of the experiences that have come my way and have always tried to do my best. I'm pleased that someone has acknowledged my efforts.

The other good news is that we'll be getting a 10 per cent pay rise from 1 January. Along with my promotion to lieutenant, that will help to pay some of the bills. So my darling, even though we feel that this last year has been a complete waste, perhaps rewards are starting to come our way.

I spent all day by the pool and playing mini golf with Karl. He's very frustrated because he's not allowed to swim, so all he can do is sleep and read. He feels like he's getting fat and lazy. After what he's been through, you'd think he wouldn't mind a bit of a rest.

A couple of nursing sisters from the Australian Field Hospital came down to the pool for a while and although they kept to themselves, it was good to have them around. They have a very difficult job working with the sick and wounded and are very restricted in where they can go, so they need as much R and C as we do. Everyone speaks very highly of the medical staff at the hospital. They do a wonderful job with our casualties and it's a comforting thought to know we're in such good hands.

The doctors and nurses over here aren't all military trained. Some of them come from major Australian city hospitals and volunteer to spend a year or two in uniform in order to gain experience treating the injuries caused by war. Some are on short term commissions and have worked in military hospitals and units in Australia before coming over here. Whatever their motives, we'd be lost without them. I hope they get the recognition they deserve.

Well my love, as it is now the last night that I'll spend in this home away from home, I'll turn in, with thoughts of you. What I need is a love-in with you, which will last for years and years. I need your tenderness and caring so much and all we need to do is be a little more patient. Our long, lonely wait is almost over.

PS I've just noticed the date I put at the top of this letter. I guess it shows how time means nothing. Here I am longing to get home and I keep putting the date back to 1970.

7 January

Our incoming mail has been delayed because the last batch finished up in Phan Rang, the major city in a province to the north and it's taken a while to get it back. However, I received your letter written on New Year's Eve, which included the letter from the Websters. I'm pleased we're in touch with Dave as he, like Guy, brings back a lot of good memories of our officer training days at Scheyville [the National Service Officer Training Unit near Windsor, New South Wales] and our time at Canungra/Main Beach.

I'm sorry you didn't have a happy New Year's Eve. There's not much to celebrate about is there!

Tomorrow we head back to the Horseshoe for a couple of weeks. I've decided to give the section 2ICs a bit more responsibility by having them take out some ambush patrols. They'll be corporals when they get back to Australia so any experiences they get over here will be very worthwhile. It'll give a few of us a bit more time to do the administration required for RTA. Recce Platoon will still be on ready reaction duty, so we won't be able to relax altogether.

I've packed my trunk and cleaned out my cupboard of all the odds and ends that have accumulated over the year. We'll be living with only the barest essentials. No more luxuries, I'm afraid we'll have to rough it for the rest of the tour.

They tell us that the *Sydney* won't be leaving Vung Tau until 26 February. That means another two days in this place. I hope that doesn't keep us on operations for another two days.

11 January. It's been suggested that the last mail to be sent to us should be on 14 February. This allows for a 10–12 day period for all our mail to work its way through the system, before we walk out of here. I'll be able to write right up to the last day and my last letter will arrive while the *Sydney* is somewhere off the Western Australian coast.

We've continued to work on improving the defences at the Horseshoe and have re-sandbagged a lot of our bunkers and fighting trenches. The diggers are getting a little tired of all the rebuilding. One placed a sign over the entrance to my bunker which read: 'On the seventh day the Lord rested ... and Recce filled sandbags.' I hope the blokes from 3RAR or whoever takes over this place from us, appreciate the hard work we've put into it. We burnt off all of the vegetation which covers the barbwire and cleared everything from the front of our area, which could provide some cover and protection to a marauding enemy. The place is quite stark, but no doubt it'll all grow back when the rains come again. We've had to replace and reposition all of our claymore mines as many of the old ones were considered to be a bit suspect. There was some doubt whether they would detonate, having been positioned in the wire for such a long time. The explosive may have deteriorated or been eaten away by ants and the electrical wiring was showing signs of wear.

7RAR has been extremely lucky lately. We've had five mine incidents in the last six weeks and in each case the mine failed to explode. They are 'Jumping Jack' mines, which when trodden on, jump about four feet in the air and then explode. Due to the heavy wet season these mines had been affected and either didn't jump, or jumped but didn't explode. If that ever happened to me I'd just sit down and refuse to take another step until the *Sydney* had anchored at Vung Tau.

A Company are at Brigid but we will replace them on the seventeenth, as they have to return to the Dat for some RTA administration. B Company are here at the Horseshoe. C Company has been on rest and convalescence but are now preparing to go bush for five weeks. D Company are in the Phouc Buu area and have found several caches amounting to 10,000 pounds of unpolished rice which no doubt were gathered as taxes from the local farmers during this last harvest. Civil Aid have been distributing it among the villages.

Support Company will mostly be operating out of Brigid until RTA. There will be some operations of six-day duration, but generally it'll be the night ambush routines.

Karl is here at the 'Shoe working in the command post. Doug is still Intelligence Officer. Greg has been given a liaison officer job with a US Training Team, somewhere to our north. Owen will RTA on 26 January, as will Terry Howard. They, together with several NCOs, have to organise for our return to Finschaffen Lines at Holsworthy. When you get back to Holsworthy you may see a few familiar faces.

16 January. B Company had two blokes killed today in a heavy contact which resulted in seven Viet Cong being killed. George's 6 Platoon was in the thick of things again, this time near the Long Hais. Colonel Grey got involved with the action by flying over the contact area and spotting for the artillery and mortars which fired in support of the platoon. He also landed his chopper in the contact area, so that it could be used to get a badly wounded digger out. He's quite an amazing boss.

23 January

We're back at Brigid. I'd forgotten what a wind blown, sand-blasting place this is. Anyway it'll only be till the third. With only 33 days to go, we'll put up with anything.

Our routine remains much the same, with night ambushes and the odd two or three day operation which takes us into the Long and Light Green. I've got a short 'op' coming up within the next five days, to go to the Phouc Buu area where D Company have been operating recently.

Whenever I get back from being out in the bush for a while, I'm handed a whole pile of letters. This time I got three from you, one from Mum and another from Grandma and Grandpa Pollard. It's difficult to work out which of your letters were written first, as you don't put a date on them. I also forget what I've written in my letters to you, so when you ask for some details of something I wrote a couple of weeks ago, I'm at a loss to work out what it is I said. Wouldn't it be good if I could just go down to the corner telephone box, drop in a few coins and ring you up. We could certainly keep up with everything that is happening in our two worlds.

Karl will certainly appreciate your letter, as I'm sure Doug will too. Neither of them receive as much mail as I do and you know how great it is to get unexpected letters.

It's funny that you should mention taking up a sport, when I return. I was thinking the same a couple of days ago. Of course, it would be outside the army because we'd be able to meet other people, just like when we were at Rockdale, during my National Service days. Perhaps both of us could take up squash. Once a week we could get out together, perhaps get a group of neighbours interested too.

I've re-read your letters and can't think of much to add except that I appreciate how you are feeling about the situation at No. 33. It's hard to live with other people (even if they are family), having to keep to their routines and be nice to everyone all the time, regardless of how you are feeling. You've got no privacy and without a car you'd have little chance to get away for a while. Hang in there love, we'll soon have the world all to ourselves.

Right now it's extremely unpleasant, with sand being blown everywhere by a gale force wind. It's been like this for the last three days and we've been forced to huddle inside our bunkers. Even in here the sand covers everything and it's impossible to escape it.

I'm reading *Little Big Man* by Thomas Berger. It has been made into a film starring Dustin Hoffman. I'm only into the third chapter and it's hilarious, so I hope I get to see the film.

On the last operation the platoon went extremely well and I was really pleased with my NCOs. Everyone was in good spirits and I couldn't fault their patrolling and ambushing. It makes it so much easier for me when everyone is switched on. I'm very proud of the way they have tackled every task, regardless of how difficult it is.

28 January

I bet you thought that I had forgotten that this is a very special day in our lives. Well, even if this letter arrives a couple of days late you can be assured that I was thinking of you. I've been trying to work out where we have been at this time, over the last five years.

28 January 1967 – Elcho Island (together) living in the converted store room beneath the Mission House.

1968 – Adelaide (together) living in a caravan in your parent's front garden.

1969 – Canungra (separated) you were at Main Beach and I was on duty at Jungle Training Centre.

1970 – Holsworthy (together) on pre-embarkation leave in Adelaide.

Happy Anniversary darling. We'll celebrate when I return, together with every other important occasion that we've missed out on in the past eleven and a half months.

Darling, I love you so very much. I love our son very much too, and soon it will be a closely shared love, not just words on paper. When I get home I'll put all writing pads and pens away and I'll express my love by actions, every day, so that there will be no doubt at all. No delays between expressing and receiving.

Your letter describing M-J's amazing sayings and doings arrived today by Possum, as road vehicle movement is being restricted because of Tet. Dear little M-J, how I long to see and play with him again. He seems to be so grown up now and yet he was just a tiny little baby when I left. The photos I have are a wonderful record of his growing up. I wish I had been part of it.

Sorry that there will be no flowers or presents to celebrate our anniversary this year. I will be thinking of you tonight and hope that you will be thinking of me.

PS As you realise by now, we didn't go to Nui Dat after our bush time because the Pioneer Platoon had to go bush and we were called to defend Brigid. There has been all kinds of changes to plans because of the need for companies to get back to the Dat and commence their RTA procedures. We will be going out bush for six days shortly and should be back at the Dat from 4 to 8 February. Perhaps I'll be able to celebrate my birthday in peace and comfort.

5 February

I've got such a huge pile of letters and cards scattered on my desk that I know I won't be able to reply to them all. While we've got a few days here at the Dat we are so busy packing, rebuilding and renovating that even at night there are few spare minutes to attend to our personal things.

We've been invited by C Company to dine with them and we have extended a similar invitation to those who have supported us throughout the tour, so even the nights will be taken up. The dinners will be a good opportunity to catch up with a lot of mates who I haven't seen for most of the year.

Ray, remember the letter I wrote describing Jones's section and how well the platoon was working in the bush ... Without going into detail, I must now tell you that we suffered one killed (Private Alan Talbot) and four wounded as the result of a mine incident on 1 February. I need to tell you this, as I wouldn't want you to read about it in the newspaper without knowing that I'm OK. I may tell you about it some other time, but for now please don't get worried for my safety, because I'll be home soon to love you forever.

The whole platoon is still in shock and while we go about our duty as if nothing happened, you can't help but feel the tension when we call a parade at the start of the day and there is almost one whole section missing. It was a shocking thing to happen but I'm so proud of how everyone reacted and the way they are taking it. It was their swift actions that had the casualties in hospital 35 minutes after the mine was tripped.

I now have only 18 blokes and as my sergeant was one of those wounded, we've all got additional duties to perform. Few orders have to be issued, as everyone is pulling their weight and helping out wherever needed. I guess we just want all of this to finish so we can get out of here.

Now that you are back at Holsworthy, you should be feeling more settled. I've been really worried about you lately because you seemed so unhappy and the pressures of staying with your family were beginning to show. Now there is so much to look forward to and prepare for. I'm sure the remaining time will just fly by.

All my gear has been packed and I've posted off a parcel of gifts for you and our families. There is another $50 in it to help keep the wolves from the door. I've also remitted $600 to you from my pay book but I'm not sure how long it will take to get to you. I'll have another few hundred dollars in my pay book by the time we get back to Sydney, so the pressure of outstanding bills will be over, at least for a little while.

We'll discuss our planned holiday when I return, but some of the blokes are going to Townsville and have said they'd like to see us there. We'll have to invite them all around to our place for drinks before we all split up and go our own ways. You'd be flattered at how many of them ask about you and M-J.

In your last letter you described the conversation that you had to put up with. Darling, I understand completely and I'm so pleased to know that you were able to put it out of your mind. It's comforting to know that you are home now, among friends and supporters.

I'll sign off now and pray that you will not be worried about the news of our tragedy. Please remember that I'm with a great mob of fellows, we all look after each other and I'm being extremely careful.

6 February

I really haven't much to say, but I'm feeling lonely and depressed and it'll help if I write to you. I've just heard that song: 'Today I killed a man I didn't know, I aimed my rifle high and shot him low' ... not a very appropriate song for the mood that I'm in.

We have reached the stage where all of our gear is packed into bags, kits and boxes and stored in large containers ready to be loaded onto the *Sydney*. I've got all my personal gear in my carryall and kitbag, except for a set of greens which I'll wear on the March-Out Parade to be held here at Nui Dat, on the twenty-fourth.

You know that we leave here on the twenty-fifth but won't get to Sydney till 10 March, because we'll be stopping in Perth for 24 hours – an invitation from the mayor. 8RAR stayed there too on their way home and were treated to a welcome home luncheon.

We go bush on the eighth until the twenty-first. This time we will be north of Xuyen Moc along with C and D companies. Even though we'll have plenty of troops in the area, none of us are looking forward to it. Still, once out there we'll all switch on and the adrenalin will start pumping once again. Like all other operations, the time will go pretty fast.

Our mine incident still hangs over our head. Private Ray Patten, one of three in the gun group that tripped the mine, died last night. The news has really hit us hard and the platoon lines are much quieter tonight.

For the last few days we've been rebuilding our tents, re-sand-bagging our bunkers and CPs, re-painting all of the main structures and generally cleaning up the place. 3RAR's advance party will be here on the thirteenth and as soon as their troops arrive they'll be going out to the Horseshoe and Brigid. Poor buggers, at least we had a few weeks to get acclimatised and 'shake down'. Best of luck to them all.

Now I can say that the time has gone fairly fast for me, but I'd never want to do it again. I feel totally drained by all of the effort. It's not so much the physical side of things. While that was hard enough, it was the emotional and psychological tension that has finally taken its toll. It's not that we're all falling in a heap or anything like that, it's just that the energy and spark isn't there anymore. You just have to look at any of the diggers. Their faces tell you how tired they are feeling. They're a lot quieter than they use to be too.

I certainly hope everything is OK with you. That's my main worry now. We've been apart for too long.

All the diggers have been congratulating me on my promotion to lieutenant. I've only just started to wear my new pips. Captain Thompson didn't know until three days ago and was a little angry at the adjutant for giving me the news, before him.

Support Company had a formal Dining-In last night. One hundred and twenty-seven diggers got dressed up in their polyester uniforms (with ribbons too) and we were treated to a four-course meal, together with wines. All the procedures of an officers Dining-In were followed, seating arrangements, menu, and toasts, and the commanding officer was our special guest. It went off really well and everyone, including Colonel Grey, had a great time.

I'll sign off for now. With the morning I hope to be feeling brighter and as each day passes, I'll start feeling better, knowing we are getting closer to our glorious meeting.

PS Please give M-J a big kiss and hug for me.

PPS I had actually forgotten that my birthday was today. It seems such an insignificant reason to celebrate.

7 February

Dear Pop, this – thankfully – will be the last time I will write to you from South Vietnam. The battalion has packed all non essential gear and apart from personal equipment we need for one last operation, our worldly possessions are stacked into several large containers ready to be loaded onto the *Sydney*. We've spent the last few days painting, re-sandbagging and generally cleaning up our Nui Dat area in preparation for 3RAR's arrival. Their advance party will arrive next week and the rest will come in on the *Sydney* a few days before we embark for our journey home. They won't get any time to settle in, as I believe they will be deployed into the field almost immediately. I hope that those who occupy our tent lines here at the Dat and our bunkers at the Horseshoe and Brigid appreciate all the work and effort that my platoon has done.

The battalion's farewell parade will be held on the twenty-fourth and I guess that will be our very last South Vietnam military duty. I'm not sure how I will feel. I'm sure I'll be relieved and very happy to have seen the end of it all. I'll be excited, because I'll be one step closer to being with my family again. I'll be proud too, because we have been a very professional unit and have completed a difficult job with excellent results, regardless of what some people think. I know also that I'll feel sad, because too many good, young blokes have died and been injured. So, it will be with mixed feelings that I'll say a fond farewell to this place.

I had a very difficult task to perform recently. I had to go down to the Australian Field Hospital in Vung Tau and go to the morgue to identify the bodies of two of my soldiers (Ray Patten and Alan Talbot) who had been killed on our last operation. After that, I went into a hospital ward to see the three others who had been wounded (Sergeant Williams, Corporal Godbold and Private Ryan). One of them had lost a leg. It wasn't the best experience I've had and I came away fairly depressed.

The incident that caused all of this occurred on 1 February. Recce Platoon had been sent into an area called Phouc Buu. We knew the place pretty well as we had patrolled there on a number of occasions. It was a well known area for mines but we knew if we stayed off roads (especially an overgrown one known as Route 328) and tracks, the likelihood of coming across one was remote. Moving through the bush is at times very difficult because in places it is very thick and there are huge areas of impenetrable bamboo and thorn thickets. However, after all of this time in country we were well used to patrolling through this kind of terrain. There have been several pretty big stoushes in the area over the past years and a number of bunker systems are scattered through the area. Our job was to check some of these out and see if there were any signs of reconstruction and to look for recent signs of enemy moving through the area.

We had been out for a couple of days and hadn't come across anything, but that was to be expected because one of the other companies had been in the area only a few weeks back. I decided to call a brief pause to our patrolling while my signaller and I got in touch with company HQ, to give them our hourly report and find out what else was happening around us.

I put the platoon down in some scrub which overlooked an open old paddy area to our west and at the same time gave us good observation of the unused, single lane road running north-south through the area (Route 328). While my sig got in touch with HQ, I positioned a gun group (a lance corporal, the machine gunner and his number two) to cover the main track and briefed them on the most likely enemy approach from the north. At the same time I sent a young lad, who had only been with us for a few days, out as sentry, to cover any approach from a small track which came in from the south. I then checked out the remainder of the platoon and rejoined my sig to see if he had established radio contact.

I was standing there with him checking our encoded report when an enormous explosion occurred about 10 metres from us. My sig's immediate reaction was to call our HQ 'Contact, Wait Out'. This alerts them that we were in some kind of trouble and keeps the radio net clear of traffic, in case we needed immediate support.

Following the explosion all went quiet. There was no follow-up gunfire or further explosions as you would expect if we were being hit by a group of enemy. The smell of explosive and a cloud of black smoke and dust hung in the air and everything seemed to be moving in slow motion. My mind was trying to come to grips with what had happened. Perhaps a rocket propelled grenade had been fired at us? No, I didn't hear any primary. It must have been a grenade thrown into our position. Perhaps one of our own grenades fell loose from someone's webbing and detonated.

Still everything remained quiet. Now the dust had cleared I could see that it was the gun group that I had only just positioned, that had been hit. There was no movement or sound from them, so I knew things were pretty bad. My sergeant too remained where he had been, sitting beside a small tree just behind the gun group, so I assumed he too had been injured.

As I went to take the radio handset to report the situation, the sig who had been taking in all of this with me made the call 'Standby Dust Off'. This informed headquarters that we had received casualties and needed helicopter casualty evacuation. I looked about me and could see our medic getting his first aid bag and others helping to assemble the mine detector we always carried with us. I called to the section commanders to check their security, to keep everyone alert and not to move.

Just then the young lad I had placed as sentry came up the small track that led right into the gun position. He looked quite dazed and must have been wondering what had happened, when he was stopped in his tracks by all the carnage before him. I called at him to stay right where he was, not to move any further then to retrace his steps back to his position and to remain alert. If this tragedy had been caused by a mine (M16 jumping mine), then we could expect to have others in the vicinity. The last thing we needed right now was someone to trigger another.

I then notified company HQ of what had happened although at that early stage I was still unsure of what had caused the explosion. As I discussed the situation with my boss, two soldiers moved forward with the mine detector to clear the way and allow our medic to get into the area to treat the casualties.

Soon after, one of them returned and handed me a piece of metal which looked very much like it was a striker pin which fires the main charge of an M16 mine. He informed me that five blokes had been injured; the three-man gun group were all in a bad way. I passed this information to company HQ and when the mine detector team returned from the blast sight, I got them to continue to check for mines within our position.

As this was occurring I received a call from an Australian casevac helicopter that was in-bound and he indicated that he would be in our location within minutes, but would be unable to land unless I could assure him that there were no enemy in the area and all mines had been cleared. This wasn't what I wanted to hear and was expressing my anger in the crudest of terms when an American voice announced that he was just passing by and would be happy to lend a hand. I'd never been so happy to hear a Yank before and immediately took back all derogatory comments I had ever made about them. His drawl was just music to my ears.

He proceeded to ask me information about our injured and our situation and we had only just thrown coloured smoke to identify our location when the US helicopter came charging in to land within 20 metres of us. The crew, together with our medic and some of the diggers helped load our three most critically injured and within minutes they were off, heading towards the Australian Field Hospital in Vung Tau. Even before the dust had settled, the Aussie casevac helicopter landed in similar style, to receive our other two wounded (Sergeant Dick Williams and Private Phillip Ryan).

When the last sounds of the helicopter faded away we were left to the silence of the bush once again. I felt very exhausted but was amazed to see that the whole incident had lasted no more than 35 minutes.

There wasn't much more we could do, so the remaining 18 of us headed off into the deepest part of the jungle to hide away for a while, catch our breath and think about our mates.

Even now, in the relative comfort of my sandbagged tent in Nui Dat, my mind is a real jumble of events. I'm sure that my whole reaction to the explosion was controlled by my training and experience. It was as if I was in automatic gear as the events unfolded. No emotion, no fear, no panic, some confusion, but mainly just a sequence of actions that took us through the whole sad episode. My diggers were exceptional. They too must have been feeling as terrible as I was and yet their actions were nothing short of heroic. Many of them had been through something similar, just before I joined the platoon in October, so they must be feeling particularly bad right now.

Two scenes have been branded on my brain for all time; the first was the cloud of black dust and smoke that enveloped us and the dreadful silence that followed the explosion. The second was giving the thumbs up to the Dust Off crew, to thank them for their great response and seeing 'Shorty' Godbold, whose leg had been badly smashed, sitting between his two unconscious mates. He waved back and gave me a grin.

When I visited him in hospital, they had removed his leg, but there he was sitting up in bed with the same cheery grin.

In my quiet moments I thank my guardian angel for getting me through another difficult situation. I must have been so close to that mine when I placed the lads down in their position. It must have been no more than a few inches from where we squatted together to get a view of the road that I wanted them to cover. Any one of us could have tripped it.

Now I must take my platoon out one more time. We have one last operation to conduct somewhere to the east, near a place called Xuyen Moc. I'm not worried about it, the mine incident hasn't turned me into a gibbering wreck and I know everyone will do the job expected of them, without complaint and to the very best of their ability. The problem is Pop that I, like all my mates and my diggers, am feeling very tired.

Perhaps I'm getting a little worried. After all, things are still happening each time we go out and after being here for so long, it wouldn't be very nice to cop it at this stage.

Thanks for giving me the opportunity to let off a bit of steam with this letter. It's great to know you understand why I need an outlet like this and it's great to have someone who is willing to share these difficulties with me.

There's no time for you to respond to this letter so we'll have to save our father/son chat till I get home. Thanks for everything.

22 February

My love, I received six letters from you on return from the bush and what a mixed set of feelings they present. Love, hate, happiness, confusion, insecurity. It's a lot to get my mind around in one sitting, however I appreciate that you wrote daily and especially that you expressed your feelings. I know the news about the mine incident didn't help and I'm sorry for putting you through such a terrible ordeal.

I've gathered the 23 pages together and will try to answer your questions, if I can.

Your first letter sounded as if you were extremely happy to be home. Please give my congratulations to the Dibbles for the birth of their daughter. As usual the weather sounds awful, so I hope it fines up for our holidays. Anyway if not, we'll just head north and follow the sun.

Letter No. 3, regarding the allotment change, was a bit of a shock. I knew the pay details would be changed and the allotment would be cancelled, but I didn't think it would be so early. You certainly made it clear that you wouldn't be able to survive without the income and I was really upset to think that the system would allow such a vital link to be severed, just so they could reorganise our pay procedures and allowances back to the Australian system. I'm sorry to have put you in such a position.

You wrote some time back that we've gained nothing from this last 12 months and perhaps you're right. Financially, it's always been a struggle and I know it's been a constant worry, much more for you than for me. A second lieutenant's pay currently is $160.16 a fortnight ($4164 a year). A lieutenant's pay is a further $5.18 per fortnight. A temporary captain receives $205.93 a fortnight or $5354 a year. From March this will go up another $18 a fortnight. The point I want to make is that this terrible year has given me an opportunity to set us up for the future. We have struggled and we'll have to do more of it for a few more years, but we are in a better position than we would have been otherwise. The future is not all doom and gloom.

The unit has always been a problem for you but I see it as a good investment for the future. If we can hang on to it for a little while longer, despite the problems in payments, it will provide a steady income and when M-J reaches school age we can always sell it to help with those costs.

Darling, I know it's been hard and I've been proud of what you have done.

No sooner had I finished reading about the latest financial disaster I had caused, that I read of your intention to purchase a TV set, on weekly terms. I'm a little bit confused but will not try and sort it out at this time, except to say: ... I'll have $1000 in my pay book when I leave Vietnam and I've remitted $800 to you (not $600 as I indicated in my last letter), so that you can live a little more at ease in the weeks to come ... the car's final payments should be cleared shortly after my return ... there will be a pay rise for all military ranks in March ... my promotion to temporary captain will help boost the coffers (Colonel Grey announced that George Wenhlowskyj, Dave Kibby and I would each be promoted to captain on return to 7RAR, after leave) ... we'll sell the unit and pay out all of those longstanding and embarrassing loans provided by family and friends. With these actions, we should start to feel a little more secure about our financial future. More importantly, you won't feel that this last long, lonely and terrible year has been a total waste.

A later letter related your ongoing fear and insecurity about being alone in the house at nights. I didn't realise that you still felt this way, as the military police had resolved the situation with the peeping Tom, some months ago. There are few words of encouragement I can give you from here, except to say that it won't be long now and your big, pale, pimply soldier will be there to protect you. Well anyway, I'll be able to back you up.

Later ... Tonight we'll attend a 7RAR Officers Farewell Dinner. Then tomorrow we have our rehearsals for our farewell parade on the twenty-fourth.

I met Major Barry Petersen for a few minutes yesterday. He's looking very well.

23 February

It's all over. At long last we will spend no more nights in ambush, no more days patrolling and no more anxious hours wondering what awaits us tomorrow. We can turn our minds to more pleasant activities.

Already I feel that a huge weight has been lifted from my heart. My body, though, feels very tired and I feel like I could sleep for a week. The trip home will give us time to relax, put on a bit of weight and prepare ourselves for whatever awaits us.

I can't help but think about those who died, especially Ray Patten and Alan Talbot who were the last casualties of the battalion's tour. I feel for their families, who must have been devastated. Like us, they would have been counting the days, excited about the happy homecoming and looking forward to getting back to a normal family routine. All their hopes and dreams were shattered, at the very last minute.

This last letter of mine is very short, but so it should be ... after all, there is nothing left to say except that, I'm coming home.

Goodbye Vietnam.

The Following Years

I have almost no recollection of my journey home. Until recently, I couldn't remember whether the Battalion flew out of Nui Dat to HMAS *Sydney* or travelled by road convoy to Vung Tau and then boarded the ship from landing craft. (Having read Michael O'Brien's *Conscripts and Regulars*, a history of the battalion, I now know that we were taken by Chinook helicopters direct to the ship on 25 February). My only memory of our departure is standing on the Officer's Deck – an open patio-type area located below the top deck and at the stern – watching two sailors in a powered rubber boat race to and fro, dragging a coil of concertina barbwire behind them and throwing grenades into the sea, as a deterrent to would-be Viet Cong underwater sabotage teams.

The journey to Fremantle took about seven days and yet I can't remember anything about the ship's routine, the quarters, the meal arrangements or how we spent our days and nights. I don't remember if I joined those who went into Perth to enjoy the hospitality of the mayor, although I still have the leave pass that was issued to me. It may have been that I wasn't in much of a mood to celebrate, so I probably stayed on board to read and relax.

Strangely enough, I can vividly remember our departure from Fremantle Harbour. I was standing on the Officer's Deck as the great ship reversed out of its berth; moving slowly but powerfully backwards towards the wharf opposite. When it was within a few metres of the pylons and decking and I was sure that I was about to witness a terribly embarrassing collision, the ship began to shudder

MHAS Sydney *docking in Sydney Harbour*

beneath my feet. The sea at the stern erupted and ever so slowly the great ship began to move forward and recommence our homeward journey.

On our way across the Bight, a severe outbreak of diarrhoea among the soldiers caused the ship to seek medical assistance from Adelaide. My final recollection of this phantom journey home was standing on the flight deck one early morning, looking at the familiar landscape of the Adelaide Hills as the ship waited off Port Noarlunga. A massive dose of home sickness flooded over me and I longed to share some quiet times with Mum and Dad. I stayed up on deck until the ship, now restocked with medicines, steamed south and left Gulf St Vincent far behind.

You would think that entering Sydney Harbour would be an unforgettable experience, but I can honestly say I don't remember anything. How we disembarked, the long awaited meeting with my family and how we assembled to march through the city, is all a blank.

Some parts of the march I can remember. Such as the way we placed our tallest and strongest soldiers to protect our precious colours (unit flags) from any possible attack by protesters. It's just as well nothing eventuated because many angry diggers carrying months of pent-up emotions would have found it difficult to control themselves if some fool had attempted to disrupt our parade.

I also remember the crowd that lined the streets. Not everyone was there to celebrate our homecoming. Many were distracted from their day's work and just stood and watched, others looked out of their office windows and waved. There was even some ticker tape floating down from the tops of the buildings, but generally it was rather subdued. Family and friends of the soldiers however were there in force and every now and then a call from the crowd indicated that they had spotted their man in uniform and he came in for some special cheer. A group of dignitaries stood on a dais at the Town Hall to take the salute. Thankfully, there were no welcoming speeches.

For me it wasn't a welcome home parade, it was simply an opportunity to show the citizens of Sydney that my mates and I were back. It was the formal end to the whole adventure and as far as I was concerned, the moment we were dismissed from the parade, I could get on with my life.

I didn't know it then, but when I said goodbye to my loved ones in February 1970, I also said goodbye to the life that I had known and the future I had hoped for. Looking back now, I realise that the experience had a profound effect on me and my attitude to many things. I'm not sure what would have happened in my life had I not spent that year in Vietnam, but I returned a very disillusioned soldier and it has taken all these years to come to grips with many issues. Like all veterans, I felt betrayed, and so I withdrew into myself and mistrusted anyone other than my immediate circle of family and friends.

Raylene, M-J and I returned to Adelaide for my leave. There were very few questions asked of me, because when someone did say 'What was it like?' I just smiled and shook my head and the conversation was dropped. It wasn't that I didn't want to tell them, it was just ... where do you start? How could I possibly put it into words? Those sounds, the smells, the feelings, the excitement, the sadness? Such mixed up emotions. Anyway, they would never be able to relate it to their lives and probably didn't care anyway. I'd only finish up having to justify the whole bloody war, so why bother . . .!

So I never said anything to anybody, even Raylene. (I now realise that I never asked Raylene about her experiences either. Perhaps she would have welcomed the opportunity to shed some of the difficult times she had been through.) The only people I could talk to were other Vietnam veterans. Then the stories, the experiences, the humour, the tragedy, would flow freely. Even to this day I am reluctant to get too deep into any conversation about the war with anyone other than a veteran. At least they understand.

Following my period of leave we returned to our cosy little married quarter at 501 Lighthorse Parade, Holsworthy, and I returned to duty with the 7th as a newly promoted captain. I was initially going to be the Mortar Platoon commander but ended up in charge of the Signals Platoon, where I stayed for the next two years. It was an interesting time as the battalion was rebuilding and retraining. Several officers who had just graduated from

Portsea and Duntroon were posted in, but many familiar faces remained. It must have been a little difficult for the young subalterns coming into a battalion where many of the NCOs and diggers were wearing ribbons and the combat badge.

The veterans who stayed on in the military were the lucky ones, because they were surrounded by familiar faces and places, did familiar things and were understood by their mates, if things got a bit 'heavy'. There was a lot of support and understanding given by all ranks to anyone who appeared to be having difficulty settling down. Even so, some weren't at ease with the peacetime routines of army and family life and faced a lot of problems. Too many marriages and careers crashed in the first few years after returning from Vietnam.

Those who came back and were, within days, discharged from the army had to readjust to life in Australia without the support of their digger mates. They must have struggled in what they saw as an unfamiliar, uncaring and sometimes hostile environment.

To the best of my understanding, I readjusted pretty well, although I found it very difficult to be at ease in a crowd. I wasn't a very social person, and felt especially uncomfortable in the company of strangers. My usual response to a domestic argument was to withdraw into myself and remain that way for a number of days. I never reached the depths of depression, but even so, really struggled to understand why I couldn't relate to others in an open and friendly manner. Despite all we had been through, even my relationship with Raylene was at times, constrained. It was as if I was keeping everyone beyond arms length.

Our second son James, was born on 6 September 1972 while we were still at Holsworthy and although duty still took me away for weeks at a time, I enjoyed the life of a peacetime soldier and learning at last about the delights and difficulties of being a father.

It was general army practice to be posted to a new unit every two years and while this suited most soldiers, it was hard on the families. The upheaval and uncertainty it caused was sometimes quite traumatic as it often meant a period of separation. Having to pack up all belongings, leave friends behind, move to another area, find suitable accommodation, enrol the kids at school and generally start family life all over again, was not always easy.

As the years passed, I was reminded that some in the community remained hostile towards our involvement in Vietnam. Even Raylene and the boys were tarnished by association and would receive abuse from some. At the very least, there was a 'coolness' towards any army family that moved into the neighbourhood. There was a reluctance to accept them into local institutions, organisations and family circles and it was only through the extreme efforts of the army wives that this prejudice was eventually broken down.

Initially, we enjoyed moving around and Raylene did a marvellous job getting us all settled into our new surroundings and turning the latest house into a home. The boys didn't seem to mind the experience as they very quickly established new friends, adapted to the surroundings and even enjoyed the challenges of a new school system.

On leaving the 7th Battalion in 1973, we moved into a married quarter in Willoughby (one of Sydney's lovely northern suburbs), while I did two years as the Adjutant/Quarter Master of 1 Commando Company. Two years later, we went off to Singleton, in the Hunter Valley, New South Wales, where I took up an appointment as senior instructor of Signals Wing at the School of Infantry. Then, from December 1978 to December 1980 we lived in Coromandel Valley in the Adelaide Hills while I worked at Keswick Barracks in Adelaide. This posting finally gave us the opportunity to be close to our families and for the boys to have uncles, aunties and grandparents close at hand.

An exciting two year posting to Lae in Papua New Guinea followed but even though the living conditions were to our liking, Raylene was clearly tired of this gypsy way of life and wanted to settle down in Adelaide where she could be close to her family. She saw out the overseas posting but that was it. She had had enough. In January 1983 when the time came to move yet again to another posting (this time in Victoria), Raylene stayed in Adelaide with the boys and I went off by myself.

This was the separation that had been threatening for some time, so when it came it was no surprise to either of us. After a year of separation, we were divorced.

In December 1984, I married Anne Hart, who was the teacher of a small country school a little way from the Monegeeta Trials and Proving Ground, where I was serving as the Officer Commanding. A further posting to an Army Reserve unit in Melbourne brought up my 21 years in the army and I felt I'd had enough, so I took discharge in 1986.

Annie and I moved to South Australia, where we settled in the Nairne area of the Adelaide Hills. Following the birth of our son Ryan on 12 June 1987, Annie returned to teaching and I gained employment as the Executive Officer of the State's Forest Industries Training Council, a position I held for the next 11 years. This was followed by a few years as the Operations And Training Manager of a small clothing manufacturing business in Adelaide. I am currently working on the staff of the Woodside Primary School, assisting defence force families and their children to settle into the school community.

Mark-John is married, has three young children, lives in Adelaide, and has established a successful career in primary school education. James has recently moved to Sydney to pursue his interests in the theatre.

We keep in close contact and I follow their careers with much pride. They keep me in touch with their mother's amazing exploits, as she travels the world as the personnel director for an international media company.

It wasn't until 1998, when I re-opened the shoe box full of musty smelling letters and began to read letter 'number one', that I commenced a journey which I should have taken years before. With support from my wife, Anne, I began the first tentative steps of collating this book. I have shed many tears, felt every emotion and in effect relived each moment, but in doing so I have come to accept the reasons why that year had a significant influence on my life. With the publication of this book I have at long last said my final goodbye. This time to my ghosts of Vietnam.

Mark-John's Recollections

I didn't get to wave goodbye to my Dad as he climbed aboard the Qantas jet that took him to Vietnam. After all, I was only 10 months old and I wouldn't have remembered, let alone understood what was going on.

As we celebrated my first birthday with relatives in Adelaide, Dad was on patrol somewhere in that hostile land. As each of the milestones in my little life were being recorded ... my first words, taking my first steps, my first hospital visit ... my Dad wasn't there. Vietnam robbed us of a good start to our relationship. It created a distance between us that was more than a physical one.

It is true that everything we experience in life goes into shaping our character. There is no point wondering what things would have been like for our family had my Dad not been in the army. But it is obvious that a year of separation, so early in my parent's marriage and particularly in the first year of my life, had an impact on our future as a family. Even more so, the experiences he went through only served to alienate him from those who did not share in his tour of duty.

My first memories of Dad are of him teaching me to swim at Bondi beach. We were living at Holsworthy and I remember ours was a fibro house that looked identical to the other 40 in the street. Other memories include the constant moving from place to place ... uprooting and re-establishing every two years. I took it for granted that it was a natural part of life. In many ways army life was an exciting environment for a boy to grow up in. For starters, Father

Christmas always arrived in a Chinook helicopter or an armoured personnel carrier. Then there were the family barbecues at the officers mess on Friday nights and every now and then, when we were in Papua New Guinea, we would spend weekends exploring the old battlefields around Lae, Nadzab and Madang. All the time I felt my Dad was an important person, a war hero even. I was proud of him, but I didn't really know him.

As I grew up Dad was involved in my life, like most fathers are with their kids. He coached my soccer team and helped me build a cubby house in the backyard. Sometimes we'd go orienteering and he'd show me how to find compass direction by the sun and stars. Occasionally he would mention a funny thing that had happened to him in Vietnam and once he gave me one of the maps he had used so I could take it to school for 'show and tell'. But he never talked about his experiences with us. He kept them totally to himself.

I certainly didn't see the divorce coming. My parents rarely fought, but they didn't publicly express affection to each other. Dad never got angry at my brother James or me, but whenever there was any hint of conflict in the family, he'd leave the house and we wouldn't see him for hours. I still remember the day when Mum told me that we wouldn't be going to join Dad in Victoria. I cried all the way to school on the bus. At the age of 12, just when an adolescent needs a father the most, he was gone again.

It was a few years later, while I was visiting him at Woodend, Victoria, that I made a profound discovery. We were cleaning up his study when I came upon a shoe box in his old army trunk. This contained more than 100 letters, all in their original envelopes and neatly organised in chronological order. As I opened the first one I realised that I was reading letters my father wrote to my mum while he was in Vietnam. Mum had saved them all and had taken great care to keep them in their original state.

I never knew of their existence, so for the next week I spent my time reading of the experiences of a family torn apart by a conflict I knew little about. I read of their efforts to keep their love alive and how a naive and zealous young man serving his country, became bitter and disillusioned as his country seemed to abandon him and his fellow servicemen. I read of my parents commitment to each other, despite the hardship and separation. I read of their hopes and dreams for the future and their fear that at any time these could be dashed by some horrible tragedy.

I read of my first year of life and how my Mum coped so well with her loneliness and the stresses of having to care for a constantly sick toddler. I read of my father's traumatic experiences and for the first time understood something of the horror that he had been through. Significantly, I read of his anguish as he realised he was missing out on sharing special moments with his son.

As Dad and I sat on the floor reliving that year, we talked; and for the first time we actually connected on a deep level. The letters opened up emotions that had been locked away for decades. In a way, I felt I was meeting him for the first time.

And since that day, these letters have continued to have a healing effect on our relationship, which has never been as close or solid as it is today.

Mark-John and his son Edward, 2002

Military Terms and Abbreviations

1 ATF – First Australian Task Force (Nui Dat).

2IC – Second-in-Command.

AK47 – Soviet/Chinese 7.62 millimetre automatic rifle used by the VC and North Vietnamese Forces.

Ammo – Ammunition.

APC – Armoured Personnel Carrier. Used as a troop carrier, lightly armoured, tracked vehicle, armed with 30 millimetre or 50 millimetre machine guns.

'Awakey' – a term every Vietnam veteran knows. Awakey is 'awake'; '33 and awakey' is 33 days before one 'awakes', or departs for home.

AWOL – Absent without leave

Batman – a private soldier, an officer's personal assistant.

Brigid – A company-size fire support base located in the sand dunes 500 metres north of Lang Phouc Hai.

Bund – An earth mound, about 50 centimetres high, surrounding a rice paddy field.

Bushranger – Armed Iroquois helicopter (UH 1H). Armed with rockets and mini-guns (multi-barrelled machine guns). Operated in pairs (Light Fire Team) or in threes (Heavy Fire Team).

Casevac – Casualty Evacuation.

Charlie – Viet Cong. Also known as VC or Victor Charlie.

Chopper – Helicopter.

Claymore – Portable, above ground, directional, command detonated mine, loaded with hundreds of small steel balls.

CO – The battalion's Commanding Officer (Lieutenant Colonel).

Coy – Company.

CP – Command Post.

Dust off – Casualty evacuation by helicopter.

Elcho Island – Off northern Australian coast, Aboriginal mission station.

FSB – Fire Support Base.

GP boot – general purpose, issued army boot.

GPMG – General Purpose Machine Gun. A 7.62 millimetre, belt-fed machine gun. The principle infantry section weapon.

Grid Reference (GR) – A set of six numbers denoting a location on a map.

Harbour – An all-round defensive position adopted by infantry units during an extended stop, while on operations.

Holsworthy – A military camp near Liverpool, New South Wales which included Finschaffen Lines, the home of 7RAR.

Hootchie – A nylon, individual soldier's shelter.

Horseshoe – An extinct volcano used by 7RAR as its Operational FSB. Located to the north of the village of Dat Do.

HQ – Headquarters.

In country – In Vietnam.

In the field – On Operations. 'Outside the wire'.

M16 – 5.56 millimetre US automatic rifle.

M16 mine – US antipersonnel mine (Jumping Jack). It was buried in the ground and when tripped would jump one to two metres into the air before exploding.

Maintdem – Maintenance Demand. A re-supply of rations, ammo and equipment. Usually carried out by helicopters.

Mils – The metric equivalent of degrees. Used for measuring angles and for navigating (compass bearing).

MPC – Paper money issued by the South Vietnamese Government. Diggers referred to it as Monopoly money.

NCO – Non-Commissioned Officer (Lance Corporal, Corporal, Sergeant and Warrant Officer ranks).

Nui Dat – Australian Task Force Base located two and a half kilometres north of the village of Hoa Long.

NVA – North Vietnamese Army.

OC – Officer Commanding. Company Commander (Major).

Paludrin – Anti-malarial tablet taken twice daily.

Picket – Duty. Radio picket, sentry picket, telephone picket.

Pogo – Term given to a soldier serving in a main base area ('behind the wire').

Possum – Sioux helicopter (OH 13). Mainly used by the CO to keep in touch with his units in the field.

R and C – Rest and Convalescence. Two days leave between operations, taken at the Peter Badcoe (VC) Club located within the Australian Logistics base in Vung Tau.

R and R – Rest and Recreation. One week's leave, taken outside of Vietnam, once during the tour.

RAR – Royal Australian Regiment.

Recce – Reconnaissance.

Roseworthy College – agricultural college north of Adelaide, South Australia.

RPG – Rocket Propelled Grenade. Shoulder fired, anti-armour – anti-personnel weapon (RPG7, PRG2), used by the VC/NVA.

RTA – Return To Australia.

SAS – Special Air Service.

'Shoe – short for Horseshoe, the ballation's forward operational base.

Sig – Signaller. Radio operator.

Sign – Indication of enemy movement (e.g. footprints).

Silk – A lightweight sleeping sheet.

Slick – Grouping of helicopters.

Stand to – The practice of having the whole unit on alert, especially just before sunset and sunrise.

Tet – Chinese National New Year celebrations.

VC – The enemy. Viet Cong. VC units were often bolstered by North Vietnamese regular forces (NVA).

Infantry Battalion Ranks

Officers

Lieutenant Colonel

Major

Captain

Lieutenant

Second Lieutenant

Non-Commissioned Officers

Warrant Officer Class One
Warrant Officer Class Two
Staff Sergeant
Sergeant
Corporal
Lance Corporal
Private Soldier

Infantry Organisation

Section – Ten men with a corporal in command.

Platoon – Three sections and a small command group. Led by a second lieutenant with a sergeant as 2IC.

Company – Three platoons and a HQ group. About 120 soldiers, led by a major with a captain as 2IC.

Battalion – Four rifle companies (A, B, C and D), Administration Company and Support Company (Mortar Platoon, Recce Platoon, Pioneer Platoon and Signals Platoon), and a HQ Group. About 800 in all, commanded by a lieutenant colonel.

For most of the tour, 7RAR was operating below strength. Due to illness, leave, training and other duties, most sections could muster only six or seven soldiers. Platoons were often operating at about 60 per cent.

It is important to remember that on average, during a calendar year, most soldiers spent about 320 days on operations.

Thanks

To Raylene and Mark-John for providing the love and inspiration for these letters and to Raylene, especially, for having the foresight to keep them.

To Heather, my real life guardian angel.

To all those I served with in the 7th Battalion during 1970–71. Thanks for the experience, the mateship and the memories.

To my wife Anne for her inquisitiveness, understanding and insistence that these letters be recorded in this manner. Her unselfish love has helped me come to grips with much of my past.

To all who edited the early drafts and supported my efforts . . . my sons Mark-John and James, my wife Anne, her brother Allen and his daughter Georgina, our close friends Julie Ratcliffe and Kathy Hart and my workmates Jill, Marleen and Veronica. Also to Sue and Ray Shillabeer who as a young married couple also experienced Vietnam. Your comments and endorsement were especially important.

Finally, to the families of Alan Talbot and Ray Patten. I'm so very sorry for what happened on that terrible day in February 1971. I have shed many lonely tears these past 30-odd years and as each Anzac Day and Remembrance Day arrives, I especially remember their sacrifice and your sadness.

Also from Wakefield Press

On My Brothers' Shoulders

Ty André with Allen McMahon

One evening in 1952, a young woman walked down to the Mekong River carrying her baby boy in a home-made basket. She lit a candle and stood it in the basket, then set her baby adrift on the stream.

Miraculously, the child was rescued by a fisherman and taken to a Catholic mission on the island of Cu Lao Gient. The little boy was named 'Ty', meaning 'billion', because the odds against his survival were a billion to one.

This is a story of that one-in-a-billion chance. For six long years Ty lived with hunger and pain. His arms and legs were crippled by polio, and he was so starved of human company that he did not know his own name. Then a young man who was visiting the mission caught sight of the tiny youngster wriggling along the ground to take a drink at the river. From that chance encounter was born a relationship that would transform both their lives, and a personal crusade that would give new hope to thousands of other children in war-torn Vietnam.

For more information visit www.wakefieldpress.com.au

Also from Wakefield Press

Prisoner of Two Wars

An Australian Soldier's Story

Sherriff Probert and John Probert

1914 *'In case I have been notified as missing . . . I was captured when wounded.'*

1942 *'My dear wife, I am a prisoner of war . . .'*

'Set against the turbulent backdrop of armed conflict and a crippling depression, *Prisoner of Two Wars* is far more than simply the story of an Australian – possibly the only Australian – to become a prisoner in two World Wars. Following the faintest of footprints, the authors embark on a journey to uncover the life and times of a man they barely knew – their father, Jack Probert, a knockabout, everyday Australian. In so doing, they reveal a dramatic tale of high adventure, perseverance, courage and ultimate tragedy. Spanning four decades, this is a compelling saga of a very ordinary man whose destiny and fate is shaped by extraordinary circumstances.'

Lynette Silver, Official Historian, Eighth Australian Division

'It has taken the Probert brothers all their lifetimes to find their father, and to discover just how rare an Australian he was. Theirs is a powerful, poignant and very Australian story.'

Tony Stephens, *Sydney Morning Herald*

For more information visit www.wakefieldpress.com.au

Wakefield Press is an independent publishing and distribution company based in Adelaide, South Australia. We love good stories and publish beautiful books. To see our full range of titles, please visit our website at www.wakefieldpress.com.au.

Wakefield Press thanks Fox Creek Wines and Arts South Australia for their support.